# THE RISE OF FRENCH NEW BRUNSWICK

RICHARD WILBUR

Copyright © 1989 by Richard Wilbur

No part of this publication may be reproduced or transmitted in any form or by any means, electronic or mechanical, including photocopying recording or any information storage and retrieval system now known or to be invented, without permission in writing from the publisher, except by a reviewer who wishes to quote in brief passages in connection with a review written for inclusion in a magazine, newspaper or broadcast.

---

Canadian Cataloguing in Publication Data

Wilbur, J.R.H. (Richard), 1926-

The Rise of French New Brunswick
Includes index.
ISBN 0-88780-070-x
1. Acadians — New Brunswick — Politics and government.
2. Acadians — New Brunswick — Ethnic Identity.
3. Canada — English-French relations. I. Title.
FC2500.6.W54 1989   971.5'004114   C88-098615-8
F1045.F83.W54 1989

---

Front cover photo: Bruce Atkinson, Harvey Studios

Published with the assistance of the Nova Scotia Department of Tourism and Culture

Formac Publishing Company Limited
5502 Atlantic Street
Halifax, Nova Scotia
B3H 3G4

Printed and bound in Canada

---

*To the Gionet and Lanteigne families*
*of Middle Caraquet*
**TRUE NEIGHBOURS**

# CONTENTS

Introduction     v
1. The Stirrings for a New Acadia: 1864 - 1868     1
2. Battles Against the Schools Act: 1869 - 1874     12
3. The Caraquet Riots of 1875     23
4. Aftermath of the Caraquet Riots: 1875     31
5. Claiming Their Birthright: 1866 - 1885     40
6. The Fight for a French Diocese: 1870 - 1881     53
7. Winning Rome's Approval: 1881 - 1912     64
8. A Protestant Backlash in Bathurst: 1890 - 1896     79
9. Coping with Industrialization and War: 1880 - 1918     99
10. P.J. Veniot, Prohibition and Pulp Mills: 1919 - 1929     117
11. The Sormany-Savoie Education Lobby: 1922 - 1939     134
12. Waiting for P'Tit Louis: 1939 - 1952     159
13. Apprenticing for Power: 1952 - 1960     182
14. The Road Towards Equal Opportunity: 1960 - 1967     200
15. The New Generation and the Assimilating Sixties     222
16. Hatfield Woos French New Brunswick: 1970 - 1982     243

Conclusion     271
Bibliography     275
Index     279

# INTRODUCTION

This is an English New Brunswicker's attempt to trace the story of French New Brunswickers as they struggled toward cultural autonomy and political equality in a world that was increasingly English and urban. That story belongs to them, and it is mostly drawn from their own accounts, supplemented by those references to the French found at first infrequently in English newspapers and the Debates of the Legislative Assembly. It is a story that few English citizens have heard, even though an increasing number of them are wondering how the French came to play such a vital part in today's New Brunswick.

It is important to note there are two components to French New Brunswick. There are the Acadians, descendants of the earliest European settlers in the Maritimes, the hardy survivors of the 1755 Expulsion who returned north to settle once again in remote river and coastal communities along the Northumberland Strait and Chaleur Bay. Most of the other French came over the border from Québec to dominate, numerically at least, the northern counties of Madawaska and Restigouche.

In the 1860s, when this story begins, the Acadians had achieved a subsistence economy based on fishing, farming and lumbering — usually a combination of all three. English entrepreneurs dominated this resource-based economy and frequently held the Acadians in economic bondage. The activities of the handful of Acadian businessmen were restricted to their own localities.

Their Roman Catholic Church was led by Irish bishops determined that English should remain the dominant language even though their Acadian adherents usually spoke French. Their only post-secondary school was struggling to survive.

Those other French in mid-19th century New Brunswick were mostly land-hungry *habitants* who were rapidly moving into what soon would become Madawaska County in the colony's northwest corner. While they shared the same religion and language as the Acadians, these French could not claim the Expulsion as part of their heritage.

Both of these French elements did share a common goal: to maintain their language while striving for a measure of political recognition from the all-powerful and indifferent English. This meant establishing their own school system, their own French diocese and their own political lobby. How they achieved these objectives is the thrust of this story.

With few exceptions, the story's framework is chronological.

It is also told as objectively as possible, using accounts by energetic and perceptive writers such as the late Alexandre Savoie and Senator Calixte Savoie. As events enter the 1960s, the author relied as well on his own material, compiled as a freelance journalist based first in Fredericton and later in the village of Middle Caraquet.

This is meant to be a sympathetic study of the rise of French New Brunswickers to a fairer place in the sun. It is not an apology for the way the English majority regarded and treated French-speaking citizens. My sole aim was to trace the way French New Brunswickers mounted a successful crusade toward equal opportunity in our province.

This work had a long gestation period. It started in 1970 when the six Wilburs resided in the old Gionet homestead in Middle Caraquet. It was continued when we moved to Outremont in 1973, where we had a front-row seat for the triumphant rise of René Lévesque's Parti Québécois. The first of four drafts was completed in 1982, a year after the Wilburs, with one left in the nest, had taken up residence in St. Andrews, about the maximum distance from Caraquet one could get and still be in New Brunswick. The cultural differences are greater still.

Most credit for the fact this book was completed goes to my wife, Marlene, a daughter of the Prairies, who declared in 1969, "you can't write about the real New Brunswick sitting in Fredericton"; so we moved to Caraquet. She also helped with the early research, working at our favourite library, in the provincial Legislature, and at my former place of employment, the University of New Brunswick. Our youngest daughter Sarah practised her typing while helping to prepare the first drafts.

A colleague at the latter institution, Dr. Murray Young, read the first attempts and provided valuable clues and insights drawn from his formidable storehouse of New Brunswick political lore. A UNB graduate student who later became a close colleague, Dr. Peter Toner, also gave of his time and knowledge, especially about New Brunswick's Irish and Catholic communities.

Both Drs. Young and Toner read and commented upon the fourth and final draft as did Wendell Fulton, an awesome authority on the inner workings of recent New Brunswick politics. I hope I have done justice to their marginal suggestions.

By a fortunate coincidence, my textual editor turned out to be Rebecca Leaman, who performed the same task in an earlier work that I co-authored. Both she and Lynn McGregor at Formac Publishing showed great patience and formidable skills, especially with word processors, as they tried (and hopefully succeeded) to clean up my messy flow of words.

I would also like to thank two Acadian colleagues, Jeannelle Haché and Jean Martin of the Legislative Research Service for their careful reading of the final draft.

Two people I corresponded with but have yet to meet were kind enough to send me draft copies of their research work, which proved very useful: Raymond Mailhôt and Dr. Robert Young.

I am also indebted, as so many have been, to the Canada Council, for a research grant that enabled me to hire two students in the summer of 1973. Six years later, Concordia University in Montréal granted me a sabbatical which was spent poring through the Debates of the New Brunswick Legislative Assembly, which I located both in Fredericton and at McGill University, Montréal.

Most of all, I thank our neighbours, the Gionet and Lanteigne clans of Middle Caraquet, who inspired me to trace their people's story. I could only use the printed word as my source; they have the real history ingrained in their everyday lives.

Richard Wilbur,<br>Fredericton, 1988

# ONE

# THE STIRRINGS FOR A NEW ACADIA: 1864-1868

In 1867, as New Brunswickers, many with great reluctance, threw in their lot with the unknown Canadians, French-speaking citizens of this small colony were coming under influences that soon would fan a nationalist movement of their own. Just as the Confederation movement had its origins among forces and circumstances outside of what would be Canada, so did the new sense of Acadian identity.

It was a French scholar and historian, Rameau de Saint-Père who first enunciated the goals that the emerging leaders among New Brunswick Acadians would take as their own. In 1859, his work *La France aux Colonies Études sur le développement de la race française hors de l'Europe (Acadiens et Canadiens)* was published in Paris. This was the first work in French which separated Acadians and Québécois from the larger theme of French imperial history.[1]

Rameau encouraged Acadians to follow the Québécois example by having their own national day and patron saint, their own distinctive flag, their own schools, clergy and press. He thought this was the only way they could change what he

---

[1] Raymond Mailhôt, *La Renaissance acadienne (1864-1888): L'Interprétation traditionnelle et le Moniteur Acadien*, Thèse, de Diplôme en Études Supérieures présenté au Département d'Histoire de l'Université de Montréal, 1969, p. 19. [Hereafter cited as Mailhôt. I am indebted to the author for sending me a copy of this scholarly work.]

obviously considered their lowly state — one based on a subsistence economy and lacking cohesive organizations and communication systems.

In 1860, Rameau came back to British North America, touring both Québec and New Brunswick and later writing his impressions for a Paris journal.[2] Considering the timing of his visit, he might even have influenced Les Pères de St. Croix in Montréal to send Père Lefebvre to revitalize a small college at Memramcook in the southeastern corner of New Brunswick.

It had begun as Le Séminaire Saint-Thomas in 1854 but lack of money forced its closure two years later. Father Lefebvre's arrival in 1864 opened a new and vigorous chapter in Acadian history. This small institution soon had permanent stone buildings to accommodate the Acadian and Irish young men (and later young women) who sought its Catholic and increasingly Acadian-oriented curriculum.[3]

From Memramcook would go forth new leaders who became the front-line fighters in the cultural battles that raged over the next three decades. At first the French and Irish stood together but gradually the Acadian priests and teachers increasingly embraced the Acadian cause. The Irish graduates of Memramcook were equally strong in their Catholic faith, but their mother tongue, English, would separate them from the Acadian world they had known as students. That distinction became crucial when the growing corps of Acadian priests began pressing for their own French-speaking bishop.

In 1860, the Roman Catholic Church in New Brunswick was tightly controlled by two Irish-born bishops, James Rogers, whose Chatham diocese included all of northern New Brunswick, and John Sweeney, bishop of Saint John. Both were fluently bilingual but conducted their pastoral affairs in English. Each would hold office until the twentieth century and each was able to ensure that his successor would be Irish-Canadian.

---

[2] Mailhôt, p. 20.
[3] Alexandre -J.Savoie, "L'énseignement, 1604-1970," in *Les Acadiens des Maritimes,* (ed. Jean Daigle) (Moncton, 1980) p. 437.

In those days, the dominant political forces within religious dioceses carried over into supposedly secular politics. Irishmen often represented predominantly French-speaking constituencies. In Gloucester County, which did have a significant English population around Bathurst, this tradition was well established by William End, a native of Limerick, Ireland, who was first elected to the New Brunswick legislature in 1830.

During his first campaign, End, according to one modern writer, made "astute use of the religious and patriotic emotions of the country's Acadian and Irish populations."[4] Once elected, End became increasingly an opportunist and supporter of those in power. Rarely did he champion the Acadian cause, probably because neither End nor his English colleagues considered that Acadians really mattered. During the 1860s, as a group they did not figure in the debates.

An exception occurred in June, 1867, when the House received a petition filed on behalf of Robert Young of Gloucester.

He was the spokesman for a small English clique of merchants and office-holders who kept a tight political and economic rein on the Acadian fishing community of Caraquet.

The petition, signed by Fabien Haché (spelled "Ache" in the document) and 173 others, requested that the debates of the Assembly be published in French. A subsequent motion tabled by Dr. Dow on behalf of Young (absent on business) called for all public notices from heads of government departments to be published in French in a French newspaper "if found practicable."[5]

Three weeks later, the Saint John *Morning Freeman*, edited by a native of Ireland, Timothy Warren Anglin, carried this item from the Chatham *Gleaner:* "*We have a good authority to state that Mr. Anglin has complied with numerously-signed requisi-*

---

[4] Bernard Poirier, "William End", in *Dictionary of Canadian Biography*, Vol. X, p. 437.
[5] *Synoptic Reports of the Legislative Assembly of New Brunswick*, June 12, 1867. Hereafter *Debates*

*tions from the Electors of Gloucester to allow them to put him in nomination as a candidate to represent their county at Ottawa."*[6]

Anglin's cause was supported by a letter signed "Acadiens de Gloucester" and carried in *Le Moniteur Acadien*, Westmorland County's newest publication and New Brunswick's first French newspaper. The letter said Mr. Anglin had always been a brave man, a sincere Catholic and an inflexible defender of his Christian beliefs. It predicted his election by acclamation.[7]

It turned out to be more difficult, despite the open support of priests in lower Gloucester who introduced him after mass and appeared beside him at public meetings. Anglin defeated his fellow Irishman, John Meehan, 1061-671, but only after he had spent (according to his opponents) heavily for carriages on the various voting days.

Another candidate in that first federal election was the young editor of *Le Moniteur Acadien*, Québec-born Israël Landry.

He probably knew he had little chance against his experienced opponent, Albert J. Smith, the Dorchester politician who had led the anti-Confederation forces to victory in the 1865 provincial election.

As Landry later admitted to his friend and frequent correspondent Rameau de Saint-Père, he would get no support from the Irish clergy. They had tried to discourage him from starting his newspaper, arguing that it would create a division among New Brunswick Catholics; also, the province had enough newspapers.

Landry's editorial appearing in the second issue, July 18, 1867, shed more light on his decision to run in the federal contest. "For the past several days, many people have been discussing about choosing a French candidate to represent the county in Ottawa. A movement of dissatisfaction has been noted because of some remarks made in a Saint John newspaper that the election of Mr. Smith should not be contested, seeing that the French were obliged to vote for him and being certain of their votes, no one else would dare offer himself.

[6] Saint John *Morning Freeman*, July 4, 1867.
[7] *Le Moniteur Acadien*, July 18, 1867.

"It seems," continued his editorial, "that French Acadians of this county found it insulting that they should be regarded as slaves, so they are determined to show that they are free and independent and that they will vote as they wish." He noted that people had been talking about George Pelletier, a Shédiac merchant, as one who should run against Smith. "They assure us that if this gentleman wishes to accept the nomination, he would be elected without difficulty for he can count on numerous supporters, not only among the French but among English in different parts of this county."

Much of this was probably so much political "puffery," reflecting Landry's youthful enthusiasm (he was still in his mid-twenties) for his newfound Acadian cause and his meagre knowledge of the political realities of Westmorland county in 1867. The Shédiac merchant Pelletier apparently valued his livelihood more than a new political career: he did not respond to Landry's editorial lure. In the end, Landry entered his own name.

The results, published September 14 in the Saint John *Telegraph*, revealed how badly Landry fared:

|  | Smith | Landry |
|---|---|---|
| Dorchester | 478 | 84 |
| Moncton | 349 | 74 |
| Salisbury | 258 | 2 |
| Sackville | 288 | 55 |
| Shédiac | 361 | 130 |
| Westmorland | 202 | 63 |
| Botsford | 280 | 46 |
| TOTALS | 2,216 | 454 |

The Saint John paper's accompanying editorial noted that Landry had received "very few French votes, probably not a third of the whole number thrown for him, so that the statements so frequently written to Saint John in reference to Mr. Landry being supported by the French clergy must be classed among fictitious things."[8]

[8] Saint John *Telegraph*, Sept. 14, 1867.

Members of Saint John's Catholic community soon would be hearing more from Israël Landry. Within the year, he left his editor's desk for a seat in front of the organ gracing Bishop Sweeney's cathedral. He would remain in that job for the next forty years. The job offer may have been a shrewd move to silence Acadian aspirations for their own newspaper. If so, it failed. *Le Moniteur Acadien* found another Québec-born editor and it would continue its self-appointed role of guardian of all Acadian causes for the next sixty years.

Over in Kent County, another Frenchman ran as a pro-Confederation Conservative MP. Auguste Renaud, a school teacher, had arrived some time earlier from his native France. His campaign, according to Landry's description contained in his letters to Rameau in Paris, was bitter but successful. Renaud defeated his English Protestant and Irish Catholic opponents to become the Maritimes' only French-speaking Member in that first House of Commons.

The bitterness generated by this campaign was evident on Declaration Day when Renaud appeared at the county court house in Richibucto, along with the other candidates. Four individuals (paid by Renaud's opponents, according to Landry) tried to seize and destroy the ballot boxes. The correspondent for the Saint John *Telegraph* gave this version:

> Four persons went into the Court House and broke into the Grand Jury Room. One of them picked up one of the Ballot boxes and tried to break it or throw it out of the window, but he was caught in the act and the box taken from him. Had he succeeded, we would have had another election. You will always see a Frenchman go from this county in future, unless the Protestants and Irish Catholics unite, which they never will ... Renaud was used most disgracefully. He was not allowed to speak at first, but finally managed a few words of thanks to supporters. He speaks very well in his own language.

The reporter concluded that after his brief speech, Renaud left for home in Buctouche "as if the old fellow was after him." Contrary to this impression, Renaud soon proved he was not one to run from a fight. During his Ottawa career, he waged many a verbal battle for the Acadian cause.

The Acadians' biggest struggles would be back in New Brunswick and many of them involved the twin causes of religion and education. Initially, these two emotional issues were championed by Bishops Rogers and Sweeney and by Archbishop Connolly in Halifax. They rightly regarded changes in New Brunswick's education system as serious encroachments to the denominational schools.

In the spring of 1866, Archbishop Connolly accompanied the Maritime delegation to London in an effort to have educational guarantees already promised to Québec extended to Maritime Roman Catholics. This proved fruitless. Even though Connolly returned overseas in a later effort to gain the support of Québec's delegates, the final document, Section 93 of the British North America Act, applied only to Québec and Ontario.

This meant that New Brunswick's Catholic citizens entered Confederation without constitutional protection for their separate schools. Financial support for these schools depended on small annual grants from the provincial legislature, a body that was dominated by English-speaking Protestants.

There were plenty of signs in the mid-1860s that New Brunswick's schools were due for major changes. In Great Britain, two commissions of inquiry into the education system had been held in 1861 and 1864. In the latter year in Nova Scotia, the Conservative government of Charles Tupper passed a Free School Act that jeopardized the continued state support for denominational schools. The Nova Scotia move was publicly praised by the principal of the Bathurst Grammar School, George Parkin, a young man whose oratorical powers would help him earn a knighthood. Speaking in the Bathurst Court House in 1868, Parkin deplored what he termed New Brunswick's neglect of education while he praised Tupper for staking his political career on the cause of free public schools.

"It needs no prophet's eye," Parkin declared, "to see that the day is not far distant when the people of this Province will be asked to declare if they wish the last barrier which separates the son of the poor man from the son of the rich man to be broken down."[9]

A few weeks earlier at the 1868 session of the Legislature, a freshman back-bencher from York County, James Hartley, had introduced four resolutions calling for direct taxation on education. They were defeated after a lively debate that revealed the views contained in school inspectors' reports that New Brunswick's school system ranked far below the standards of Nova Scotia, Québec and Ontario.

The handful of literate Acadian subscribers to *Le Moniteur Acadien* were getting a slightly different message at this time from Rameau de Saint-Père in Paris. He had continued his correspondence with Israël Landry and shortly before the fledgling editor quit to become an organist, he published Rameau's letters.

One appearing in the July 21, 1868 edition urged New Brunswick Acadians to try to form adjoining parishes that would create a solid block unbroken by intervening English communities.[10] Considering the political realities of that day, this was not likely to happen. Oddly enough, it would be exactly one hundred years later when this same goal was expressed by young militant Acadians writing in *Le Moniteur*'s successor as the voice of Acadian nationalism, *L'Évangéline*.

The small Acadian elite growing in eastern New Brunswick would soon be taking up less modest but more attainable goals that Rameau had suggested: a flag, a patron saint, a motto. The vast majority of their neighbours had a more practical objective. They desperately wanted jobs.

In 1868, railway construction held out big hopes, especially in contracts for the Intercolonial. The bitter debate about its route had just been decided: it would pass through the most French part of New Brunswick, the eastern counties along the Northumberland Strait and Chaleur Bay.

---

[9] Cited in K.F.C. MacNaughton, *The Development of the Theory and Practice of Education in New Brunswick, 1784-1900* (Fredericton, 1947), p. 185-6.
[10] Cited in Mailhôt, p. 21.

While hundreds of Acadians joined Irish New Brunswickers in front of railroad contractors' employment offices, far more were leaving the province. The Saint John *Globe*, a persistent critic of Confederation, almost gleefully reported on the daily exodus. In late October, 1869, it noted that several families and individuals, young and old, numbering nearly 60 from the North Shore, had just left for California.[11]

By the late 1860s, signs of New Brunswick's desperate economic plight were everywhere. In mid-November of 1868, two local banks closed their doors. The Commercial Bank of Saint John failed on November 13 when its chief cashier vanished along with $90,000. Eight days later the larger Bank of St. Stephen ceased operations when the Bank of Montréal and the Bank of New Brunswick refused to honour its paper currency.[12]

Bank closures rarely affected Acadian fishermen and marginal farmers. For them, cash was a rare commodity. Theirs was largely a subsistence economy, or at best a barter system. No matter what they did — cutting lumber or fishing for cod and herring — they were usually in debt to *les anglais*.

The sprawling, isolated fishing community of Caraquet, fifty miles down shore from Gloucester County's shiretown of Bathurst, was a case in point. Several hundred families lived in small neat houses along a twenty-mile stretch of coastal road overlooking Chaleur Bay. The tiny English minority's power was best illustrated by James G.C. Blackhall.

Blackhall's father had arrived in Caraquet in 1822 to represent a Jersey fish-packing and exporting firm and he soon held most of the government patronage positions in the community. The

---

[11] Saint John *Globe*, October 30, 1869.
[12] See Chatham *Gleaner*, November 14, 1868, Saint John *Globe*, November 21, 1868, Fredericton *Head Quarters*, November 4, 1868. Stories in the *Gleaner* were also carried in the Saint John *Morning Freeman*.

most prestigious one was Justice of the Peace, but Blackhall was also a member of the local school board. He was Caraquet's harbour-master, customs inspector, highway commissioner, tax-collector, inspector of weights and measures, member of the local board of health, the town clerk and property assessor. [13]

In 1826, James Blackhall married an Irish girl in a civil ceremony. He adhered to his Presbyterian faith and she remained a Roman Catholic. They had three daughters, who were raised Catholics, and three sons, reared as Presbyterians. Their eldest son, James George Canning Blackhall, was born in 1827. By the 1860s, he had assumed all of his late father's offices and had added several more: the postmaster, coroner and magistrate. He married the daughter of the Caraquet manager of the Robin Collas Fish Company. His brother Richard had marriage links with another Jersey-owned fish company based in Caraquet.

A close friend of the Blackhalls was another member of Caraquet's tiny English minority, Robert Young. He was a member of the Executive Council of the Province of New Brunswick — an appointed position — and owned a large general store and a fish exporting business.

By the late 1860s, the region's federal member of Parliament was Timothy Warren Anglin, who served from 1867 to 1878. During his last four years in Ottawa, Anglin was Speaker of the House of Commons, a position he filled with considerable success. He did have one handicap. In 1877 he admitted his inability to read the opening prayers in French. As he explained to his parliamentary colleagues, "any attempt to do so would be ludicrous."[14]

Blackhall, Young and Anglin. This English trio with close links to the overwhelmingly French lower Gloucester coast would play key roles in New Brunswick's first cultural conflict

---

[13] Clarence LeBreton, *Les Blackhalls: Histoire d'une famille et son influence*, in Fischer and Sager (eds.) *The Enterprising Canadians* [Maritime History Group, Memorial University, Newfoundland, 1979], pp. 23-33. This is also the main source for subsequent references to the Blackhall family influences in Caraquet.

[14] William M. Baker, *Timothy Warren Anglin, 1822-96: Irish-Catholic Canadian* (Toronto, 1977) p. 169.

since Confederation — a conflict that helped spawn the Acadian Renaissance.

# TWO

# The Battles Against the Common Schools Act: 1869-1874

By 1869, New Brunswick's school system was in a deplorable state, even for the low standards of that day. The glaring inadequacies in teacher-training, the poor and scarce textbooks, the dilapidated buildings — all had been described year after year by the handful of officials paid to keep the system going.

"In some parts of Kent, in the rural districts of Northumberland and in the lower parishes of Gloucester," wrote the Chief Inspector of Schools in his 1869 Annual report, "the aspects of educational matters is perfectly appalling and nothing short of Direct Taxation will put even the elements of school knowledge within reach of a larger proportion of the children of the country."[1]

The handful of New Brunswickers who ever got to read this familiar lament knew that the areas most frequently referred to in this reports were predominantly Roman Catholic and French-speaking. With today's hindsight, one might wonder how these poor regions could be expected to raise the taxes to upgrade their local school systems.

---

[1] *Journals of the Legislative Council of New Brunswick, 1870*, Report of the Inspector of Schools for Kent, Northumberland, Gloucester and Restigouche, (D.Morrison), p. 25.

This was the intent of the legislation first introduced by George King soon after he was elected in 1869 as a member for Saint John. His bill would also establish a non-denominational school system. Any religious instruction would have to be given outside school hours at additional expense to the parents. No wonder the subsequent debate was so bitter and so long. While it raged for six years, another issue was rarely mentioned. As if by common consent, the language question was not considered, especially by the Irish bishops and their public organ, the Saint John *Morning Freeman*.

They could safely ignore the French fact because the New Brunswick English held it in such contempt. Both English Protestants and Catholics seemed to assume that in due time, just as Lord Durham had predicted, the French would be assimilated.

Some idea of how English politicians regarded their few French colleagues can be seen in this account of a Saturday session of the legislature, carried in the March 11, 1869 edition of the Fredericton *Head Quarters*:

> So exhausted were the members by their great efforts on Thursday and Friday afternoons that they appeared incapable of anything but play on Saturday. In the morning, the House, in the absence of the Speaker ... gave way to its humour and held a mock session in which the Provincial Secretary Mr. [Pierre-Amand] Landry took a prominent part, discoursing in French, much to the astonishment if not the delight of the galleries.
>
> The Hon. Member for Westmorland [Landry] representing the habitants, spoke, by the way, quite fluently, and proved that it is only native modesty and inaptitude in the use of the general language that keeps him so silent. Among other serious subjects touched upon was an Hon. Member's nose, which principal feature of his face bears a scar ... The House then amused itself over a bill against cheese manufacturies.[2]

---

[2] Fredericton *Head Quarters*, March 11, 1869.

Once in 1867 and again in 1869, the French MLAs asked to have the Debates printed in their language, but they received little support. In 1870, when the editor of *Le Moniteur Acadien* had agreed to provide a translation, the House approved a distribution based on the 1861 census. When the motion came up for second reading a week later, the Official Reporter noted that a larger portion of the remarks on this issue had not been noted "because they were not considered of general interest."[3]

Exactly one month later, on St. Patrick's Day, 1870, George King moved that the House go into Committee to consider a bill "relating to Common Schools." As *Le Moniteur Acadien* correctly observed, the government, which had published some details of the King bill the previous December, did not intend to pass it at this session. It merely wanted a general discussion. It was also preparing for a general election.

Whatever King's motives were, he and his colleagues, including Lieutenant-Governor L.A.Wilmot (who seemed to be directing the political scene) played their cards well. The heated campaign following dissolution of the House in June, 1870 produced more than the usual deals and manoeuvres, especially in constituencies delicately balanced between Protestant and Catholic voters.

A candidate's card appearing in the Chatham *Gleaner* caught the flavour of the election spirit in Gloucester. Justinian Savoy promised to give the present government his "most determined opposition." Then he went into details:

> They have abused the public confidence and plundered the public treasury to bribe members ... $2, 000 to one man and $1, 200 to another and $22, 000 to a Railway Company are a few ways your money has been wasted and shews why the money for your roads and bridges is so much less this year ... and also shows why this Govt. tried to burthen you by direct taxation to keep up your

---

[3] *Synoptic Reports of the New Brunswick Legislative Assembly, 1870*, February 11. Hereafter *Debates*.

schools. If useless offices and salaries were cut off and even moderate economy used, we would have plenty of money for all our schools, roads and bridges.[4]

Despite these revelations, the incubant, William Taylor, won.

Voters in other areas of Gloucester responded differently. They elected two anti-school bill candidates, Samuel Napier of Bathurst and Théotime Blanchard of Caraquet.

Another mixed county, Westmorland, also returned an Acadian opponent to the new school bill. Pierre-Amand Landry, regarded as the Acadian spokesman for his area, had been approached by William Caie of Kent, a member of the government's Executive Council. Caie had tried to win Landry's support for the school bill by offering him the post of Commissioner of Public Works. He also promised to name Landry's father, Amand, a former MLA, to the Legislative Council. The younger Landry, as he remembered this stormy election years later, refused these temptations and despite fierce opposition, kept his Westmorland seat.[5]

Two other French candidates, Antoine Girouard of Kent and Levite Thériault of Victoria may have succumbed to the lures. They won their elections and later supported the school bill when it was re-introduced for serious debate in 1871. In July of that year, Thériault was named to the Executive Council, a move that the Saint John *Morning News* strongly disapproved:

> He is a French Roman Catholic. He does not oppose the School law, but he does not manfully stand up for what he holds to be right and for the public good either. Under what influence did he succumb at the critical moment? Will he be unassailable to that influence in critical emergencies, now that he is a member of the Local Govern-

---

[4] Chatham *Gleaner,* June 18, 1871.
[5] D.M.M. Stanley, *Au service de deux peuples: Pierre-Amand Landry* (Moncton NB: Éditions d'Acadie, 1977,) p. 58.

ment to whose hand is entrusted the working of the New School Law?[6]

In 1870 and in every provincial election down to 1960, the English remained in control. This contest just before the bitter school bill debate was no exception. King and his supporters took 24 of the 40 seats.

Their victory depended on two veteran politicians, George L. Hatheway of York and Benjamin Stevenson of Charlotte. Shortly after the Throne Speech, the King government resigned and was replaced by another led by Hatheway. It soon became clear that King was still the guiding spirit. On April 12, 1871, he once again introduced a school bill.

The Opposition was ready. Strongly supported outside the House by Bishops Sweeney and Rogers, it had done its homework. Nine days after King tabled his second version, Pierre-Amand Landry presented a petition with the names of 108 Roman Catholics from the parish of Dundas, Kent, asking Lieutenant-Governor Wilmot to incorporate in the new law the same privileges to protect Catholic rights that had been given to Québec's Protestant minority under section 93 of the British North America Act.

Similar petitions came in rapid succession from Saint John and Gloucester County. Bishop Sweeney's name headed the 2,000 signatures on the Saint John document. None of these petitions mentioned language rights, in sharp contrast to the cultural struggle that had been raging in the new province of Manitoba.

Most New Brunswickers concerned with minority rights must have been acutely aware how the government of Sir John A. Macdonald had settled the question in Manitoba. He had given in to the demands of Bishop Taché allowing for special provisions for French as well as denominational schools in the new province.

---

[6] Saint John *Morning News*, July 18, 1871. [No official reports of the Legislative Assembly *Debates* exist for 1871, but the local newspapers carried extensive albeit highly partisan views and accounts.]

We have to assume that New Brunswick's Irish bishops were just as opposed to extending French language privileges as they had been a few years earlier when they advised Israël Landry not to begin *Le Moniteur Acadien*. They were determined to keep New Brunswick's Roman Catholics under the English linguistic umbrella. By fighting the Commons Schools Act only on religious grounds, they hoped to avoid an open split between their adherents. It would be easier, or so they must have concluded, to fight the King bill on the double-taxation issue.

As if to emphasize how scarce money was among ordinary citizens in 1870, the *Morning Freeman* carried this item on the same page reporting the election of Samuel Napier of Bathurst and Théotime Blanchard of Caraquet, both strongly opposed to the school bill:

> Yesterday a large body of fine-looking men evidently from the country were observed walking from the direction of the Railway Station down Germain Street. A gentleman asked one of them what so unusual a spectacle meant and was told that these men had all come from Kent County and were going to seek in the United States the bread they were no longer able to earn in this Province .... They numbered 53 and intended to leave ... on the steamer this morning. What a dreadful commentary on the present state of things is this wholesale exodus of the people.[7]

As these New Brunswickers (and many more like them) took this drastic action to solve their personal economic problems, others reacted to the new school bill. On January 14, 1873, the Chatham District School Board passed this resolution that was immediately published in the Chatham *Gleaner*:

> Whereas we, the rate-payers of District number seven, particularly of Chatham, feeling it our duty to manifest our disapprobation of this iniquitous School Act, cannot let the opportunity pass without signifying our un-

---

[7] Saint John *Morning Freeman*, June 30, 1870.

qualified dissent therefrom. Therefore resolve, first that the present school act grossly invades and sets at naught the conscientious convictions of all true lovers of religion; And secondly, resolved that it is the indispensable obligation of every parent to teach his child his duty toward God that he may therefore walk in the way to which he should go; and as the present School Act is, in its very essence, opposed to this, inasmuch as it would deprive the child of all religious instruction whatever in school, it is therefore worthy of the censure and disapproval of all true men; Thirdly, resolved, that as we cannot conscientiously avail ourselves of the privileges afforded by the Act, we shall take other and more legitimate means of giving our children that education they require.[8]

The Bathurst School Board took more direct action. After defeating a motion for new school tax assessments, it passed a resolution condemning the law and unanimously decided not to impose any school tax for the coming year. Over the next few months, this tactic was adopted by most Acadian and Irish communities along the north shore.

By the summer of 1873, the school issue was still hot. One Sunday evening in mid-August, hundreds of Acadians crowded into their parish church at Caraquet to discuss the school question and to hear speeches. Their local MLA, Théotime Blanchard, delivered the first one and he was followed by three Bathurst Irishmen, P. J. McManus, Kennedy Burns and J.E. O'Brien. Among the resolutions passed were several condemning the school law and the government that had introduced it.

Robert Young, their member to the appointed Executive Council, was roundly criticized for abandoning his previous stand in favour of denominational schools supported by public taxes. He was accused of joining a party of "fanatics and bigots." The gathering went on record as regretting having supported Young in the past. Everyone was urged to take all legal means

[8] Chatham *Gleaner*, January 18, 1873.

to avoid paying the school tax. They should also keep their children away from school.

This particular meeting obviously had been well planned.

Young knew about it but his letter read at the church said he wouldn't be there because he had not received an invitation. He also objected to political meetings held on Sunday and did not think it proper to hold such discussions "in a House of God."

The correspondent for the Chatham *Gleaner* who had sent in a report on this unusual gathering said Caraquet citizens had regarded Young's explanations and comments as "most insulting."[9]

Similar meetings held during this same month of August, 1873, in Neguac, northeast of Chatham, and in St. Charles, Kent County, suggest an organized campaign was underway. Each meeting passed similar resolutions urging non-payment of school taxes and in a couple of cases deploring court action already taken against tax-resisters.

Not one of these resolutions or supporting editorials in the *Morning Freeman* and *Le Moniteur Acadien* mentioned language rights. In a typical editorial, *Le Moniteur*'s Fernand Robidoux thought the "King Bill" was out to establish an American system of education — one he concluded was already leading to immorality.[10]

As organized as it obviously was, this combined press, clerical and citizens' campaign against the Common Schools Act was doomed to fail. Proof of the kind of opposition they faced came in 1872 when a test case, instigated by August Renaud, MP for Kent, to uphold the legality of an Acadian Catholic school in his constituency, was lost in the lower courts.

If Québec's French and Catholic establishment had gone to bat for their cultural cousins in New Brunswick, it would have been a different ball-game. Alas, the inward-looking Québécois more or less ignored the parliamentary fight championed by

---

[9] Chatham *Gleaner*, August 16, 1873. See also *Le Moniteur Acadien*, 28 août 1873.

[10] *Le Moniteur Acadien* 21 & 28, août, 1873.

Renaud and his New Brunswick colleague, John Costigan, MP for Victoria.

It was the same story at the polls. The Catholic opponents to the King bill were out-numbered and hence out-voted. In the federal election of 1872, New Brunswick's lone French MP, Renaud, lost his seat in Kent to anglophone R.B. Cutler. In another try in 1874, Renaud lost again, this time to George McLeod. Anglophone Catholics T.W. Anglin and John Costigan, were both re-elected with ease. Could part of the explanation be that they had the silent support of Bishops Sweeney and Rogers?

"Vote for the Queen and Against the Pope!" That was Premier George King's battle cry in the provincial election of 1874. He won an impressive victory. Thirty-four pro-Schools Act candidates were returned compared to only five who opposed it. These five included two Irish Catholics, Henry O'Leary of Richibucto and Kennedy Burns of Bathurst, and three francophones: Théotime Blanchard of Caraquet, Urbain Johnson of Buctouche, and Lévite Thériault from Edmundston.

It was one of the bitterest campaigns in provincial history, providing convincing proof of Protestant political power.

Writing in his final edition before voting day, editor George Day of the Saint John weekly *New Dominion and True Humorist* urged his readers to "resist the interference of Québec priests and demagogues in our provincial affairs; resist the effort to make the Roman Catholic Church the State Church of New Brunswick."[11] Above all, voters were to ignore the views of Anglin's *Morning Freeman*, "the hireling organ of a despotic and alien hierarchy."

This same issue had another editorial entitled "Westmorland Forever." It hailed the defeat of Pierre-Amand Landry and directed some barbs at *Le Moniteur Acadien*. "That miserable, wretched, vindictive, conscience-enslaved propaganda of corruption can now weep in sackcloth and ashes over the defeat of its men and measures."

Why this outpouring of venom against the Roman Catholic and to a lesser extent French New Brunswickers? Any attempt

---

[11] *New Dominion and True Humorist*, June 20, 1874.

at a balanced answer would have to consider Protestant Canadians' real and imagined fears over a militant Catholic community spurred on by the recent (1869-70) debate at Rome's Lateran Council over Papal Infallibility. But perhaps the main cause of religious and cultural suspicion throughout the young nation of Canada could be traced to the terrible struggles over control of Ireland.

This debate was raging throughout the British Isles and the Protestant side was championed in Canada by the Orange Lodge. In 1874, George King probably owed a huge political debt to New Brunswick Orangemen. Once his victory was assured, his government began applying the regulations of the Common Schools Act with great vigour. It also made a crucial change in the tiny educational bureaucracy.

The Chief Superintendent of Education, John Bennet, had always had a good rapport with Catholic school officials and educators. Premier King replaced him with Theodore Rand, the former Chief Superintendent of Schools in Nova Scotia. Rand was a devout Baptist and a strong advocate of a state-directed school system.[12]

After the Conservatives' 1874 electoral sweep, "neither religious principles nor private conscience," as one modern writer put it, "deterred the tax collector."[13] Throughout the summer and autumn of that year, *Le Moniteur Acadien* reported on numerous cases where farm animals and equipment had been seized for non-payment of school taxes. Included were Bishop Sweeney's horse and carriage — gifts from the City of Saint John. The fact he was able to buy them back for one dollar at a public auction did not silence his parishioners' outcries at this insult.

More moderate members of the new legislature (and there were a few) deplored such harsh measures. They introduced a motion to repeal the school act, but were defeated 25 to 13. For

---

[12] K.F.C. MacNaughton, *The Development of the Theory and Practice of Education in New Brunswick, 1784-1900* (Fredericton 1947) p. 197.

[13] George F.G. Stanley, "The Caraquet Riots of 1875" in *Acadiensis* (Autumn 1972) p. 23.

George King, attorney-general as well as premier, there would be no backing down, especially when two months after his electoral sweep, the Judicial Committee of the Imperial Privy Council in London ruled that the Common Schools Act was within the constitutional rights of the New Brunswick government.

New Brunswickers opposed to the act did more than withhold their school tax payments. Many followed the other suggestion of the Catholic lobby and kept their children away from schools. While school attendance rose steadily after 1872 in the ten predominantly Protestant counties, it was a different story in the others. Inspectors' reports for Kent, Northumberland and Victoria showed almost no increase; state-run schools in Gloucester reported sharp drops. The new county of Madawaska, created from Victoria in 1873 after waves of settlers swept down from Québec, did not have a single public school operating as late as 1876.

In December, 1873, the Sackville *Borderer* noted that since the passage of the school act, thirty French school districts in Westmorland had no schools. Its editor thought this was "cheering news." "Cheering News!! replied the editor of *Le Moniteur Acadien. "Vraiment! Pour vous autres communs qui vous dépouilles pour faire instruire vos enfants! Dignes filles des persécuteurs des héros de Grand Pré et de Beau Bassin!"*[14]

Most did not realize it then, but these harsh events had a positive side for French New Brunswickers. They were being forced to establish their own French-speaking school system. The Act meant that Collège Saint-Joseph in Memramcook, for example, lost a $400 provincial grant. Late in 1873, Father Lefebvre launched a public campaign to build a new and larger campus. Bishop Sweeney sent a cheque for $500 and other contributions began pouring in from around the province, especially from Kent and Westmorland. Each issue of *Le Moniteur Acadien* carried lists of new donors: the campaign had become a French rallying (battle?) cry.

---

[14] *Le Moniteur Acadien,* 18 décembre 1873.

In September 1872, les Soeurs de la Congrégation de Notre-Dame took over a convent in Bathurst and a few months later other members of that order moved to Memramcook to open a convent near the all-male institution. On July 30, 1874, *Le Moniteur Acadien* reported that September would see two more convents open at St. Louis-de-Kent and Caraquet.

In the short space of three years, George King's Common Schools Act had all but wiped out the old public school system that had served French and Catholic children. In its place, a new system was quickly emerging — one more militant and much more French.

This was the situation on the eve of a series of events that would give New Brunswick Acadians a powerful rallying cause.

It produced such an uproar that a furious but embarrassed King government was forced to concede major amendments to the Common Schools Act.

# THREE

## THE CARAQUET RIOTS OF 1875

Early in January, 1875, in the windswept and isolated fishing community of Caraquet, the local MLA, Théotime Blanchard, chaired a meeting called to nominate citizens to fill the various parish offices. It was an annual ritual, but this year was different. Blanchard and several others had refused to pay their school taxes and therefore were ineligible to serve as members of their district school board. They were named anyway.

As member of the Legislative Council and acknowledged spokesman for the area's tiny English minority, Robert Young objected. He knew the letter of the law. He set up another meeting to select a "legal" slate of officers and to approve a new school tax rate. You could almost feel the tension in that cold night air as Caraquet citizens once again filled the parish hall for the meeting called by James Blackhall, the man of many offices, and his brother-in-law Phillip Rive, manager of Caraquet's largest fish plant.

Blackhall rose to address his fellow townfolk, but they weren't about to listen. Angry shouts greeted his first words. Someone rushed forward and grabbed the papers from his hands. Then he and Rive were ordered to leave. Young was not present: he was in Fredericton, as he often was, attending a cabinet meeting.

The next day, January 15, about thirty Acadians went to the school. It was locked. They headed for Blackhall's office. As secretary of the school board, he had a key. He refused to give it to them, so they went over to Robin's store near the wharf, where they bought a gallon of rum. The weather was bitterly cold and the rum probably did as much for their blood as it did for their courage. While some began singing *La Marseillaise*, they returned to confront Blackhall once again.

What happened next depended on which newspaper report was read. According to the Saint John *News*, which seemed to have scooped its competitors, "a mob" forced its way into Blackhall's office, turned over a stove, tore papers from the wall, broke some windows and ordered a terrified Blackhall to sign a statement promising to have nothing more to do with school meetings or enforcing the school act.[1]

Another version reported in Anglin's *Morning Freeman* was much closer to Blackhall's statement given later under oath. Denying that he had been beaten or that he had been afraid, he admitted to a slight sense of danger when he signed the citizens' document. The "mob" had stayed in his office for some time while he worked on his accounts. Now and then he told them to quiet down.

The stove was damaged after about forty men had squeezed into a space meant for ten. Blackhall remembered seeing one fisherman kick at the stove and then others brought in snow to put on the hot coals that had spilled on the floor. After that, Blackhall went into his inner office and took a drink offered by Joseph Chiasson, one of the "mob's" leaders. Chiasson thought the rum would help as Blackhall looked pale and nervous. A short time later, the office was empty once again as the "mob" headed for Young's house to see if he had come back from Fredericton. He was still away.

Mrs. Young seemed to panic at the sight of the approaching crowd and quickly bolted her doors to protect her children. Next

---

[1] The various versions relating these events generally agree on what took place up to the riots. See George F.G. Stanley, "The Caraquet Riots of 1875" in *Acadiensis* (Autumn, 1972), an account based on reports appearing in *Le Moniteur Acadien* and the Saint John *Telegraph*. My account is based on the *verbatim* evidence given at the Acadians' trial and carried in the Saint John *Morning Freeman*. This appears to have been the only publication that carried the trial evidence as it was copied down by court reporters.

door at Young's store, an equally frightened clerk, Colson Hubbard, gave a few provisions requested by Chiasson and his four companions, including the burly Mailloux brothers.

No damage done, the Acadians began moving down the street, knocking on the doors of *"Les Bourbons."* They were the few citizens known to favour the school act. One by one, they all signed statements promising to withdraw their support from the hated law.

One man, Haché, called out as they passed his house: "Hey Joseph ! Aren't you going to get me?" Chiasson came up and Haché seemed happy to sign.

The short January day was ending. The rum had disappeared some time before. The "mob" broke up. The "riot" was over.

After they had left her house and moved off down the town's one main street, Mrs. Young ran to a nearby telegraph office and sent a frantic message to her husband to return home. He had already left Fredericton and did not receive the telegram until he arrived at Sackville.

Young's nerves seemed to be better than his wife's. He took his time moving north, arriving in Chatham by train two days later. A second telegram warned that his life was in danger and that a mob was about to burn the store and all his records.

Even this was not enough to stir the Hon. Robert Young. He stayed in Chatham four days, consulting with William Kelly, the Commissioner of Public Works. Then he headed for Bathurst, where he probably had more discussions with Senator John Ferguson and Sheriff Vail. He reached Caraquet on Friday, January 22 and found his family safe, his store undisturbed.

Saint John's partisan newspapers refused to let these events disappear without a trace. Thundered *The Freeman*:

> Mr. Young has done mischief enough in Gloucester and he and his colleagues should be satisfied. For three years the number of schools in the County has been so reduced that hundreds of children have been deprived of all chance of literary introduction. For three years the people have been harassed, insulted and annoyed, maligned and

misrepresented by persons owing them gratitude and paying them hatred.

For any repetition of such demonstrations ... not they but the remorseless faction which strives to trample upon them and to rob them, will be held accountable. They want peace.[2]

Editor George Day in his *New Dominion* asked "the good and intelligent in the City of St. John to calmly weigh the importance of the disturbance."

Straws tell us how the wind blows and were the Anglin-Sweeney party as strong, in proportion to the population in New Brunswick, as it is in the benighted, priest-ridden, Anglin-blighted, ignorant County of Gloucester, it would enforce its power with just the same brute force. It is priestly interference and jesuitical counsel; it is the miniature vatican and poison-producing newspaper distillery at Saint John that are preventing the wretched savages of that northern district of our province from becoming civilized and enlightened — that are hindering these poor untutored slaves of ignorance, from the enjoyments and blessings which are offered through a free education.[3]

On the Sunday following Robert Young's return to Caraquet, Father Joseph Pelletier read two statements to his congregation. The first expressed his disapproval of the events over the past ten days. The second, he explained, had been handed to the sexton just minutes before mass by Colson Hubbard, Young's clerk. It ordered Father Pelletier to stop "the band of pirates" responsible for the trouble or else the presbytery would be burned to the ground.

Even as he was reading this remarkable document to his amazed flock, the Sisters at the convent next door were hurriedly packing their meagre belongings, prepared to leave at a moment's notice. Angry as most of the citizens must have been

[2] *Morning Freeman*, January 19, 1875.
[3] *The New Dominion*, January 23, 1875.

at this threatening and insulting message, they did nothing immediately, probably out of respect for the Sabbath and Father Pelletier.

About ten o'clock the next morning, nearly a hundred men began to gather outside Young's store. They were unarmed, sober and angry. They found the store barricaded. Inside were Young and a few friends, apparently ready for the worst.

They asked Young to step outside. He refused. The crowd stood around for a while longer, and then began to break up. Most wandered back to their homes, but a few gathered in the kitchen of André Albert's to decide what, if anything, they should do.

Robert Young had already decided his course of action. Two days earlier, Colson Hubbard had given him the names of the apparent ring-leaders. Young sent this list to Sheriff Robert Vail in Bathurst and requested him to come to Caraquet and arrest them.

On this fateful Monday, even while the crowd stood outside Young's store, Vail and four constables were on their way. When they reached New Bandon, they swore in two more constables and arriving at Caraquet, they recruited John and Richard Sewell. Vail's entire force was made up of English-speaking Protestants. Quickly they arrested several Caraquet men and locked them inside Young's store.

Vail might have stopped at this point. All had gone smoothly. The prisoners had offered little or no resistance. Instead, he telegraphed William Kelly in Chatham to send more men. This was illegal because Vail's jurisdiction was restricted to Gloucester.

Kelly quickly complied with Vail's request. Soon a force of twenty men, mostly from Chatham and Newcastle, was heading for Caraquet. Like Vail's men, these were all English and Protestant and many were members of the Orange Order. Their sleighs arrived over the snow-clogged Caraquet roads early on Wednesday morning, January 27.

"Imagine if you can," asked a *Freeman* editorial three days later, "such a raid made in Portland [Saint John] or in Carleton or in Gagetown or in Woodstock by a body of armed Frenchmen brought suddenly from a great distance and led by some person whose authority the people knew nothing of, and fancy what the consequences would be?"[4]

The editor's worst fears would soon be realized. Resistence began to stiffen as the English made more arrests. Gervais Chiasson fought fiercely before being bound and dragged inside Young's make-shift jail. Rumours spread that "Young's Army" planned to arrest anyone it could find. Even then, the Caraquet fishermen remained calm.

Some of them must have suspected they were on Young's list.

Once again, as they had done Monday morning, they gathered at André Albert's house at the other end of the straggling village. A few settled down to play cards around the big kitchen table. Others talked and glanced every now and then down the road. All the while, Mrs. Albert worked at her big stove and kept an eye on her children.

Suddenly, Télesphore Brideau rushed in. Young's army was just approaching Séraphin Albert's house and they were all armed. Several Acadians rushed out of André Albert's but most stayed. They talked in noisy confusion.

Now English voices could be heard. A mad scramble followed. Some frantically climbed the ladder into the attic while the rest hid in other rooms. Then James Blackhall, the "army's" interpreter, knocked loudly on the door. André Albert cautiously opened it.

"Is Charles Parisé there? Sheriff Cable has a warrant for his arrest." The confused Albert thought he said Xavier Parisé and said he didn't know. Some of Cable's men pushed him aside and went in.

Seeing Mrs. Albert stirring a pot on the stove, they somehow thought she was about to throw the contents at them. Waving a gun in her face, they shoved her and another woman into an adjoining room.

Suddenly they heard a noise from the attic. Constable Ramsay raised his rifle and fired point-blank through the ceiling trapdoor. Two others rushed up the ladder but the Acadians pushed them

[4] *Morning Freeman*, January 30, 1875.

back. Bayonets were thrust into the ceiling planks. A shot rang out from the attic and a bullet glanced off Mrs. Albert's stove.

Frantic and angry cries filled the crowded kitchen. Two more constables stormed up the ladder and John Gifford fired blindly into the dark. Another shot rang out. Gifford fell back to the kitchen floor, a bullet in his head.

The other constables began firing wildly into the ceiling and through the attic opening, even though by this time one of their own men was up there too. Gunsmoke was everywhere, helping to conceal the Acadians and allowing two more to escape.

Another shot was fired and Louis Mailloux fell to the attic floor. Then it was over. The Acadians finally convinced *les anglais* that they wanted to surrender — something they had been trying to do since the fracas began. They were quickly marched off down the road to Young's jail, two of them holding rags to their bleeding faces.

Behind them in the Albert attic, Louis Mailloux was breathing his last. Gifford had died instantly.

The next morning, Thursday, January 27, 1875, thirteen prisoners were loaded aboard sleighs for the fifty-mile run to Bathurst jail. When they arrived several hours later, some Acadians were badly frost-bitten.

Alarmed at the news that two men had died, Senator John Ferguson and two Justices of the Peace in Bathurst convinced William Kelly to send an organized militia force from Chatham. Later that same day, two officers and 41 other ranks of the Newcastle Field Battery left for Bathurst. They took with them two nine-pound cannon.

They were soon followed by a second unit of four officers and 46 men. Despite having to shovel through immense snowbanks, they managed to reach Bathurst the next day. The gunners remained there to guard the prisoners. The infantrymen went on to Caraquet. They found everything peaceful and immediately returned to their homes in Chatham.

The Caraquet Riots were over. The courts would now take over.

# FOUR

## Aftermath of the Caraquet Riots: 1875

Less than one week after the tragic deaths in Caraquet, an involved and lop-sided legal process began. James Blackhall assumed his coroner's role to conduct the inquest into the deaths of John Gifford and Louis Mailloux.

His hand-picked jury found that Mailloux had been killed by a "leaden" bullet fired by a person unknown. No charges should be laid. Nine rioters already being held in the Bathurst jail were blamed for Gifford's death. On February 1, 1875, they appeared in a Bathurst court before an English magistrate. John Young, Robert's brother, acted as court interpreter. They were all formally charged with murder and were ordered held until the next sitting of the court. That would take place in September.

A few days after these wheels of justice began turning in Bathurst, the provincial legislative session got underway in Fredericton. Considering the recent events in Caraquet and Bathurst, the elected representatives might have been expected to step around issues likely to arouse more cultural animosity. Instead, the dominant group of English Protestants seemed determined to show the world that they were in control.

Their actions should be judged in the harsh light of their own day — when Protestants and Catholics seemed in a perpetual state of war. The bitter 1874 election campaign had produced a Protestant sweep; most of them now adjusting to their surroundings in the old legislative building were rabid anti-Catholics.

Typical of the members of this new House was John A. Humphrey, one of four Protestant Englishmen elected to represent Westmorland. He came from a proud Methodist tradition and ran for public office to further his commercial interests and those of an enterprising group of Monctonians leading their community into the industrial age. A millwright by profession, he was in the process of establishing a woolen mill on the outskirts of Moncton that soon would be a large employer of Acadian and Irish Catholics. Like most aspiring entrepreneurs of his generation, Humphrey was convinced that a few bosses and many marginally-paid workers represented the natural order.

Each had his place. Pre-eminence belonged to those with capital and the nerve to risk it in new ventures. In Moncton in the 1870s, that group was mostly Protestant. They effectively closed their ranks to the French and barely admitted the Irish.[1] Why? Because this "lesser" breed was hampered by a religion that ignored the virtues of individualism and free enterprise.

These were virtues that the supporters of the Common Schools Act hoped would be instilled in the minds of future New Brunswickers. Give them the kind of schooling available to white children in the great republic to the south. Above all, let it be an education unhampered by what they believed were the backward teachings of the Church of Rome.

Men like Humphrey were more at home with their ledgers and legal books but they had run for office to ensure the passage of laws that would help them create the new society. They were practical men with little time for philosophizing. Still, the partisan newspapers they supported with their advertising and readership kept them in touch with some of the larger issues.

One was a debate currently raging in neighbouring Québec. At the heart of it was control of public education. It involved the Institut Canadien and conservative forces within the Church led by Bishop Bourget.

In 1844 about 200 young Montréalers formed the institute as a free discussion group that would operate outside the existing structure of elementary schools and classical colleges. As one

---

[1] See J.E. Belliveau, *The Monctonians: Citizens, Saints and Scoundrels* (Hantsport, N.S., 1981) Vol. I, pp. 230-231. [J.A. Humphrey is the author's great-grandfather.]

modern historian describes it, the institute was "an adult education centre with a library, a reading room and an organized program of debates and lectures on the intellectual, economic and political questions of the day, both European and North American."[2] Members of the institute "were free-thinkers in an era of increasing Catholic conservatism." Constant pressure directed mostly by Bishop Bourget had reduced the institute's membership.

By 1865 the hardy survivors (including Wilfrid Laurier) appealed to Rome, asking whether they as Catholics could belong to a literary society that included Protestants among its members and books banned by the Church's Index.

When one of the Institute's most active members, Joseph Guibord, died in 1869, Bishop Bourget refused his widow's request to have him buried in consecrated ground. A lengthy legal battle began — one that would travel the same route and at almost the same time as another establishing the constitutionality of New Brunswick's Common Schools Act. In November, 1874, the Judicial Committee of the Imperial Privy Council decreed that the parish and the Montréal cemetery must bury Guibord in consecrated ground. It would be another year before this court order was carried out.

Many members of New Brunswick's English Protestant community must have applauded the court's decision. At issue was the same question posed by the Common School Act: which was supreme in lay matters, the State or the Church? Both the Guibord affair and the same court's decision upholding the legality of the Common Schools Act were regarded by most liberal-minded citizens as great victories.

In 1875, few would have considered the Loyal Orange Association as part of those liberal forces at work in New Brunswick, Québec or anywhere else. It represented the ultra-conservative Protestant tradition of Ulster in strife-torn Ireland. When migrating Ulstermen established their farming communities in the lower Saint John river valley, they brought with

---

[2] S. M. Trofimenkoff, *The Dream of Nation: A Social and Intellectual History of Québec* (Toronto, 1983), p. 93.

them this historic cultural baggage. At its core was an undying hatred and deep suspicion of all things Catholic and papist. By 1875 this group had become a powerful political force, one that could be counted on to support the new Common Schools Act.

When the New Brunswick legislature began debating the bill incorporating the Orange Lodges in March 1875, the member for Bathurst, Kennedy Burns, arose to point out the lodges' anti-Catholic bias. Calling the bill offensive to 100,000 New Brunswickers, Burns moved for a three-month postponement.[3]

In an effort to defuse this emotional issue, Henry O'Leary of Kent, one of the few Celts present as he reminded his newly-elected colleagues, gave a witty and urbane speech describing all the trouble the Orange Order had caused for so long in the old country.

A prominent Orangeman and editor of the Saint John *News*, Edward Willis, was in no mood to treat the matter lightly.

"What class of people," he wanted to know, "gave evidence of special loyalty when rioters rose against their neighbours and the law in this Province, when bodies of men were required to go from their homes for the protection of their fellow citizens?"

This was too much for Kennedy Burns. He accused Willis of raising the Caraquet matter "to arouse a feeling and prejudice to assist the passage of the bill." It could be shown "at the proper time that the party with whom the Hon. Gentleman was associated had concocted a scheme which brought about the Caraquet troubles and that it was done for the express purpose of getting the poor French people of that district in the meshes of the law."

Burns also charged that some members of the Orange Lodge "lately established in Chatham" had gone to Caraquet with rifles and pistols "and committed breaches of the peace and thereby exasperated the people." Such groups were "dangerous to the best interests of the community."

The member for Restigouche, Alex McKenzie, made this eloquent plea:

---

[3] *Debates*, March 3, 1875.

Can I make enemies of my neighbours because Sir Phelim O'Neil massacred Protestants in Ireland? Let by-gones be by-gones. This free country acted no part in them. Free then it should be from British religious prejudices. Here on Canada's free soil persecuted and persecutors meet on equal terms ... Sink the past, then, and let all unite to be Canadians first ... We are not here to legislate as Catholics or Protestants, but as New Brunswickers, and assist the approach of that time when there will be "on earth peace and goodwill towards men."[4]

The house majority ignored McKenzie's plea. It defeated Burn's motion for a three-month postponement and passed the Orange Bill 25 votes to ten.

Like a dog worrying a bone, the Government members were determined to go at the Caraquet affair. On April 8, 1875, William Kelly of Chatham introduced a bill to establish a police force and a lock-up in Caraquet. It was needed, he argued, because the Acadian community was 40 miles from the nearest jail in Bathurst. Kelly also tabled two petitions in favour of his bill signed by "persons who pay a large amount of the taxation of the district." Théotime Blanchard tabled an opposing petition signed by 1,500 citizens. The Kelly bill passed easily.[5]

The next day, the Provincial Secretary, John Fraser, told the House that $10,000 had been needed in supplementary estimates to cover the cost of quelling the Caraquet riots. Legally, he said the county of Gloucester should pay, but "the Government felt it would perhaps fall too heavily on it and concluded it should be a provincial charge for the present."

Théotime Blanchard now had the floor. He wanted to say "a few words in defence of what was called the Rioters of Caraquet."

The riot act had never been read and he saw no reason for "the calling of the Prussian Army to Caraquet by the Bismarcks and

---

[4] *Debates,* March 3, 1875.
[5] *Debates,* April 8, 1875.

Kaisers of Gloucester." The whole affair had been caused by an attempt to fasten the school tax on the people against their wishes "at the bid of a few" led by "a gentleman who a few years ago, sitting at the priest's pew in the chapel at Caraquet, advised the people not to pay the school tax." Blanchard concluded that if that gentleman had stuck to that policy, there would have been no trouble.

Even as he spoke, nine of his fellow townsmen were languishing in their Bathurst jail cells. Outside, a small band of supporters led by Pierre-Amand Landry and Kennedy Burns worked to arrange their legal defence. A prominent Saint John lawyer, S.R. Thompson, would be their attorney and the bilingual Landry would act as his assistant. Heading a fund-raising campaign was Pascal Poirier, a future senator, who was aided by Gloucester's Liberal Member of Parliament, T.W. Anglin, now Speaker of the House of Commons.

At the same time, readers of Anglin's *Morning Freeman* were kept informed about government attempts to pack the Bathurst jury. In its September 11 issue (which began with Anglin's editorial on Montréal's Guibord affair) the *Freeman* noted that only four of the 23 names on the selecton list for the grand jury were Roman Catholic.[6] It also pointed out that, of the Catholics named for possible jury duty, two were relatives of the Hon. Robert Young and the others were "partisans of Mr. Young in other matters." The defence tried unsuccessfully to throw out the grand jury indictment because five of the jury members were close relatives of constables involved in the riot. At the end of September, the final jury included three Protestants, seven French and two Irish Catholics.

From the start of the proceedings, the defence managed to place the King government on trial. Defence attorney Thompson's questions to Robert Young were often ruled out of order, but the "King of Caraquet" rarely budged from his seat beside the Crown Attorney. Close by was Premier King, acting in his capacity of Attorney-General, who often directed the prosecution.

[6] Saint John *Morning Freeman*, September 11, 1875.

The entire testimony was printed verbatim each day by the *Freeman*. Extensive coverage was also given by *Le Moniteur Acadien* while central Canadian newspapers, including the French press in Montréal and Québec City, carried lengthy reports. Montréal's influential *La Minerve* had one editorial written by Pascal Poirier, who was helping the defence committee's fund-raising drive in Montréal and Ottawa. From the present perspective, the whole effort could have been a dress rehearsal for the Liberal defence on behalf of Louis Riel ten years later.

Early December, 1875, brought the expected verdict: guilty of wilful murder, with recommendation for mercy. Judge John Allen was not prepared to pass sentence on Joseph Chiasson, the first Acadian to stand trial. With the defence counsel's agreement, he arranged that if the other eight agreed to plead guilty to manslaughter, Judge Allen would send Chiasson's case to the Supreme Court for a ruling. The following June, their Lordships, who now included Judge Allen, concluded that several procedural errors had been made at Chiasson's trial. They recommended the charges be dismissed.

What a victory! Justice had been done! What celebrations for the joyful fishermen and their families in Caraquet! It was a great day for other Acadians too — people like Pierre-Amand Landry and Pascal Poirier, on the threshold of illustrious public careers. In a short time, Landry would be again back in the legislature while Poirier would soon be named Senator at the age of thirty-two.

After the celebrations, the Acadians along the Caraquet coast woke up to a continuing reality: Robert Young's economic clout was as strong as ever. He and the other English bosses would still set fish prices. Acadian fishermen remained in their debt.

They would tell their grandchildren how Louis Mailloux died, but the sad events of that cold January 1875 would not be acknowledged officially for another hundred years. In 1972, a new school complex in Caraquet would be called Polyvalente Louis Mailloux.

Mailloux's death had not been in vain. The school system for French and Catholic New Brunswickers changed significantly within months. During the summer of 1875, Premier King and his cabinet agreed to several concessions requested by Bishops Sweeney and Rodgers.

The state school system would remain, but in Catholic areas the teachers could be nuns and brothers dressed in their traditional religious habits. The English in Fredericton would have the final say on textbooks, but promised to remove all anti-Catholic biases. Buildings such as convents could be leased to the public school system and no restrictions on their use would be made after school hours.[7]

The storm was over — for now. The new secular school system was firmly in place, maintained by local taxes. George King's premiership would end in 1878, but his successors would continue to be English Protestants for another forty-five years.

This perpetuating English elite largely failed to note that the old order was changing. More and more young French New Brunswickers were graduating along with Irish Catholics from the little Collège Saint-Joseph at Memramcook. Most would return to their home parishes as priests, lawyers, teachers — even a few doctors and dentists.

This group soon would spearhead a drive for more recognition of the French fact. It would be a drive organized and directed by the college and *Le Moniteur Acadien*. It would take time, but time — and patience — these Acadians had.

Young English New Brunswickers were on the move too, — most succumbing to the lure of good jobs in the new factory towns of New England, and the many opportunities offered by Montréal and Toronto. The youth of French New Brunswick were leaving too, but for every one joining this exodus, several more stayed behind to carve out new homesteads along the coastal roads, in the settlement tracts being opened in Gloucester,

---

[7] The details of *The Compromise*, as it became known, were not made public until J.J. Fraser investigated the Bathurst Affair in 1896. [See Chapter 8]. See also K.F.C. MacNaughton, *The Development of the theory and practice of education in New Brunswick 1784-1900* (Fredericton, 1947.)

Restigouche, Kent and Madawaska. Settlement: that was how to create a new Acadia.

# FIVE

## CLAIMING THEIR BIRTHRIGHT: 1866-1875

Getting farmland in post-Confederation New Brunswick was a big obstacle course for both French and English. Those who succeeded needed great determination to make up for minimal government aid. What they wanted most were roads. Instead, they usually had a choice to work as cheap labour building the politicians' railroads or filling the lumber barons' isolated camps.

How much good farmland was there in New Brunswick? The most intensive study had been done in 1849 by a three-member team led by Professor James F.W. Johnston of Britain's Royal Agricultural Society. Like many later efforts, this study told New Brunswickers things they already knew. And it was very optimistic.

The best farmland was along the Saint John River. The poorest covered much of the eastern counties, home of the Acadians. The professor saw some hope for five million acres in Kent, Westmorland and Gloucester. Once cleared of hemlock and other softwoods, he thought they might "prove productive when submitted fairly to the plough." His optimistic conclusion: New Brunswick's potential farmland could grow enough food for 3.5 million people, an estimate one of his fellow commissioners thought too high.[1]

---

[1] J.F.W. Johnston *Report on the Agricultural Capabilities of the Province of New Brunswick* (Fredericton, 1850), p. 25.

As soon as the Confederation furor had died down, New Brunswick's legislators started up-dating land settlement regulations. Until 1866, citizens could get crown land either by paying cash or by promising to clear so much a year. Many, with the silent backing of lumber mill owners, moved into the virgin forests, where they cut the most accessible and largest trees. Then they left for Upper Canada, New England or even the far west.

A few new areas opened in the late 1860s managed to hold most of their settlers. One was a 10,000-acre tract between Caraquet and Pokemouche. Surveyed in 1866, it laid out scores of 100-acre lots around the Paquetville area.

Two years later, the secretary of the Board of Agriculture asked the deputy surveyors about the suitability of land in their areas. How many farmers were actually taking up lots?

James Battimer referred to 1,000 acres in the parish of Beresford north of Bathurst which he said was "mostly occupied by squatters and others." He commented favourably on two other surveyed tracts yet didn't mention the largest in his jurisdiction: Paquetville was rapidly becoming the most successful new settlement in the entire province.

Battimer and the two other deputy-surveyors for Gloucester were English and resided either in or near Bathurst. Given the cultural biases of their day, they probably had little contact with what the French were doing in the lower part of their county. Or perhaps they preferred to ignore them.

A report from Northumberland did mention the Paquetville tract, but in rather negative terms. The people "chiefly follow the cod-fishing and do not wish to move away from the sea-shore; therefore our best land is still a wilderness."[2]

Surveyor Douglas of Buctouche noted in his report that the area closer to Moncton had been surveyed in 1852 and was now well-supplied with roads. It was nearly all filled, especially a 20,000-acre tract along the Buctouche river. The new settlers filling up the first and second tiers on each side of the river were either from Prince Edward Island or Westmorland County.

[2] *Journals of the Legislative Assembly of New Brunswick, 1869*, Report of the Board of Agriculture, Appendix V, pp. 117-125

Douglas reported that the "French settlers that come here from the Island are rather of a poor class. A good many of them are not able to pay for their petition, and still they go on and settle for a short time on a lot, make a clearing and then sell out to another." He noted that English settlers avoided the area "because it is impossible to get an English school."

Douglas thought the new settlement act recently passed by the legislature would work "if the parties taking land under it would perform the labour." This they seemed reluctant to do.

"After they pay one instalment on the roads, they slacken up and it is almost impossible to get them to work again. They think then that they have got a hold of the lot, and Government will not trouble them."

The lack of roads posed a major deterrent for would-be settlers in northwestern New Brunswick. By 1868, the upper sections of Victoria were attracting Québécois, but as Charles Beckwith noted in his report for that year, they rarely stayed. Finding no roads, they "pass on into the State of Maine where they find roads and lots ready to choose — located and survey paid for by the State." He thought they would have preferred to settle in New Brunswick, "as they prefer our laws, but have not the means to pay for the survey."

Beckwith's French counterpart, F.A. Têtu of Edmundston, was even more critical. Noting that a few tracts had been surveyed years earlier, Têtu said that "those hundred acre lots have been divided and subdivided into fourths and even eighths of 100-acres to meet the home increase of our population."

> But yesterday, four French families inquired from me if I had from the Government any good lots to sell. My answer was, "There are no surveyed lots, but you will get some if you will apply first, and then wait till the spring to have your lots surveyed." What had they to do till then? The ice on the river is very strong just now. They went across and will find plenty of lots in the back settlements of Madawaska Plantation.

Têtu said that by such "an injudicious system of administering the public lands, we have lost ... during the last fifteen years no less than eight hundred French immigrants with their families, cattle, horses and what generally accompanies the poor immigrant."

Têtu's blunt comments got results. By 1869, with a larger budget, he was able to survey 206 lots "of fine settlement land" in the parishes of St. Francis and St. Basil. He reported that 173 of these lots had been occupied by "Canadian Frenchmen" and others who had returned from Maine.

They were probably taking advantage of a new act passed in March 1868. It enabled a settler "to obtain land as it were, *free*, for the merely nominal price of twenty cents per acre cash, or thirty cents by labour, if applied to the making of roads in his immediate neighbourhood for his own advantage."

In his annual report for 1869, Surveyor-General Flewelling noted that his department had issued three times as many land grants as the previous six-year average of 348. Besides the great activity reported by deputy-surveyor Têtu in the northwest, a land rush had started in Kent and Northumberland. All told, 150,000 acres had been taken up under the new legislation.

Annual receipts for crown land sold at public auction showed that some Acadians and Québécois were involved, but the vast majority got title by working on the roads. It was the English who had the cash to buy their land.

In the period 1866-1872, a total of 631 English New Brunswickers bought 129,215 acres, compared to 59 French who took up 938 acres. Both groups preferred to pledge their labour. In this same period, 1,121 took up crown land in the English counties with promises to work on the roads.[3]

In the mixed counties of Gloucester, Kent, Northumberland, Restigouche, Victoria and Westmorland, a total of 648 French citizens got acreage using the labour clause. In Victoria, which still included what would soon become Madawaska, 496 French-speaking settlers took up land, compared to 193 English.

All this settlement activity seemed to go on in spite of what the politicians wanted. Their spending priorities continued to be

---

[3] These figures are based on the author's analysis of the annual listings of grants given by the Surveyor-General in each of the years noted.

railroads; at least they didn't see much need to spend public funds to entice immigrants to come to New Brunswick.

When the Provincial Secretary, John Beckwith, proposed in 1870 that the immigration allotment be increased by $1,000, to the princely sum of $4,000, he was reminded that the previous year's money had not been spent.[4] Beckwith's motive might have stemmed from the fact he was also manager of the New Brunswick and Nova Scotia Land Company, a speculative firm organized to sell colonial lands especially in York County. Conflict of interest was rarely an issue back then. Most of Beckwith's colleagues in the legislature, notably those holding cabinet positons, were also directors of railroad companies. Still, they refused to support his motion: it was defeated. The 1870-71 immigration allocation remained at $3,000.

The following year, New Brunswick's actual spending for immigration reached a record low. Circulars and a report cost $572; another $147 went to direct settlement aid to bring the annual total to $715. Of course, Ottawa continued to pay most of the costs for New Brunswick's immigration effort, by maintaining an official in London who was supposed to act for both levels of government.

Judging by the sporadic press reports, native-born New Brunswickers were on the move, *leaving* the province. The exact number will never be known, but Victoria County seemed to provide an exception to this exodus. A total of 44,848 acres were taken up there from 1870-1872 and, of the 509 occupying lots under the Act to Facilitate Settlement, 396 were French, mostly from Québec.

The Surveyor-General noted this trend in his annual report for 1871. He also commissioned a special study of Victoria, probably to prepare the way for the creation of Madawaska County.

"Notwithstanding the disadvantages of its position," the report noted, Victoria County's population had increased "over fifty percent in the last decade." This was a more rapid rise than in

---

[4] *Synoptic Reports of the Debates of the Legislative Assembly of New Brunswick, 1870*, March 24. Hereafter *Debates*.

any other part of the province and was four times the average for the new Dominion of Canada.

The greatest barrier to further settlement was still the lack of good roads. As for railways, the report predicted that "much of the land to be granted to the Rivière du Loup Railway company will be taken from this County." As a result, the New Brunswick government would lose control of some of the best settling districts in the province.

Even though this rail line was not completed until 1889, work on the New Brunswick section northeast of Edmundston was well underway by 1872. At the same time, the New Brunswick Railway, more commonly referred to as the Gibson line, after its principal owner Alexander "Boss" Gibson, was approaching Edmundston from the south. In January, 1874, the government engineer reporting on its progress, so that it could comply with the generous legislative grants, said that 76 1/2 miles had been completed. This entitled the line's promoters to receive 765,000 acres of land!

Railway demands for land grants were only part of the reason for large-scale government surveys. A Free Grant Land Act similar to the 1872 Dominion Land Act was passsed by the New Brunswick legislature that same year. It brought the province into line with the land policies of Ontario and Québec.

Under this new act's terms, "ten or more young men, or heads of families, may procure homes on tracts of land selected by themselves or the Government through which roads are made for them free." Married men would get a free grant of 200 acres and "when they chop 2 acres, $15 are given and $15 more when a log or other house is built."[5]

Meanwhile, the New Brunswick government, largely through the efforts of Thomas Potts, the Dominion Land Agent in London, was actively encouraging a group of Danish citizens to settle in Victoria County.

It may have been pure coincidence that these Protestant people were being enticed to come to a province currently in the throes

---

[5] *Journals of the Legislative Council of New Brunswick 1873*, Report of the Surveyor-General, iv.

of a religious tug-of-war over the recently-passed Common Schools Act. It also could have been a deliberate attempt to stop Québec settlers from moving any further south into New Brunswick settlement lands. Whatever its motives, the predominantly English and Protestant Legislative Assembly bent over backwards to help these Danes.[6]

Along with the usual free land and access roads, they got temporary housing and the promise of railroad and other jobs to help them through their first years. The New Brunswick government spent $10,656 on their passage and another $2,400 for building and furnishing their houses. For the fiscal year 1872, the government spent a total of $20,000 on immigration — roughly seven times the amount spent two years earlier. By 1874, this expenditure had reached $61,000, or $49,466 more than had been budgetted.

In May 10, 1873, nearly 600 natives of Kincardinshire and Aberdeenshire in Scotland arrived in Saint John. Like the Danes, they would settle in Victoria County and would soon establish communities named after those they had left behind.

In several legislative debates the following year, the tiny Opposition, composed of five French and/or Irish Liberal members, expressed its growing concern over the government's immigration policies. On February 27, 1874, Théotime Blanchard of Caraquet moved that certain government departments publish their reports in French. Noting that the province now had 45,000 French citizens, he claimed that "the treatment they received at the hands of the Government was a lesson to them." He predicted that the government would soon feel the "increasing power of his people."

In the debate that followed, the Attorney-General said he had been informed that all French citizens could read English. Not so replied Henry O'Leary, recently elected in Kent as an anti-school bill member. He also told the House that the French

---

[6] *Journals of the Legislative Council 1873*, Report of the Surveyor-General. A good running account of the early progress of the New Denmark settlement is found in the *Reports of Free Grants Commissioners, 1873-1878*.

settlers in one Kent parish had to build over thirty miles of roads and a large bridge "and they have not been given one cent by the Government towards either."

The Blanchard motion was easily defeated but the fiery Caraquet member was soon pressing the attack from another angle. Two weeks later, he zeroed in on his neighbour and political foe the Hon. Robert Young, claiming that the wealthy member had never accounted for $3,000 supposedly spent on Caraquet area roads. Not only that, Blanchard charged that after Acadians had done the work on roads around Paquetville, they were told that instead of cash from Fredericton they would get credit to buy their supplies from Young's stores. Blanchard referred to them as "government stores" and said it was part of a system that "bore hard on the people."[7]

Four days later, Blanchard was on his feet once again. The Surveyor-General had just admitted that 45 Scots had moved on to the American West. So had several Danes who had been "injudiciously selected." Did the government intend to bring out immigrants from France? asked Blanchard. Definitely not; the government had made its plans for 1874 and had no more money for "any new undertakings."

Lack of ready cash did not stop this government from spending. In the fiscal year 1874-75, it went over its immigration budget by nearly $50,000 — a huge amount for that day. It probably took what it needed from Education, which had been underspent by $55,000.

By 1875, New Brunswick, along with the rest of the young country, was mired in a worldwide depression. During the budget debate for that year, Provincial-Secretary John Fraser criticized Ottawa for ending its $10,000 immigration subsidy "without due notice." The federal government had also refused to pay more than $24,000 subsidy to the Eastern Railway Extension, which had under-estimated its costs by 25-33 percent.

Many ordinary New Brunswickers continued to find their solution by leaving. A special survey of the farming lands appendixed to the 1877 report of the Secretary of the Board of

[7] *Debates*, March 14, 1875.

Agriculture noted that "among the Acadian French ... there are many young men who leave their own country, either for the West or for the manufacturing towns of the East."[8]

This report was signed with a "J", indicating it probably had been written by Edward Jack, a deputy-surveyor in the Crown Lands Department who also wrote promotion articles for the railroad developers, especially "Boss" Gibson.

"Our French fellow citizens," claimed Jack's report, "are prudent and economical, having but few wants and these easily satisfied. The forest is to them what the city is to the merchant or manufacturer, and although they are indifferent farmers, they cannot be excelled as bold and economic forest pioneers." He concluded his survey with a rosy picture of northwestern New Brunswick once Gibson's New Brunswick Railway was completed.

This was accomplished in October 1878 and the following May Edward Jack wrote a feature article for the Saint John *Daily Telegraph* on the inaugural trip. After the predictable glowing paragraphs on the scenery and the region's economic potential, he gave his readers the standard English Canadian view of the simple and pure life enjoyed by *les habitants*:

> The Madawaska Acadian French have been living for more than a century remote from the world, with scarcely any means of communication with a market and with but indifferent opportunities of education. They are, therefore, a backward people, content to pursue the methods of agriculture employed by their fathers and with but little taste for modern innovations.[9]

As for what they thought of the new railway, Jack concluded that if it had "depended on the aid or even the goodwill of the French inhabitants, it would never have been constructed." In

---

[8] *Journals of the Legislative Council, 1878.* Appendix to Report of Secretary to the Board of Agriculture. See also *Public Archives of New Brunswick*, microfilm #130 (Clippings collected by David Jack entitled "Mainly about Railways", by Edward Jack. Hereafter *Jack.*

[9] *Jack.*

fact, most of them had been "openly hostile to this attempt to introduce the arts of civilization amongst them, and some of them went so far as to attempt to oppose the building of the line by forcible means."

In 1880, Edward Jack toured Northumberland and Kent counties and reported that most of the settlers there had come from the sea coast or from Prince Edward Island. He repeated his view that the French were "good persons to clear land" but were not good farmers. "They do not seem to understand the necessity of restoring to the soil that which is taken from it by the crops."[10]

Jack would have learned more about the Acadians if he had talked with the Revs. Joseph Ouellet of Buctouche and F.X. Joseph Michaud of nearby Sainte Marie. They were president and secretary-treasurer of the Société agricole de Sainte Marie and along with their pastoral duties they ran their own farms. These Acadian priests were among the first to take advantage of government-purchased breeding stock. They had also been spreading their land with mud from the nearby mussel beds — obviously they were aware of its uses as a fertilizer.

In their society's report of 1882, sent to the provincial Board of Agriculture in Fredericton, Fathers Ouellet and Michaud had criticized their fellow Acadians for their poor attitude toward their profession and urged them to follow the example of their more resourceful ancestors. This same report was the first one published by the Board in French.[11]

Edward Jack also knew a few things about soils. He stated bluntly in his 1880 report that "from Welford Station to the settlement at Carleton Station [in Kent County], the land on the west side of the Intercolonial Railway is in general unfit for farming purposes." Referring to the 1850 survey of the area done by the Johnston Commission, Jack concluded that if one used Johnston's yardstick of fertility — the quantity of hay a section of land could produce — the soil in this area was "very generally

---

[10] *Journals of the Legislative Council 1880, Report of Secretary to Board of Agriculture.*
[11] *Journals of the Legislative Council 1885.*

of inferior quality." Yet settlers "will continue to locate themselves upon it."

What these Acadians were after was the bark of the hemlock tree. It was used by the tanning industry and was in great demand by American buyers. With the opening of the Intercolonial Railway in 1876, these Americans saw the chance to broaden their supply lines. The Acadian settlers eagerly complied, but their haphazard method of harvesting left the landscape scarred with rotting hemlock trunks. It also caused a rash of forest fires.

Edward Jack urged the government to "sell and dispose of these hemlock and inferior settling lands to the highest bidder, at public auction, rather than give them away." He believed such a cash purchaser (a railway developer perhaps?) would conserve the land and be more careful of fires than these "reckless settlers who consider these trees but waste products of the soil and only there for the purpose of being cut down and burnt."

Jack's superiors in Fredericton ignored his suggestions. They seemed pleased that the land was being settled. In 1882, members of the legislature were told that nearly all the lots in the Acadiaville block in northeastern Kent were occupied. "Some settlers left for other parts, but these lots were at once taken by other and better settlers who will improve the settlement."

From nearby Northumberland, Free Grant Commissioner Doolan reported that Rogersville was "improving rapidly" while in Gloucester "the opening of the rich silver and lead mine within two miles" of the new settlement of Robertville had "created a new market for the produce raised" by the settlers. It also had given them chances for jobs.

Reading between the lines of these annual reports, it seems that most New Brunswickers, English as well as French, were moving either to the nearest urban centre or were quitting the province altogether. Yet, in some areas, the land rush continued.

One report noted that those taking up lots in the new settlement of Canoose in Charlotte County were men "chiefly from the lumber mills who have found steady employment with good wages at Milltown. Therefore, little attention has been paid to their new farms during season."

Twelve settlers had arrived in Kintore, Victoria County, but "some have left the place." Eighty-one new immigrants were reported in New Denmark but for a time "the western fever raged badly: two families and a few young men were lured away."

*Le Moniteur Acadien,* provided more evidence of the restless population. A November 1882 issue noted the return of fifty Acadians who had worked in the United States during the summer.[12]

The secretary of the Kingston [Rexton] Agricultural Society reported that "a migration to a small extent" had taken place from his Kent County parish. "Some of the farmers, principally among the French residents, becoming discontented with their "paternal acres" had sold out. Most had moved to the new districts of Acadiaville and Rogersville "near the Inter-Colonial Railway, where besides obtaining a good-sized wilderness farm *gratis* under the Free Grants Act, they are tempted by prospects of money to be made in picking hemlock bark, getting out railway ties and cutting and hauling saw logs."

By the spring of 1885, the hemlock bark bonanza was over. The *Moncton Transcript* of May 6 reported that 350 families in the Rogersville area were in "an emergency state of destitution." The American bark buyers, faced with a glutted market, had refused to pay the settlers for 5,000 cords of bark "now stacked in the settlement." The tone of the report implied that they should not have neglected their farms to collect bark.

Later stories included charity appeals for these unfortunate victims of distant market fluctuations. On May 21, Saint John citizens held a fund-raising drive, while in Rogersville, the parish priest, Father Marcel-François Richard, negotiated two bank loans totalling $1800 to relieve the suffering of his people. Farther south in Welford, a large bark extract factory remained closed throughout the summer of 1885.[13]

New railroad construction that year helped to ease the situation. Track-laying on the St. Louis branch of the Kent-Northern line began July 7, while the first sod for its rival, the Moncton-

[12] *Le Moniteur Acadien* November 23, 1882.
[13] Moncton *Transcript*, May 6, May 22, July 8, 1885.

Buctouche Railway, was turned November 5. Soon, a veritable army of labourers began streaming out of their frontier homes to build these and other government-subsidized rail lines.

The short-term results provided desperately-needed cash for these would-be and sometime farmers. Over the longer run, these and similar activities would help hundreds of families stay in rural surroundings for a generation or more.

After the decline in railway construction, scores of small saw mills and lobster canning plants provided the economic underpinnings for much of eastern New Brunswick. In the early years of the twentieth century, the construction of giant pulp and paper mills at Bathurst and Dalhousie created new jobs.

For those living along the sea coast, fishing remained the mainstay.

Such varied activities kept up the facade of rural life, even though these people, especially the Acadians, were grossly under paid and often crassly exploited. Except for the rich farmlands of the upper Saint John River valley and along the banks of the rivers flowing into the Northumberland Strait, New Brunswick Acadians were unable to develop an agricultural economy. More importantly, they clung tenaciously to their "paternal acres" and even as more and more of their sons and daughters moved to nearby villages and expanding centres like Moncton, they remained rooted in their Acadian and Catholic heritage.

In so doing, they enabled a new generation of leaders to create an Acadian renaissance.

# SIX

# The Fight for a French Diocese: 1870-1881

The emerging group of Acadian leaders had been on a collision course with their Irish bishops since Confederation. The big issue was language. The Acadians wanted their own French-speaking diocese and one of their own people as bishop. The Irish-dominated Catholic leaders refused to tolerate such ideas. What made the clash so bitter and so prolonged was the longevity of both Bishop Rogers in Chatham and Sweeney in Saint John.

Consecrated in 1860, both men remained in their positions until the twentieth century. Although each could converse in French (Bishop Rogers spoke it fluently) neither would use it when communicating with Acadians. For them, the new nation of Canada was English-speaking.

Throughout their long reigns, these powerful personalities were closely supported by a growing number of Irish businessmen and politicians. Westmorland had the Friels and the McSweeneys, Kent the O'Learys and the McInerneys. In Northumberland, the O'Briens and Creaghans were gaining commercial prominence, while in Gloucester the Byrnes and McManus families were firmly established in Bathurst.

Most of them sent their sons to bilingual Catholic colleges. These young Irish came through these institutions with two things intact: their Catholic religion and their first language, English. Many of them proved excellent students.

A glance through the names of the academic prize-winners of the Class of 1889, Collège Saint-Joseph at Memramcook, shows that James Friel and E.A. Reilly took most of the honours. Other prominent names were Ed J. Byrne, W.O. McInerney and Daniel Gallagher.[1] Most were staunch Liberals, the party favoured as well by more and more Acadians, especially after Louis Riel's execution in 1885 and the advent of young Wilfrid Laurier as the national party leader in 1887.

While law and politics were attracting these young New Brunswick Irish, their Acadian contemporaries (and in many cases their former classmates) often took religious orders. Why? For one thing, a clerical career was more attainable. For another, the Catholic way and the French language were the twin pillars of emerging Acadian society. Together they provided Acadian leaders with a common goal: New Brunswick's first French diocese. It was an objective not easily achieved. Bishop Rogers in particular fought against it with all his influence and skills. Despite mounting Acadian pressure this doughty bishop held out for forty years.

Like the military battles of old, this one did not involve great numbers of people. Most Acadians watched from the sidelines, allowing themselves to be dragged in only when their schools and local parishes were caught in the middle. But the outcome of this battle would have a profound effect on French New Brunswickers.

The shock-troops in this prolonged struggle were New Brunswick-born and usually Memramcook-trained priests and teachers. They were becoming politicized by what they read in *Le Moniteur Acadien* and more culturally-militant publications from Québec. They identified with the historical and geneological articles sent to *Le Moniteur* by Pascal Poirier in Ottawa. They noted and discussed the occasional piece boosting the Acadian cause by Rameau de Saint-Père in Paris.

Most ordinary Acadians were too busy making a living to bother much about things. Many were illiterate and few had the time and money to subscribe to *Le Moniteur Acadien*. Nevertheless, through the pulpit and increasingly in the classroom, they and their children began hearing about these cultural issues. The

[1] *Le Moniteur Acadien,* July 9, 1889

details may have escaped them, but one thing was obvious: their new core of leaders had taken on their Irish bishop.

These leaders included a growing number of young Acadian doctors and lawyers, as well as priests and teachers. But one figure emerged who rightly earned his unofficial title: "The Father of Modern Acadia."[2]

Marcel-François Richard was a typical New Brunswick Acadian. His ancestors arrived from France in 1649. When the British tried to expell all Acadians in 1755, the Richards were among those who escaped by fleeing north into what soon would become New Brunswick. His grandfather Joseph Richard helped found St. Louis-de-Kent near the mouth of the Kouchibouquac river a few miles north of Richibucto. He arrived there in 1798. His son Pierre-Luc established a homestead nearby, shortly after marrying Marie-Tharsile Barriault, who bore him ten children.[3] Marcel, the youngest, was born in 1847 and when he proved to be an apt student he was encouraged to enter the priesthood. He completed his local schooling in 1860, four years before the opening of Le Collège Saint Joseph in Memramcook. The nearest French college for training priests was in Québec — too far away and too expensive an undertaking for the Richards to consider.

Instead, they enrolled thirteen-year-old Marcel in St. Dunstan's College, an English institution at Charlottetown, where he emerged as a bilingual graduate in 1867. Somehow, funds were found to send him to Le Grand Seminaire in Montréal, where he met other Acadian novitiates. One of them, Stanislas-Joseph Doucet of Gloucester County, would become his life-long friend and ally in their common struggle to "Acadienize" their Church in New Brunswick.

---

[2] Emery LeBlanc, *Les Acadiens: La Tentative de génocide d'un peuple* (Ottawa, 1963), p. 31.

[3] The definitive study of Father Richard is Camille-Antonio Doucet's *Une Étoile s'est levée en Acadie: Marcel-François Richard* (Ottawa 1973). Father Doucet is a member of the Trappist Order, which established a branch in Rogersville with the encouragement of Father Richard. See Chapter I of Doucet's study for details of Richard's life. Hereafter *Doucet*.

Marcel-François Richard was ordained in July, 1870, by Msgr. Peter McIntyre, Bishop of Charlottetown, who was acting in place of Bishop Rogers, absent in Rome attending the Vatican Council.

The young priest was assigned to his home parish as assistant to the curé, Father Hugh McGuirk.

What should have been an exciting and pleasant experience for young Marcel proved just the opposite. Shortly after settling in, he noticed the strange behaviour of his superior and realized that Father McGuirk was suffering a severe mental breakdown. When he did not improve, Bishop Rogers named Father Richard curé of St. Louis parish.[4]

That should have ended the affair, but during his temporary recoveries Father McGuirk threatened the new priest and often interrupted the mass. At one point he locked himself inside the church. In January, 1871, Bishop Rogers told Father Richard that for his own protection he might have to resort to civil law and the office of the local magistrate.

When the tension and confusion continued, Father Richard sought the advice of the local justice of the peace. He was told Bishop Roger had to be present before a court order could be issued declaring Father McGuirk insane. Fearing for his personal safety, Richard got the English-speaking sheriff of Richibucto to issue a warrant to arrest Father McGuirk as an "irresponsible" citizen.

At this point, McGuirk regained his sanity once again and convinced the court officials that his young assistant was plotting against him. Suddenly, the roles were reversed. McGuirk hired as his lawyer a prominent Protestant Conservative politician, C.J. Sayer, and accused Father Richard of defamation.

In the 1870s, religious issues and controversies seemed to mesmerize the ordinary citizens. This was made to order, especially for rabidly partisan newspapers like the Moncton *Times*, which quickly put its editorial weight behind the McGuirk cause. Bishop Rogers countered with a brochure he called "A Statement of the Case McGuirk versus Richard." He challenged McGuirk's

---

[4] *Doucet*, chapters II and III for details of "l'affaire McGuirk."

attempt to use a 1862 provincial statute to argue that the church was legally his because he had built it.

The case dragged on for months and finally in June, 1874, it was decided against Father Richard. The court ordered him to pay McGuirk $1200 in damages plus another $500 in legal fees. Richard refused to consider paying the lawyers — a stand that brought a quick response.

While passing through Moncton, the young priest was arrested and taken to the county jail in Dorchester. That happened to be the home town of Acadian champion Pierre-Amand Landry. He had little trouble persuading Westmorland's federal Member of Parliament, Albert J. Smith, the Dominion Minister of Fisheries, to put up Father Richard's bail.

Back in St. Louis, irate parishioners, already upset over the Commons Schools question, quickly raised the sum owing for legal costs. Two citizens, Jacques Vautour and Michel LeBlanc, won the privilege of presenting the money to the judge in Moncton. Their beloved priest was soon free and on his way home.

From Richibucto to St.Louis, reported a triumphant editorial in *Le Moniteur Acadien*, there was a "continuous ovation."[5] As for the unfortunate McGuirk, he would spend the next fifteen years in the provincial hospital in Saint John.

Once back at his parish duties, Father Richard wrote often to Bishop Rogers, detailing his varied activities. One week he described how he convinced some idle farmers to build a new hay barn, a task they completed in two days. Another time, he travelled to the Micmac reserve of Big Cove on the Richibucto river to administer to the needs of this enclave of Catholic native people.

In 1874, largely through Father Richard's efforts, the small Académie Saint-Louis opened its doors as a bilingual school. Making no secret of his goal to create a rival to Collège Saint-Joseph in Memramcook, Richard had managed to secure a large piece of property and hired several lay professors.

[5] *Doucet*, p. 43

In 1875, Father Eugène-Raymond Biron had arrived from France to assume the directorship of the Memramcook institution. A year later he joined the staff at St. Louis. Biron, a member of a wealthy aristocratic family, had been converted to the Acadian cause by Rameau de Saint-Père. He spoke almost no English, which might explain his apparent lack of sympathy for anglophone students at Memramcook.

"Unfortunately, the Acadians are poor," Biron wrote to Rameau shortly after his arrival in August, 1875. "The English, Americans and Irish are wealthier" and in his opinion were given preferred treatment at the college.[6] He decided to accept the St. Louis position after he had heard Placide Gaudet, a friend of the young parish priest, give a glowing account of the possibilities of the new Kent County school.

Biron found things at St. Louis in a state of confusion but despite the presence of some English students, he noted that the predominant language was French. In December, 1879, he wrote Rameau of the possibility of the Jesuits seeking a place in New Brunswick. This order, renowned for its teaching tradition and feared for its lobbying skills, had been forced to leave France because of the rising Gallican or nationalist tone of the Church there.

Bishop Rogers, equally aware of the Jesuits' situation, had offered them a choice of four places in New Brunswick to establish their own school or take over an existing institution. He had suggested Petit-Rocher, Caraquet, Madawaska or St.Louis.

Father Richard apparently wanted the Jesuits to choose St. Louis, but Biron was less enthusiastic. "If they come to these provinces," he wrote to Rameau, "they would make a good college but it would not be a college for the Acadians."[7]

The Jesuits finally chose an English-speaking college in Charlottetown, where Bishop Peter McIntyre reigned. The decision sent Bishop Rogers looking for another teaching order, one that

---

[6] *Doucet*, p. 91. [The Biron correspondence is at the Centre d'Étude Acadiennes de l'Université de Moncton. See note 1, p. 89.]

[7] *Doucet*, p. 43.

might aid St. Michael's College, an English-speaking institution he had recently established in Chatham.

The existence of two colleges, one primarily to serve English students, the other just thirty miles southward for the French, might promote bilingualism. As Bishop Rogers wrote later in his memoirs, he "wished all our future priests, like those of the past, and our educated men, to know both languages." He thought such linguistic skills essential if they were to succeed professionally "in the mixed population of our diocese."[8]

A major problem was finding enough money to support the growing number of educational institutions sprouting up like mushrooms, especially in Acadian communities. Parishioners showed great ingenuity at fund-raising, as well they might: they often had to support new churches as well as new schools.

Throughout the economically depressed 1870's, *Le Moniteur Acadien* carried numerous reports of special collections and bazaars. One Sunday in October, 1873, a lottery organized at Grand Anse, a coastal community midway between Bathurst and Caraquet, offered as prizes a horse, a cow, a wagon, a gold watch, a lace handkerchief and a rifle. This particular bazaar brought in $1418.50, no small sum in those days.[9] In Moncton, a church picnic featured a beauty contest. Often the students' band from Collège Saint-Joseph was on hand at these affairs to provide music as well as publicity for their struggling institution.

Another controversy was developing on the political scene that had strong overtones of the stresses between French and Irish Catholics. It grew out of an 1877 by-election caused when T.W. Anglin, the Liberal member of Parliament for Gloucester, was voted out as Speaker of the House of Commons and had to seek re-election. As he had done in the past, Anglin sought and received the personal support of Bishop Rogers, who nevertheless warned that he could not give his public endorsement. The bishop no doubt was sensitive to the growing opposition to clerical influence in political affairs, both nationally and in New

---

[8] Cited in *Doucet*, p. 102, note 2.
[9] Léon Thériault, *L'Église catholique 1763-1953* in *Les Acadiens des Maritimes* (Moncton, 1980), pp. 323-324

Brunswick. Bishop Taché's prominent role in the recent confrontations at Red River and the religious and linguistic guarantees written into the Manitoba version of the British North America Act had angered many English Protestants. Then there was the bitter sectional rivalry caused by New Brunswick's Common Schools Act.

After much pleading from Anglin, Bishop Rogers agreed to issue a pastoral letter, one that clearly indicated his neutral ground in the forthcoming by-election.[10] He was not supporting Anglin any more than the other candidate, Onésiphore Turgeon of Bathurst, a Québec-born teacher.

Many took the letter to mean that Anglin had his bishop's support. That is how Turgeon read it, and when he lost by 500 votes, he turned to Bishop Conroy, a papal legate sent to Québec to investigate continued internal strife in the church there. Conroy advised Turgeon to consult his own bishop. Fortunately for his later political career as well as for the Church, Turgeon accepted Bishop Rogers' view that he had received widespread support among Gloucester voters.

Turgeon later won the Liberal seat for Gloucester and represented that riding from 1900 to 1923, when he was named to the Senate. He held the latter position until his death in 1944 at the age of ninety-five. Throughout this remarkably long career, his name became synonymous with the Acadian cause.

During Turgeon's first political battle, the English press in Moncton seized on his charges and for a few weeks after the by-election issued several editorials based on deeply-held English views that New Brunswick French voters were controlled by their priests.

Actually, the Turgeon affair was not so much about the priests' influence as it was the antagonism between English and French voters. Anglin was, after all, English-speaking, while Turgeon was another Québécois, who in the tradition of Israël Landry and Fernand Robidoux, editors of *Le Moniteur*, had become an enthusiastic supporter of the Acadian cause.

[10] William C. Baker, *Timothy Warren Anglin, 1822-1896: Irish Catholic Canadian* (Toronto 1977), pp. 207-208

Father Richard remained a silent observer to the Turgeon affair, but he continued to increase his public image through frequent letters to *Le Moniteur*. Most dealt with education. One entitled "The Question of Schools", published in December 1880, criticized the department of education and the Normal School in Fredericton for its training of French students. He argued they were being tested for their proficiency in English. French was regarded as just another subject, like Latin or Greek.[11]

Among Acadian educators over the next two generations, this would be an oft-repeated and justified criticism. It was a touchy question as well for Bishop Rogers — one that he refused to debate publicly. It too involved the language of instruction. One of his pet projects, the English-speaking St. Michael's College at Chatham, faced mounting financial problems and finally, in September, 1880, when there was not enough money to pay its staff of Christian Brothers, he closed it down. They were so angry when they left Chatham they took their furniture with them.[12]

St. Michael's (and Bishop Rogers') problem was the rapid decline of Irish parishioners: they were fleeing the depressed economy of the Miramichi. He must have been silently fuming at the prospect of the first Acadian Congress which opened at Memramcook in July, 1881. Here was tangible evidence that Acadians were on the march.

No English delegates were invited to this historic gathering but anyone remotely connected with the Acadian cause was there. Pierre-Amand Landry, Pascal Poirier and Urbain Johnson were the most prominent Acadian political figures. Among the large delegation of parish priests were Father Marcel-François Richard and his old friend from his days at le Grand Séminaire, Stanislas Doucet. One open-air mass was attended by 5,000 people, but the rest of the deliberations involved only the registered delegates.

[11] Cited in Alexandre-J. Savoie, *Un Siècle de revendication scolaires au Nouveau-Brunswick 1871-1971* (Edmundston 1978), p. 101. Hereafter Savoie.
[12] *Doucet*, p. 104.

A special group of Québec observers included Sir Hector Langevin, federal Minister of Public Works; Jean-Paul Rhéaume, president of the St. Jean Baptiste Society; J.-J.B. Chouinard, representing L'Institut Canadien; and reporters from several major Québec newspapers.

At the opening ceremonies, Father Richard delivered the sermon. After some appropriate religious remarks, he outlined the story of the Acadian Expulsion and the years of struggle that followed.[13] He made a strong plea for better religious instruction and paid special tribute to the role being played by Collège St. Joseph. He urged Acadians to remain on the land, where they could educate their children to assume the peaceful triumph of the Acadian cause.

Later Father Richard delivered a powerful address favouring a resolution to make August 15, the Feast of Assumption, the Acadian National Day. One of the movers of this resolution was Father Stanislas Doucet. What followed was a debate so bitter that it almost appeared that this first Acadian Congress would never be repeated.

A powerful group led by Pierre-Amand Landry and Father Bourgeois of Collège Saint-Joseph favoured instead St. Jean Baptiste Day, June 24. They argued that this would unite all French-Canadians, Québécois as well as Acadians. August 15 was the final choice and, according to a modern historian, Father Richard played the key role in this decision.[14]

It is known that it was Father Richard who later sent the letter to the episcopate in Halifax requesting its official approval. Beneath his signature were the names of five of his superior clerics — all but one of them Irish. They were Archbishop Michael Hannon, and Bishops Sweeney, McIntyre, Rogers and Cameron.

Unwittingly or reluctantly, these English-speaking Catholic leaders were helping their Acadian adherents move toward linguistic autonomy within their Church. For the next twenty-five years, the pressure would mount toward achieving that goal.

[13] *Doucet.* See appendix, pp. 282-289 for a transcript of this speech.
[14] *Thériault,* p. 327.

Some of the fiercest battles involved two clerics — Bishop James Rogers and his Acadian priest, Marcel-François Richard. One had power and tradition, but the other had two greater advantages: the rising tide of Acadian nationalism, and *time*.

# SEVEN

## Winning Rome's Approval: 1881-1912

Young Acadian leaders like Father Richard might have thought at times they were alone in their uphill struggle to gain cultural recognition. Most nationalist movements have had this inward-looking bias. Yet all, including the Acadians, continually drew their inspirations and examples from others.

The Acadians were constantly in the shadow of their more numerous and more politically-important Québécois cousins. Both French-speaking groups were struggling to stay alive religiously and linguistically in a 19th century world dominated by Anglo-Saxon Protestant England. France herself constantly felt these pressures, which helps explain the presence and efforts of people like Abbé Biron, working in remote area such as St. Louis-de-Kent. In short, English-French pressures could be found everywhere.

In September 1881, Collège Saint-Louis had more students than ever before and Father Richard and Biron, the school's director, looked forward to what Richard would describe in his memoirs as "an exceptional year." [1]

The parents of some of the new Irish students would have preferred to enrol them in St. Michael's College in Chatham, if

---

[1] Camille-Antonio Doucet, *Une Étoile s'est levée en Acadie: Marcel-François Richard* (Ottawa, 1973), ch. 8. For much of this portion of Richard's career, Doucet relied on Richard's unpublished memoirs. Hereafter *Doucet*.

it had remained open. We can also assume that Bishop Rogers was not enthused over the success of the Kent County school.

He made this clear when Father Richard was in Chatham the following January. Rogers said he had heard that the college administration was too ambitious and lacked competence. What was worse, its teachers favoured the French students and as a result he thought the Irish were not getting their money's worth. Rogers also accused Richard of lacking consideration towards himself for refusing to help reorganize the idle Chatham college. He thought the younger priest had been too busy with affairs at Saint-Louis. Other priests in the diocese had complained to their bishop that their parishes were in debt because all the money was going to Saint-Louis.

This first discussion, according to Richard's entry in his diary, continued until midnight. The next morning, Bishop Rogers showed him a letter from a fellow priest outlining the complaints of two Irish students claiming they had not received the course promised them.

Father Richard later investigated this charge and apparently resolved the problem because the two students returned the next year. Bishop Rogers continued to tolerate the college but that was about all. When Richard refused his suggestion to become director of both Collège Saint-Louis and St. Michael's, their relationship grew distinctly cool.

Biron did not help matters in 1882 when he delivered a controversial sermon in Richibucto.[2] He urged French Catholics to avoid doing business with English merchants in the town. One of these merchants, Henry O'Leary, had sent his sons to Collège Saint-Louis and both he and the priest of the Richibucto church complained to Bishop Rogers about Biron's provocative views.

At the end of the 1882 school year, Biron asked Rogers' permission to return to France to attend to some family matters. The Bishop invited him to Chatham and the lively exchange between them resulted in Biron's dismissal as director of the college.

[2] *Doucet*, p. 110.

This was a great loss to the Acadian cause. Despite his uncalled-for outburst in Richibucto, Biron had generously used his personal wealth to help finance the Saint-Louis operation. All told, he had given $4,000, "an imposing sum for that time," in the words of Richards' modern biographer.[3] Biron would never return to New Brunswick, but through his good friend Rameau managed to keep in touch with later developments.

Both Rameau and Biron were French aristocrats who apparently regarded Acadians as noble peasants striving to maintain a culturally-pure Catholic and French society in the face of tremendous pressures from what they saw as the crass and materialistic world of *les anglais*. The two Frenchmen were 19th-century romantics who thought New Brunswick Acadians had all the attributes they admired but could no longer find in their own country.

It is difficult not to sympathize with Bishop Rogers when faced with the likes of Biron. He knew far better than this wealthy and privileged Frenchman how unrealistic his views were in the context of the New Brunswick Acadians' world. It was anything but a rural Utopia. Both Rogers and Richards knew their parishioners had to survive in a rapidly-changing society, one dominated by the English. Both were aware, as obviously Biron was not, of the world represented by Rexton, just up the river from Richibucto. Here Biron would have discovered the other New Brunswick, with citizens as determinedly Protestant and English as Biron was Catholic and French.

Like some militant young Acadians of our day, Biron seemed to assume that merely by speaking French, Acadians could make their historic adversaries disappear. Reality suggested another approach, one based more on compromise than confrontation.

Those confrontations would continue, and often the school system would set them in motion. On July 5, 1882, Collège Saint-Louis held its annual closing exercises. Biron had delayed his final departure so he could take part. On the platform with him were Bishop Rogers and Father Richard.

---

[3] *Doucet* p. 116.

In the audience were Henry O'Leary and his wife, eager to hear their son Richard deliver a short speech in French. His effort earned him loud applause. A few minutes later, Bishop Rogers strode up to the podium.

Looking flushed and angry, and speaking only in English, Rogers told the assembled guests that the college administration was "too Frenchy." [4] This phrase has mystified one modern Acadian scholar: did he not mean to say "too French?" No, the bilingual bishop had chosen his words deliberately. "Frenchy" was just the right word to introduce his next remarks. The administration had incurred his displeasure because of its unfair treatment of its Irish students. If the situation did not improve, he would be obliged to withdraw his support.

He could see nothing wrong about being a patriot and defending one's nationality. "However, the Acadians should not pretend to have the same language privileges as the people of Québec who have their language guaranteed by a treaty while the Acadians, living in a conquered land, are not able to avail themselves to the same independent degree in regard to the French language."

The audience was thunderstruck. They did not applaud. Father Richard spoke next and said how grieved he was that the college and himself had caused displeasure to His Grace. He never believed it a bad thing to teach in French at a college located in a parish almost all French, where the majority of the students were Acadians. Still, he stressed that it was open to all nationalities and that French and English were on an equal footing in the classroom.

A short time later, Henry O'Leary wrote a long letter to his friend Richard in an effort to bridge this cultural gulf. He mentioned a talk he had had with Bishop Rogers the previous winter. He had learned of a quarrel between some French and Irish students that had apparently been caused by a young American. Both O'Leary and Rogers had agreed that Biron was very nationalistic but neither had directed criticism at Richard.

---

[4] *Doucet*, p. 117.

It would take more than a well-intentioned letter to heal the wounds, which soon would prove fatal to the college. Rogers refused to name a replacement for Biron. In what must have been an act of desperation, Father Richard wrote to Valentin Landry, the only Acadian school inspector, asking that the college be reclassified as a high school.

Shortly before September, 1882, Rogers told Richard to proceed with normal opening plans and prepare to welcome a new director.

He was 78-year-old Charles LaFrance, who quit after three weeks when he found the work load too heavy. Stanislas Doucet, now "curé" of Pokemouche in Gloucester County, offered his services. Rogers accepted if he would take up the same position at Saint-Louis so Richard could concentrate his efforts on the missionary parishes of Acadieville, Rogersville and Barnaby River as well as move to Chatham to revive St. Michael's College.

Richard reluctantly agreed but when his old friend Doucet arrived in Saint-Louis, their bishop had changed his mind. In disgust, Richard resigned as director of Collège Saint-Louis and by December, it had closed its doors. Its dejected founder now had little choice but to direct his talents to the mission parishes along the Intercolonial Railway in the interior of Kent County.

"Why is the Collège Saint-Louis closing?" asked a reader of *Le Moniteur Acadien*, who signed himself "an interested Acadian."[5] He suggested that either Father Richard had lost his courage or had found the task too much. If he was short of funds, why not a public appeal? After all, in the reader's opinion, the college was a national institution. He blamed Richard for the situation.

Refusing to rise to the bait, Father Richard nevertheless responded, saying that in the interests of religion, the church and Acadia, the issue should die. It would have done so except for the continued interest of several journalists in Québec.

Someone had given them a letter written by Bishop McIntyre to a Québec lawyer denying charges raised in the Québec press

[5] *Le Moniteur Acadien*, January 22, 1883.

that the Maritimes' Irish bishops had been treating the Acadians unfairly. McIntyre said Bishop Rogers had nothing to do with the closing of the college: that was entirely Richard's fault.

Again, we see outside forces, once more from Québec, taking up the Acadian cause. These interventions could not be ignored by the Maritimes' Irish Catholic leaders, undoubtedly aware that the Québeckers had their own axe to grind.

In the early 1880s, Québec nationalists, mostly young journalists and politicians, were fighting their own ultra-conservative bishops who opposed any moves that might weaken the Catholic Church's efforts to maintain a rapport and a spirit of accommodation with the English Protestant élites directing Canada's political and economic destinies.

By December, 1884, when Bishop McIntyre wrote the letter leaked to the Québec journalists, the entente so carefully built up by the late Georges Etienne Cartier was breaking down. Within a year, Catholic militants in Montréal and Québec City would be publicly voicing their outrage at the trial and execution of Louis Riel.

Former Conservative politician Honoré Mercier would emerge as the leader of Le Parti National. For a few short years he would be the René Lévesque of his day, demanding greater Québec autonomy within a young dominion facing its first testing time.

We can be reasonably certain that Acadians like Fathers Richard and Doucet were acutely aware of these rumblings in neighbouring Québec.

So were the Maritime bishops. Bishop McIntyre wrote a letter (and perhaps even arranged its wider distribution) to try and convince Québec French Catholics that all was well within the Maritime Catholic family. But McIntyre did more than write letters to head off internal dissension. It was Bishop McIntyre who deliberately called a retreat in the summer of 1884 in an apparent attempt to discourage if not to prevent his Acadian priests from attending the second Acadian Congress held at Miscouche, Prince Edward Island.

Once again, as in the first Congress held three years earlier at Memramcook, Father Richard played a key role.[6] He presided over the proceedings and proudly announced the decision of a three-member commission (all priests) on the design of a new Acadian flag. It would be a *tricolore*, with a distinctive gold star on a blue field. When it was unfurled for the first time before the assembled delegates, the enthusiasm, according to *Le Moniteur Acadien*, was universal. Everyone demanded a song. "Let it be la Marseillaise", someone called out. Then Father Richard began singing in his rich baritone voice, "L'Ave Maris Stella." All joined him.

Along with a new flag, the Acadians now had their national anthem. One by one, the nationalist symbols that Rameau had urged the Acadians to adopt were in place.

Symbols and anthems and special holidays are needed but to maintain momentum, all national movements must find issues. In 1884, *l'affaire* Collège Saint-Louis was made to order. Richard had already received Bishop Rogers' reluctant permission to go to Halifax to seek the advice of Archbishop O'Brien. Richard's request for an internal inquiry was denied. In July 1885 he was transferred to Rogersville, a move regarded by *Le Moniteur Acadien* and some Québec journalists as banishment.

The issue was now taken up by a small group of New Brunswick and Québec MPs. Pierre-Amand Landry, Conservative Member for Kent, in an attempt to answer pro-Riel agitators

---

[6] Raymond Mailhôt, *La Renaissance Acadienne (1864-1888): L'Interprétation traditionelle et Le Moniteur Acadien* (Thèse, Université de Montréal, 1969), appendix xxxix, letters from Father Richard to *Le Moniteur Acadien*, December 2, 4, 18, 1888. [While these letters touch on the Miscouche Convention, their main theme is a defence of Richard's actions in colonizing Rogersville.] Hereafter *Mailhôt*.

in Québec, told a Saint John meeting that Maritime Acadians, with much greater grievances, had remained calm.

In the spring of 1886, during the Commons debate on Riel's execution, a Liberal member for a Montréal riding answered Landry by noting that the Acadians' passivity had not prevented continued suffering.[7] The college at Saint-Louis had been closed because the French language was being used.

Not so! replied Kennedy Burns, member for Gloucester. Such remarks insulted the "ecclesiastical dignity" in charge of that diocese. Referring to Rogers by his title only, Burns credited him for "all the advancement made by Acadians in his diocese in the past 25 years." For examples, he pointed to the schools established in Chatham and Newcastle by the Sisters of the Congregation of Notre Dame. "The great majority of these ladies are French." And it was simply incorrect to say the Collège Saint-Louis had been closed because of a language conflict.

On May 29, 1886, the new Acadian senator Pascal Poirier rose in the Red Chamber on a question of privilege.[8] He wished to deny the statements made in the "other house" by Burns and Girouard. First he outlined the history of the college and the roles played by Richard and Biron. Then he gave his version of Bishop Rogers' amazing speech to the college's last graduation class and concluded with a tribute to his own alma mater, Collège Saint-Joseph — proof of the success of Acadian efforts.

However perplexing and boring this may have been to non-Maritime senators, the Collège Saint-Louis issue and the politicians' references were played up both by *Le Moniteur Acadien* and New Brunswick's second French newspaper, *Le Courrier des Provinces Maritimes*, which began publishing in Bathurst in 1885.

It is worth noting that Father Richard was anything but a passive by-stander to these Ottawa speeches. In fact, he was in the Commons visitors' gallery when the exchange between Burns and Girouard took place. Somehow he had gained Bishop

---

[7] *Canada, House of Commons Debates,* March 24, 1886, p. 332.
[8] *Canada, Senate Debates,* May 29, 1886, pp. 879-880.

Rogers' permission for the trip to lobby for a special freight rate for lumber shipped by rail from the Rogersville area.

When he returned home, his bishop wrote him a sharp note criticizing him for getting involved in secular matters. "You are a priest, not a merchant!"[9] A few months later, Rogers denied his request for a short holiday, saying he had embarrassed him further by press statements about his business plans for the Rogersville parish.

Any chance of the two men settling their differences was lost when Rameau de Saint Père arrived in 1888 to help Rogersville Acadians celebrate August 15, their *fête nationale*. Richard later wrote his bishop that he had not specifically invited the famous French writer, but added that the visit was appreciated.

By December 1888, Bishop Rogers took the unusual step of ordering Richard not to come to his New Year's Day Levee in Chatham, an event normally attended by all the priests in the diocese.

Rogers' frustration with all things Acadian probably was increased by new evidence of the widening rift throughout the Maritimes between French and English Catholics. A letter signed "Cape Breton" appearing in late December 1888 in the new French weekly *L'Évangéline,* denounced the practice of giving sermons in English to a mostly French-speaking congregation. As one modern scholar has put it, this signalled an open war between Acadian and Irish Catholics.[10]

The editor of the new publication was already widely-known. Valentin Landry had been the first French-speaking school inspector in New Brunswick history, being appointed in 1879 to serve the entire northeastern area of the province. In 1880, he had convened a Bathurst meeting of French-speaking teachers.

According to *Le Moniteur*, this was the first time they had ever been free to discuss in their own language such issues as teaching methods, curricula, textbooks and low salaries. Probably encouraged by the many signs of an Acadian renaissance in the early 1880s, Landry decided that journalism offered a better

---

[9] *Doucet*, pp. 163-4. Also *Mailhôt,* appendix xxxix.
[10] *Doucet*, p. 176.

chance to fight for the cause than an English-run public school system. Why he chose Digby and later Weymouth in southwestern Nova Scotia as the base of his operation is a mystery. That area had significant numbers of Acadians but they were a long way from the centre of Acadian militancy. It was not until 1905 that *L'Évangéline* was moved to Moncton.[11]

Certainly the time was ripe for a more militant Acadian voice. By 1887, *Le Moniteur Acadien* had become closely identified with the Conservative Party, which was fast losing support among French-speaking Canadians. What was needed, many Acadians believed, was an independent-minded newspaper able and willing to comment on such volatile issues as the rift between the Irish prelates and many of their Acadian subjects.

Proof that the Irish-Acadian battle was heating up came in 1890 when Bishop Rogers forebade Father Richard to attend the Third Acadian Congress, scheduled to begin August 15 at Church Point, Nova Scotia. His telegram read: "Leave of absence for Convention not granted, for personal reasons to yourself."[12] Richard's old friend, Stanislas Doucet of Pokemouche, also did not attend, probably for the same reason. Congress delegates went on record as deploring "the regrettable reasons beyond their control" which prevented the participation of these key figures.

By 1891, relations between bishop and priest had reached the point that Rogers refused to include Rogersville on his itinerary for confirmation cermonies, even though 200 children were involved. It is hard to imagine another decision that could have revealed so graphically to 200 Acadian families how bad relations had become between their priest and their bishop. How many ordinary Acadians became fervent nationalists by this one incident? How easy it must have been to place the blame on an Irish bishop who refused to speak French, even though he could, and who refused to travel the twenty-five miles from his palace to their own community which had been named after him.

---

[11] Alexandre-J Savoie, *Un Siècle de revendications scolaires au Nouveau-Brunswick 1871-1971* Vol. I, p. 178.

[12] *Doucet*, p. 177, n. 37.

In desperation, Richard wrote a long letter to Rome, outlining his grievances and requesting permission to appear in person. Cardinal Simeoni in his reply counselled patience. He also wrote Rogers for explanations of the eight complaints Richard had listed. The first one was that Rogers had wrongly blamed him for the closure of Collège Saint-Louis.[13]

Rogers had no difficulty refuting his priest's charges but both he and Bishop Sweeney came under more Acadian pressure in 1893 with rumours they were planning to name Irish co-adjutors who would probably succeed them.

The president and the secretary of La Société Nationale l'-Assomption, Pierre-Amand Landry (now a judge), and Senator Pascal Poirier, circulated a petition among all French-speaking priests in New Brunswick asking each "as advocates of this national and religious cause" to contribute ten dollars towards a campaign to have the future bishop of Chatham chosen from the French clergy.[14] Their request was premature because few replied.

It was not until 1896 that the aging Bishop Rogers sent Archbishop O'Brien the names of his six nominees: three English and three French. Again the Landry-Poirier team swung into action. They appealed to Mgr. Merry del Val, the special Papal envoy touring Canada in the aftermath of the Manitoba Schools controversy. When he refused to intervene, they asked Québec bishops to approach him on behalf of the Acadian cause. They too refused.

When Rome named Timothy Casey as co-adjutor in Saint John and Thomas Barry in Chatham, only one Acadian priest took part in their inauguration ceremonies at the Saint John cathedral. Judge Landry explained his absence to an English journalist by saying he did not wish to aid in "the funerals of the

---

[13] *Doucet*, pp. 180-181.
[14] *Doucet*, p. 202. Also Léon Thériault, "L'Église catholique," 1773-1953 in *Les Acadiens des Maritimes* (Moncton, 1980) p. 331. Hereafter *Thériault*.

Acadian people." [15] Valentin Landry of *L'Évangéline* told his readers it was like a day of national mourning.

By 1900, the Acadian leaders were preparing for yet another national congress, this time at Arichat, Cape Breton. They seemed to have recovered their spirits. Why not try for a new Acadian diocese in Moncton, Father Richard suggested in a letter to Judge Landry?[16] It would consist of Westmorland and Kent Counties plus other parishes, including Rogersville in Northumberland. When this request was sent to the apostalic delegate in Ottawa, he advised the Acadian leaders to wait until a new bishop was named and then make a direct request to Rome.

Predictably, the Arichat Congress called for a French bishop but a resolution to this effect sent on to the palaces in Saint John and Chatham brought a stoney silence. So Judge Landry, Senator Poirier and Dr. J.L. Belliveau of Shédiac sent a petition with 156 Acadian signatures representing a veritable who's who of the Acadian cultural and professional establishment.[17]

Bishop Sweeney, who would die within the year, did not reply. Bishop Rogers said it must be a papal decision. Archbishop O'Brien could not "make the recommendation, at present, for the dismemberment of the diocese." [18]

If the decision had to come from Rome, why not forward a request signed by all the Acadian priests in New Brunswick? That was done in May, 1901, but once again, there was no progress. Bishop Rogers's death in 1904 and Bishop Barry's elevation as his successor increased the tension, if that was possible. It was felt especially in the Moncton area, soon to be the headquarters for the Société Mutuelle l'Assomption.

This was an insurance company formed at Waltham, Massachusetts in 1903 by expatriate Acadians. It should not be confused — although it often was, at least by English New Brunswickers — with Société Nationale l'Assomption which was created in 1889 to organize the third Acadian national

---

[15] Cited in *Thériault*, p. 333.
[16] *Thériault*, p. 334.
[17] *Thériault*, p. 335.
[18] *Thériault*, p. 335. It is worth noting that this letter was in English.

convention held the next year at Church Point, Nova Scotia. Both organizations were Acadian lobbies that would wield great influence. Initially, the older one, Société Nationale l'Assomption, acted as a lay arm within the Catholic Church, while the Société Mutuelle l'Assomption assumed the financial and business responsibilities of an expanding Acadian clientele.[19]

The 1903 constitution of the American-born group outlined its aims. Its members would rally the Acadians under one flag, aid its members who became ill, provide financial benefits to families of deceased members and guard the Acadians' language, customs and religion. It also established a fund to help educate promising young Acadians.

In 1907 the Société Mutuelle l'Assomption was incorporated as a New Brunswick business and established its headquarters in Moncton. Its presence there helped make Moncton the centre of the Acadian lobby. It also eclipsed the Société Nationale l'Assomption, which continued to work closely with it.

Faced with this new and powerful pressure group, Father Savage of the Moncton parish was not enthused. In 1907, he refused to give his permission allowing the la Tour branch of Société Mutuelle to hold a "communion en corps" as it had done the previous year, on August 15, the Acadians' national day.

Editorials in *L'Évangéline* against the Irish hierarchy became so critical and aroused so much controversy that at one point Father Savage accused the newspaper and Société Mutuelle l'Assomption of being affiliated with the "Black Hand," a Maffia-like organization in the United States.[20]

Meanwhile, Father Richard had obtained permission from his new bishop for another visit to Rome, ostensibly to accompany an older priest. Once there, he obtained his third private audience with the Pope. According to Richard's memoirs, the Pontiff promised to appoint an Acadian bishop.

---

[19] Emery LeBlanc, *Les Acadiens: La tentative de génocide d'un peuple* (Ottawa, 1963) p. 95.

[20] J.E.Belliveau, *The Monctonians: Scamps, Scholars and Politicians (Hantsport, N.S., 1981)*, Vol. II, pp. 51-56 *passim*. Also *Thériault*, pp. 345-6.

Realizing the inevitable, the Maritime's Irish hierarchy began suggesting an Acadian diocese for Bathurst rather than Moncton. To promote this idea, they sent their own delegate to Rome, Father Henry O'Leary, a member of the same Richibucto family that had figured in Richard's earliest confrontations with the late Bishop Rogers.

Occasionally, this internal debate spilled over into the public domain, thanks in part to *L'Évangéline*. Editor Landry made no secret of his pro-Acadian views and in 1909 his paper was accused by Mgr. Sbaretti, the papal legate in Ottawa, of making "regrettable insinuations against religious authority." Members of the Société l'Assomption were advised to withdraw their support from *L'Évangéline*. The next year, Landry sold his interests but it would take years before the publication recovered from this blow to its credibility and circulation.

Events in 1910 indicated the widespread opposition to the Irish influence within the Catholic Church in Canada. In that year an Ontario priest, Father Fallon, joined the fight against the existing French-speaking schools in his province. On May 31, 1910, Father Richard was once again in Rome but he had to wait nearly a month for a papal audience. Once more, the pontiff gave his assurance that Acadians would soon have their bishop and at the end of the audience he presented Richard with a golden chalice "to remind Acadians that their Father loves them."

That summer, while Richard was celebrating the fortieth anniversary of his ordination, a special papal envoy visited many Acadian communities in New Brunswick. In Moncton, accompanied by Senator Poirier, he called on Father Savage. That meeting lasted only fifteen minutes: the bilingual priest refused to speak French. Prior to his Acadian tour, the papal envoy had attended the Twentieth Eucharist Congress, held for the first time in Montreal. He and thousands of other Catholics heard Henri Bourassa publicly rebuke the Archbishop of Westminster for his anti-French remarks.[21] Clearly, the time had come for the Church to give greater recognition to the French fact in Canada.

---

[21] Mason Wade, *The French Canadians* (Toronto, 1956) pp. 580-582.

During the summer of 1912, the long-awaited news came. Father Edouard Leblanc of the parish of St. Bernard in Weymouth, Nova Scotia was named Bishop of Saint John. One of his first acts was to order Father Savage to ask his French parishioners to decide to form their own parish in Moncton. Only three voted against the move.

It would take another ten years before an Acadian bishop occupied the Chatham diocese, an event that Father Richard would not live to see. He died June 18, 1915. He had played a key role in this long struggle to gain more Acadian recognition within the Church. Acadians now had their own bishop and a French parish in the increasingly important centre of Moncton. Eventually, the rest would follow: new French dioceses in Bathurst, Edmundston as well as Moncton — although it would not be until 1944 that all were in place.

One of Father Richard's most important contributions was helping to strengthen the Acadian base in southeastern New Brunswick. Early in his struggle with Bishop Rogers, he had looked to Westmorland compatriots for support rather than the more completely French communities in the north.

He recognized that Acadians were rapidly moving into the industrial town of Moncton. Even though most would take up jobs in the lower levels of the economy, their concentrated numbers in this urban setting offered more hope of achieving gains against the entrenched Irish than Acadians scattered along the coast of Gloucester.

In later years, these northern Acadians would argue that their Moncton cousins had traded some of their cultural heritage for financial security. Yet this same economic stability helped them keep alive Collège Saint Joseph at Memramcook as well as maintain two French newspapers. The Moncton-based La Société Mutuelle l'Assomption would play an increasingly powerful role in a never-ending lobbying effort that eventually would produce the Université de Moncton and a provincial government led by a southern Acadian, Louis Robichaud — like Father Richard, a son of Kent County.

# EIGHT

## A PROTESTANT BACKLASH IN BATHURST: 1890-1896

In tracing the slow climb of French New Brunswickers toward equality, it is tempting to ignore the English Protestant community. It would be wrong to assume they were too engrossed with money-making to worry about the "lowly" French.

During the 1890s, New Brunswick's "ruling class" had a constant national reminder of the province's most important cultural minority. The Manitoba Schools controversy was slowly working its way through the various courts. Thanks to the proud biases of most Canadian newspaper editors, literate Canadians were familiar with the details of Canada's first major constitutional issue.

One Fredericton editor who reflected the accepted prejudices of the day was Herman H. Pitts, editor of the *New Brunswick Reporter and Fredericton Advertiser*. He was also Grand Master of the New Brunswick Loyal Orange Association. A staunch Presbyterian caught up with the wave of moral reform gaining momentum at this time, Pitts and others, including Protestant clergymen championing the cause of temperance, seemed to be praying for their own New Brunswick version of the Manitoba issue.

As spokesman for provincial Orangemen, Pitts wanted "more religion in politics, more Christian men in public office." He thought Canada should be unilingually English, "notwithstanding Québec is largely French."[1] Applying this outlook to New Brunswick's political scene of the early 1890s, he wanted to end Premier Andrew Blair's successful coalition of English businessmen, and Irish and Acadian politicians.

Outrageous bigot though Pitts was by today's standards, he nevertheless reflected the cultural climate of his day — a climate dominated by British imperialism. The 1890s marked the high point of the greatest empire the world had known. It covered a quarter of the globe and its distant colonies produced its most fanatical defenders. They were often English Protestants. Two of the most prominent came from English New Brunswick.

The prosperous farming community of Salisbury produced George Parkin, who first distinguished himself at the University of New Brunswick and then went on to become headmaster of Bathurst Grammar School (1868-1872) before assuming a similar post at the prestigious Collegiate School in Fredericton. In 1889, Parkin's oratorical skills earned him a request to tour the Empire on behalf of the recently-formed Imperial Federation League. Later, as Sir George Parkin, he became the first secretary of the Rhodes Scholarship Trust, a vital recruiting arm for young imperialists.

Another son of the empire, George Foster, came out of Carleton County. After a distinguished undergraduate career at the University of New Brunswick, where he later taught, he entered the House of Commons. A more staunch Tory there never was. He soon became a Conservative cabinet minister and like Parkin a knight of the realm.

How eagerly editor Herman Pitts must have seized on the speeches and exploits of these native sons to further the cause of an English-speaking, British and Protestant world. Imagine his scorn for all things French and Catholic and especially Acadian.

If you cannot, just remember the out-pourings of another Fredericton editor, Michael Wardell, two generations later. He too was a fervent Imperialist who took great delight in scorning

---

[1] *The New Brunswick Reporter*, February 8, 1890, cited in Michael Hatfield, "H.H. Pitts and Race and Religion in New Brunswick Politics", *Acadiensis* (Spring, 1975), p. 47, Hereafter *Hatfield*.

the legislative reform efforts of the first Acadian to be elected premier of New Brunswick.

To Fredericton readers of Pitts' *New Brunswick Reporter*, the Imperial cause was beyond criticism, deserving of unquestioned loyalty. They hailed Pitts' idea of a new reform party, one supported by English-speaking Protestants who would end what they regarded as the special privileges of the French and Catholic minority. To launch his party, Pitts needed a issue.

It came all too conveniently and not coincidentally in 1890 from Bathurst. As in Manitoba, it involved that historically-explosive question, education. Some of Bathurst's Protestant citizens accused their Roman Catholic neighbours of conducting the village's school affairs contrary to the Common Schools Act of 1871 and the compromise regulations adopted in 1875 after the Caraquet riots.

In no other field of public endeavour are there more experts than in education. No other issue can generate as much heat and debate or produce more rumours and malicious gossip. Schools are our most familiar public institution. The fact that children are often the first transmitters of what supposedly happened or what was said in the classroom brings two results: many versions of the event and instant broadcasting of what the bearer considers the truth.

It is ever the case today and was even more so in 1890 in a society that paraded its prejudices and views, especially on religion and language. We should not be surprised, therefore, to learn that the Bathurst school controversy that rapidly developed involved Protestant and Roman Catholic clergy (including Bishop Rogers) as well as angry parents and tax payers.[2]

---

[2] Much of the material for the Bathurst controversy was taken from "Report Upon Charges relating to the Bathurst Schools and other Schools in Gloucester County" (Fredericton, 1894) by the Hon. J.J. Fraser, Judge of the Supreme Court. This information was supplemented by Hatfield's excellent article and more from K.F.C. MacNaughton's pioneer study, *The Development of the Theory and Practice of Education in New Brunswick 1784-1900* (Fredericton, 1947), especially chapter 9, Hereafter *MacNaughton*.

On the face of it, Roman Catholic residents of the Bathurst area had more legitimate complaints. From 1873 to 1890, they had maintained at their own expense two convent schools, one in the village of Bathurst and the other outside. These were attended by about 180 young girls taught by the Sisters of the Congregation of Notre Dame, an order that did not allow its members to teach boys. Throughout this period, these Catholic rate-payers also had to help pay for the public schools operating under the Common Schools Act of 1871.

In June, 1890, the Sisters informed their students' parents that they needed more money. Some was raised during the summer but it was not enough. Reluctantly, the parents decided to end their arrangement with the Sisters, who refused to teach under the Common Schools Act, and find another order that would.[3] With Bishop Rogers' help, several Sisters of Charity with teaching licenses to work in a secular school system were hired from Nova Scotia and in September, the town and village of Bathurst had a common school system like many other New Brunswick communities.

Now it was the Protestants' turn to complain. The addition of 180 students meant a sharp increase in their school taxes. But money was not their only concern. They viewed the Sisters, with their distinctive dress, as proof that Bishop Rogers and the two local priests, Fathers Barry and Varrily, planned to bring the secular schools under the control of Catholic teachers.[4] They petitioned the Board of Education in Fredericton to intervene, but the Board refused. It argued that the changes made by the Bathurst school trustees had complied with the terms of the 1875 Compromise — a document not widely understood by the average New Brunswicker.

Considering New Brunswick's past history of educational conflict and the on-going Manitoba schools debate, it seemed inevitable that this volatile Bathurst issue would spread to the larger political stage. The vehicle proved to be a Kent County by-election, called for September 1891 to replace Pierre-Amand

---

[3] *Fraser Report*, p. 8.
[4] *Fraser Report*, p. 8.

Landry, recently named to the New Brunswick Supreme Court by the federal Conservative government.

The Liberal campaign was led by Charles LaBillois, minister without portfolio in the Blair cabinet and a member from Restigouche. He was aided by Peter Veniot, a native of Richibucto and now the owner of the Bathurst *Courrier*. The campaign heated up quickly after Veniot released a pamphlet featuring remarks attributed to A.A. Stockton of Saint John, the provincial Conservative leader, that French should no longer be permitted as a language of instruction in the primary grades.[5]

The Liberal victory in Kent produced a Protestant backlash, something the *L'Évangéline* correspondent had predicted during the campaign. It appeared first in Bathurst, when a Presbyterian minister, A.F. Thomson, launched a speaking tour among Orange Lodges during the winter of 1891-92.

Thomson warned his sympathetic audiences of the dangers New Brunswick Protestants faced from militant Catholics firmly entrenched in the Blair government and the revamped Bathurst school system. His words took on more meaning midway through his tour when the Bathurst school trustees appointed a young Acadian woman licensed to teach only in French-speaking districts as the new superintendent. When angry Protestants withdrew their children from classes, she was forced to resign.[6]

At the next session of the provincial legislature in March and April, 1892, this Bathurst issue sparked a stormy debate and clearly placed the Blair government on the defensive. In a heated exchange with the Conservative leader, Stockton, Premier Blair gave his version of the Kent by-election campaign, claiming he could produce two witnesses who would make an oath that Stockton had made a "most inflammatory speech" at North Welford, "an exclusively Protestant section" of the riding. He charged that Stockton had said the government had violated the school law "in the interests of the nuns and Catholic separate schools" and that he sympathized with the Bathurst agitators.[7]

[5] *Hatfield*, p. 50; also *Debates,* March 3. 1892, p. 10.
[6] *Hatfield*, p. 50; *Fraser Report*, p. 29-30.
[7] *Debates*, March 3, 1892, p. 10.

Blair had a good political reason for not backing away from the Bathurst school issue. The continuing economic depression was more critical to most New Brunswickers as they watched the stagnant lumbering industry and lamented the departure of their young people for New England and Ontario. There was also the threat of scandal.

On March 23, 1892, the Conservative Opposition tabled a memorial charging the Blair government with election bribery involving the Central Railway and some large lumber operators. On April 4, the House passed a resolution establishing an investigating committee.

Shrewd politician that he was, Premier Blair probably realized his vulnerability on economic policies and patronage, so he may have welcomed the Bathurst controversy as a timely diversion. About the same time, Herman Pitts, through the columns of his *New Brunswick Reporter*, was concluding the Bathurst affair would make an ideal political springboard, especially if linked with the Protestant-led temperance forces.

Throughout the 1892 legislative session and into the summer, Pitts emerged as the self-appointed spokesman for what he considered the beleagured Protestant community. When Blair confirmed widespread speculation and called a general election for October, Pitts entered the lists as the independent candidate for York.

Appealing to local Orangemen and the Sons of Temperance, Pitts skillfully used the Veniot pamphlet of the Kent campaign plus new charges from Bathurst. One claimed that a teacher, under orders from his priest, was teaching catechism during regular school hours contrary to the 1875 Compromise agreement. Pitts quickly assumed the role of the *de facto* leader of the Conservative party. His image was further enhanced when Premier Blair became one of his three opponents in York. When the October 22 returns were tallied, Pitts had won easily, while Blair finished last.

"The fact has been demonstrated beyond peradventure," crowed Pitts in a post-electoral editorial, "that such open catering to the Roman Catholic vote as was made by Mr. Blair throughout his political career must in the end bring its own reward."[8]

In the overall results, the Liberals fared better than their leader, being returned by another healthy majority. Blair himself found a seat in Queen's, winning it despite more sectarian tactics by the Tories.

In December, 1892, a few weeks before the new legislative session, the Blair government, in an apparent move to spike the guns of the confident Pitts, released at long last the details of the 1875 Compromise on the Common Schools Act. They appeared as a supplement to the annual report of the Chief Superintendent of Education and were in response to a series of questions placed in the House the previous session by John Seivewright, MLA for Bathurst. He had requested copies of all orders-in-council, regulations and instructions relating to the Bathurst schools.[9]

It was at this point, to use the words of Judge J.J. Fraser who would later investigate the affair, that John E. O'Brien, a Bathurst school board trustee and its secretary, "threw a fire-brand into Bathurst Town Community."[10] Disregarding the advice of both Protestant and Catholic rate-payers expressed at two public meetings, O'Brien appointed his son to teach at the Bathurst Grammar School. Since O'Brien was Protestant and his son Roman Catholic, religion was not the central point of objection.

At issue was the fact that the younger O'Brien had been "removed from office by the Board of Education for inattention to, and gross neglect of the duties of his office as Inspector. The causes which led to this inattention and neglect," the Fraser Report would later explain, "were well known in Bathurst as were his habits of life."[11] Most Protestant rate-payers and not a few Catholics were furious. The local Methodist minister, Rev. J. Seller, had until now remained out of the simmering dispute,

[8] *The New Brunswick Reporter*, October 26, 1892, cited in *Hatfield*, p. 52.
[9] *Journals of the Legislative Assembly*, 1893; see *Appendix* dated December 21, 1892.
[10] *Fraser Report*, p. 32
[11] *Fraser Report*, p. 30

but he was so angered by the O'Brien appointment that he joined Rev. Thomson as one of the most active protestors.

Within days after the appointment, Protestant parents withdrew their children from the Grammar School and found temporary facilities in a building that had been used by the local Orange Lodge. While these new classrooms were being made ready, Herman Pitts stepped up his campaign in Fredericton. He had no trouble convincing the organizers of the annual provincial meeting of the Orange Lodges, slated for Fredericton in February, that the Bathurst school question should be the main issue.

The first speaker at that meeting was Rev. J. Seller, who gave his version of recent events in his community. He then got unanimous support for several petitions urging that certain education privileges given to Roman Catholics be revoked. Other resolutions called for the support of the alleged grievances of Bathurst's Protestants. Predictably, the Seller speech and the resolutions were widely circulated among provincial lodges.

It was now Premier Blair's turn to take the initiative. He and several cabinet ministers met in Bathurst as members of a special committee of the provincial Board of Education. At first, the chief Protestant spokesman in the community, Rev. A.F. Thomson, refused to attend the hearings.[12]

When he did, Thomson admitted his ignorance about some financial aspects of his community. He did not know, for instance, that Catholic residents paid $616 of the annual tax levy compared with $350 supplied by the Protestants. Also, he was unaware of the fact that the decision to hire the Sisters from Nova Scotia had created a budget deficit of $300. (And back in the 1890s, local school boards could not overspend.)

Premier Blair said he would take no part "in reviving the animosities and strife and struggles that were abated in 1873 and 1874 by the orders of our predecessors." Nor would he appeal the 1875 Compromise.

---

[12] *Debates* February 24, 1893; also *Supplementary Index,* Report of Special Committee of the Board of Education, p. 110-111.

"Mr. Thomson may succeed in finding somebody that will, or he may succeed in setting this country on fire, and perhaps in the consuming flames something will be evolved that will work out the problem he has in hand." The meeting then adjourned until the evening to hear other witnesses. None appeared.

Once more the scene of this on-going drama shifted to Fredericton and another session of the legislature. Armed with petitions signed by 10,000 members of the Orange Lodge, Herman Pitts, the new member for York, demanded that the government restore the original terms and intent of the 1871 Common Schools Act and withdraw the 1875 Compromise regulations.[13] What followed was a debate between two formidable adversaries.

The issue was one vital to all New Brunswickers: the public school system. At least, it was the acknowledged one. Another was the question of religious toleration. Speaking before several hundred citizens squeezed into the public galleries, Herman Pitts began his long-awaited maiden speech by referring to the recent election. He would not have done so "were it not for the libel that has been cast upon the county of York which has sent me to represent it in these halls and which sir, I am proud to believe, neither consider me a bigot, agitator nor anarchist."

His Fredericton petition of 116 names began with the signatures of three of the community's most prominent citizens, Harry Chestnut, William Lemont and J.A. Van Wart. This would suggest that the concern for the public school system went far beyond the views being expressed by the more militant Protestant groups such as the Orange Lodge and the Sons of Temperance. Using the arguments contained in this and previous petitions, Pitts conveyed the deep concerns of many Protestant communities.

They viewed recent moves to bring confessional or religious schools into the public system as a violation of section 102 of the Common Schools Act. They thought special licensing privileges granted to members of Roman Catholic teaching orders were unfair. Pitts listed four concessions made under the 1875 Compromise which he claimed had never been endorsed

[13] *Debates* 1893, March 27, pp. 54-64

by the Board of Education. Instead, he said they had been approved through interpretations by members of the Executive Council.

One allowed children from any part of one district to attend any of the schools within that district. Another exempted nuns and members of teaching orders who had been examined by their own orders from attending the training school in Fredericton. A third allowed these teachers to refrain from using texts containing material they considered objectionable. A final concession permitted religious instruction in schools "after school hours only."

"The main issue presently," Pitts argued, was whether the Sisters of Charity should be permitted to teach at all in New Brunswick schools. They had never attended the provincial Normal School. Instead, they had entered the New Brunswick system "armed with teaching licenses granted by their own religious institution in Halifax. Will the Convent at Bathurst or at Buctouche ... be next recognized as a Normal or Training School?" he asked.

Another reason for the "recent troubles" in Bathurst and Bathurst Village, according to Pitts and the petitioners, was that too many conventional buildings were being used for school purposes "while rooms in the Public Schools were unoccupied." It was an "outrage" that the Protestant minority of Bathurst Town should be "compelled to contribute largely to the support of the Roman Catholic Schools ... yet have to maintain a private school at their own expense for their own children."

Pitts had it "on good authority" that classes in both the town and village had been so graded as to place Protestant children under sisters' instruction in the convent. He added that this was neither an Orange nor a Protestant issue. "It is a question of equal rights and equal justice to all parties and individuals."

Citing a private letter from George Fowler, provincial Grand Master of the Orange Order, who had recently visited Bathurst, Pitts warned that "the half has not been told." The position of the Protestant minority in Bathurst "would make the blood boil in the veins of every true Protestant and Orangeman." Furthermore, he too had gone to Bathurst and came back with the same impressions as Fowler's.

At this point, Pitts seemed to veer from his text, based as it was on petitions, to pass on some stories he had heard. Someone at a public meeting in Bathurst claimed that a Protestant teacher had been told by a priest visiting her school to teach catechism "or be replaced by a teacher who would."

John Seivewright, the Liberal member from Bathurst, quickly rose to his feet to deny this story. He was joined by Premier Blair who wanted to know the teacher's name. "Miss Alexander," he was told.

"She volunteered freely to teach it," said Seivewright.

Pitts had other stories. "Some Protestant children have to cross themselves ... If such a report was circulated about a Roman Catholic child in one of the most remote districts of our backwoods being made to do the equivalent in Protestant terms, then how quickly there would be a cry raised by the Roman Catholic authorities."

Seivewright called out again: "State your charges."

Pitts said he had none to make, but he gained Seivewright's admission that there were problems in Bathurst schools. The Liberal member replied that they were caused by poor administration by the Bathurst school trustees. Pitts did not agree. "The Attorney General [Premier Blair] is largely responsible for all this faction. He is today reaping the fruits of his catering to keep in power." The Legislative Chambers echoed with thunderous applause as Pitts took his seat.

It was now Premier Blair's turn. The forty-nine-year-old leader was at the peak of his career and must have been keenly aware that he had to answer Pitts' charges of "selling out to the Romans."

Born of Loyalist and Scottish ancestry, educated at Fredericton's prestigious Collegiate School, this staunch Presbyterian lawyer had represented York for fourteen consecutive years, until this same Herman Pitts had soundly defeated him six months earlier.

Answering the Compromise issue first, Blair said it allowed Roman Catholic children to be taught together in populous districts. He did not think "Protestantism ... so feeble a thing that it could not stand up to such an arrangement as that." [14] As for the teaching sisters brought in from Nova Scotia, Blair observed that no one had suggested they were not fully qualified. In fact, since coming to New Brunswick, all had received good inspectors' reports. Blair defended the 1884 decision of "the present Board of Education" permitting the Sisters of Charity to take their teaching examination outside of Fredericton. "It does not detract from the non-sectarian character of the school law, nor extend any privileges that would not be readily extended to anybody in the land."

Anticipating that the House might be asked to pass regulations barring the nuns from holding their teaching licenses, Blair declared: "If that is the proposition, I want to hear somebody calmly propose to this legislature that we appeal the Catholic Emancipation Act and revive religious tests in this country."

"This was not the proposition at all," interjected Pitts. "They should be made to go to the Provincial Normal School."

"That is the proposition," maintained the Premier. "These gentlemen object because they belong to the Roman Catholic Sisterhood. Every university graduate is allowed to pass an examination who has not gone to the Normal School."

Citing cases of two Presbyterian and seven Episcopal clergymen given licenses without attending Normal School, Blair said, "Instead of granting equal rights to all, you would absolutely proscribe a particular class and create deep-seated discontent."

As to whether teachers should be able to wear religious insignia in the classroom, Blair said the framers of this law "became so ashamed of this regulation that they passed an order in 1872 that nothing should prevent the wearing of the cross as ordinarily worn by certain denominations." And he added: "The order of 1872 was published before the general election of 1874 and when [it] ... took place, they resulted in the return of the most Protestant House that ever sat in this province, with a government in power that did not contain one Roman Catholic

---

[14] *Debates* 1893, March 27, pp. 61

member, and that House ratified ... the regulation of 1872 abolishing the milinery regulation."

Blair denied charges that the Board of Education had ignored petitions protesting the Bathurst situation. He outlined the various steps the government had taken, including the appointment of a Committee of Instruction in 1890 and the cabinet visit to the area just before the present session. He blamed the Rev. A.F. Thomson for most of the trouble. "He has put forth statements which are not accurate. He has taken every means to inflame the public mind and has acted in every other way than a gentleman connected with the church and filling his high position ought to have done. I do not exonerate the Board of Trustees from all criticism."

The root of the Bathurst problem, Blair argued, was the "question of taxation. Probably the district is called upon to pay $120 to $150 more than it would if all parties would work harmoniously together." [15]

Pitts: "Mr. Seller does not say that."

Blair: "Clergymen are not trained in business."

"It is not our intention," the Premier concluded, "to ask the House to refer this petition to a special committee for the purpose of summoning witnesses from Bathurst and bringing half the community here to tell us what we already know." The House was then adjourned until March 29.

There was no adjournment for many parents and students in Bathurst. About March 20, the students whose parents had withdrawn them from the Grammar School to protest the appointment of teacher Edward O'Brien finally resumed their studies. Their "school" was located in rooms originally rented to the local Orange Lodge.[16] Within days, the building's owner, Charles Bosse, bowed to local pressure and advised the parents to find classrooms elsewhere. The parents ignored his request to move their children, even after Bosse had dismantled the stove pipe.

---

[15] *Debates* 1893, March 27; p. 70.
[16] This account is taken from *Fraser Report*, p. 32-34

On Sunday, March 25, Bosse padlocked the building as word spread of a possible confrontation the next day. About 8:30 on Monday morning, a crowd of about twenty-five gathered outside as students began to appear. Someone broke the padlock, allowing the teacher and students to enter.

Just then, a sled came by and its occupant, a Protestant named Richard Miller, who tried to goad the Catholics in the crowd. After a few words and shouts, the crowd gradually drifted away.

Two hours later, Premier Blair received this telegram:
ON VERGE OF RIOT THIS MORNING. DOOR PRIVATE SCHOOL BARRICADED
NUMBER ROMAN CATHOLICS IN VICINITY WHEN PROTESTANTS ARRIVED.
OUR LIBERTIES AND RIGHTS THREATENED. CALL UPON GOVERNMENT FOR PROTECTION.
J. SELLERS, A.F. THOMSON

Herman Pitts received one too, informing him of the contents of the one sent to Blair. What could have been a repetition of the events leading to the Caraquet Riots eighteen years earlier did not happen. The militia was not dispatched to Bathurst.

Neither was the telegram mentioned next day when A.A. Stockton resumed the House debate on the Bathurst affair. In a short speech, he repeated Pitts' demand for a seven-man commission of inquiry and placed most of the blame on the Board of Education. The chief government spokesman was the Surveyor-General, L.J. Tweedie, a Presbyterian lawyer from Chatham. He began by dismissing the charges raised in the Fredericton *Daily Gleaner* that Roman Catholics, "excited at Blair's inflammatory speech, had formed themselves into a mob and proceeded to the private Protestant school and barricaded the door." [17]

This was "wholly and absolutely untrue," said Tweedie. "The alleged mob ... was a mere dispute between landlord and tenant. The landlord was a Protestant and so were the tenants."

Loud laughter and jeers came from the government side of the house when Tweedie read the telegram sent to the Premier. He also tabled two others sent by Mary Alexander, the Bathurst

---

[17] *Debates* 1893, March 29, pp. 80-83.

teacher. The first to Pitts said she had been compelled to teach catechism in order to get and then keep her job. The second to John Seivewright said she had never been coerced and had taught it after school hours of her "own free will."

Tweedie reminded the House that he had been elected nearly twenty years earlier "on the school question." He had been in favour of the principle of free non-sectarian schools then "and by no act of his had he endeavoured to interfere ... since then." There had been religious peace "until questions had been raised by an individual in the county of York secretly aided by the Opposition."

Another Government speaker, Charles LaBillois of Restigouche, the minister without portfolio, said he was the only Roman Catholic member of the Board of Education. He denied a charge made by Rev. Thomson at a Fredericton meeting of the Orange Lodge that Protestant children in Bathurst had been forced to kneel and make the sign of the cross. He also referred to a circular Thomson had sent to New Brunswick Protestants in 1882 claiming that "most criminals in the jails ... are Roman Catholics."

Perhaps expressing his own frustration at not being placed in charge of a department, LaBillois observed that in provincial affairs in Fredericton, "not one Roman Catholic was in office." In his home town of Campbellton, where Roman Catholics formed "about one third of the population, there are six teachers and all [are] Protestant." Yet despite the provocation during the recent general election, LaBillois said there had been no Roman Catholic retaliation.

"In every Roman Catholic county, Protestants are elected. Take Kent, Gloucester and Restigouche, and you have able men well qualified to defend Protestant rights."

Confirming this ecumenical spirit, Powell, an Opposition member from Sackville, said that in the last election, "none were more steadfast than the priests of St. Joseph's College of Memramcook, who almost to a man supported me."

In the rest of the debate, which dragged on until April 6, only two francophones besides LaBillois took part. One was Goguen, the Opposition member from Kent, who accused Pitts of "trying to drag the Opposition after him." He would not follow but would "vote squarely against" his resolution. The other was the veteran Liberal member from Caraquet, Théotime Blanchard. He agreed with his leader's view that taxation was at the heart of the Bathurst affair. He also reminded the House that he had been a member when the Common Schools Act had been passed.

"I do not hesitate to say that I was strongly opposed to that Act on conscientious principles, but when the propositions made by the Catholic Members of the House ... were accepted and the regulations now in force passed, I withdrew my opposition to the law and in my humble way did all I could to bring our schools in the County of Gloucester under the law." [18]

He also admitted to his fellow members that he was wearing an emblem which bore a cross. "At the same time, I hold a school license under which I taught school for many years in this Province and under which I could yet teach if I desired ... I do not believe any law should prevent me from wearing that emblem." Blanchard concluded that in his view, "the two Bathurst gentlemen who are taking such an active part in this affair want to drive the Sisters of Charity out of Bathurst, and if they could do so, out of the Province."

On April 4, when Premier Blair began introducing the resolutions relating to the Bathurst issue, it was obvious that the outnumbered and divided Opposition could not defeat them.

The first said that Regulation 21 passed in 1875 pertaining to the wearing of religious symbols did not contravene the non-sectarian principle of the school law. It passed 28 votes to 9.

The second said that the leasing of school buildings from religious groups did not contravene the non-sectarian principle but should be subject to the limitations of a 1892 regulation that schools should be fully occupied before additional space was leased — unless special permission came from the Chief Superintendent of Education. This passed without division.

On April 6, 1893, the legislature passed a Blair resolution calling for "one of the judges of the Supreme Court or county court to be commissioned to proceed to Bathurst Town and

---

[18] *Debates* 1893, March 29, p. 100.

Village to inquire into and fully and thoroughly investigate any alleged infractions of the law." Twelve days later, Judge John J. Fraser of the Supreme Court was given the task.

A Presbyterian like Pitts and Blair, Judge Fraser had been a member of the government that had negotiated the 1875 Compromise following the Caraquet Riots. In fact, one modern scholar, in a definitive study of Fraser, credits him with being a major influence in drafting the 1875 Compromise. He suggests that Fraser, who succeeded George King as premier in 1878, did much to heal the cultural wounds resulting from the introduction of King's Common School Act. It was Fraser who chose Pierre-Amand Landry as his Minister of Public Works, a portfolio second only to the Premier's in terms of its patronage-dispensing power.[19] His 72-page report tabled the following April dismissed all the grievances submitted by Rev.Thomson. It also produced evidence suggesting that the affair had been greatly exaggerated.

Fraser criticized the local school board for poor judgment but he found no evidence of clerical interference in the schools or that the Sisters had forced Protestant children to kneel or to cross themselves.[20] As for the teaching of catechism, "the evidence established" that several had done so during the noon-hour break on the assumption that this was not part of the teaching day. Although an infringement on the regulations, it was not a "wilful" one.

The tabling of the *Fraser Report* more or less ended the Bathurst Affair, even though Pitts and other militant Orangemen managed to keep it alive a little longer. His motion to nullify it was soundly defeated.

Next, five directors of the Bathurst Orange Lodge filed a suit against the Bathurst School Trustees on the ground they had no right to levy taxes on the lodge's premises.[21] Taking a leaf from their brothers in Ontario and Manitoba, Pitts and his fellow

---

[19] Dr.D.M. Young of the University of New Brunswick prepared the J.J. Fraser entry for the *Dictionary of Canadian Biography*. I am indebted to him for this information.

[20] *Fraser Report*, p. 60

[21] *Hatfield*, p. 56

Orangemen now turned to the Manitoba schools controversy in an obvious effort to keep alive sectarian unrest.

At the 1894 annual meeting of the New Brunswick Orange Lodges, delegates unanimously endorsed a resolution to oppose any political candidate refusing to vote against remedial legislation. Three months later, a Presbyterian clergyman in Moncton denounced separate schools in one of his Sunday sermons.

These tactics made little impact on New Brunswick voters. In the 1895 provincial election, the Blair forces won 37 of the 46 seats. Among the victorious candidates were seven Acadians, a record. They included Peter Veniot, the Bathurst publisher who was probably aided by Blair's announcement a week before voting day that a compromise had been reached in the Bathurst affair, one acceptable to the Orange Lodge.

Undoubtedly, another factor helping both the Liberals and their Acadian supporters was a redistribution bill passed in March, 1895. It added three additional seats to the legislature — one each to Kent, Gloucester and Madawaska.

The dogged Pitts would not give up, but in the new legislature he seemed a lonely figure. When he introduced a resolution opposing any move by the federal government for a remedial bill in the Manitoba Schools case, he asked nine members, one after the other, to second his motion. Each one refused.

The *coup de grâce* for the Bathurst affair came on March 17, 1896 — St. Patrick's Day — when Judge Barker of the New Brunswick Supreme Court dismissed the suit launched by the Bathurst Orangemen.

One of the positive results of this cultural clash was the clarification of certain aspects of the 1875 Compromise. During the height of the controversy, the Board of Education decreed that trustees no longer could permit teachers to use any prayer in opening the school day. It had to be the Lord's Prayer.

"School Hours" were defined as "all the time between the opening and the close of the school for the day." This ended the practice in Bathurst schools where a teacher taught catechism during the noon-hour break. Also, public school buildings had to be fully occupied before additional premises could be leased.[22]

What did this Bathurst Affair do for the cause of New Brunswick Acadians? Very little. Once or twice in editorials and speeches, Herman Pitts and his Orangemen supporters mentioned the French language. But for them, the real danger was Catholicism.

For Pitts and others of like mind, the Bathurst Affair was yet another chapter in the long struggle between the Orange and the Green — one their ancestors assumed they had won at the Battle of the Boyne. New Brunswickers like Pitts were prisoners of their colonial mentality, one tied to ideological rigidities and stereotypes the Lodge had carried from "the old country." For Orangemen in the 1890s, the real enemy were the Catholic Irish, not Acadians.

Was it not an Irish-born bishop, James Rogers, who had invited the anglophone Sisters of Charity to leave Nova Scotia and teach in Bathurst? It was all part of an Irish plot to indoctrinate helpless Protestant children.

Nowhere in the speeches, editorials or documents relating to this affair was there an awareness that Bathurst was becoming a French-speaking community. A year after Judge Fraser filed his report, Premier Blair remarked in the legislature "that the school difficulties at Bathurst had arisen from the fact of there being not merely two religious persuasions in that locality but also two nationalities." He was probably referring to English Protestant and Irish Catholic "nationalities" — not English and French.

The wily Liberal leader, as well as many Acadians, must have been secretly pleased to see the Irish Catholics bearing the brunt of the struggle against angry Protestants. New Brunswick's Irish population was not growing as fast as the French and hence was potentially a weakening force. Because of a higher birthrate and a less mobile population, Acadians were filling a vacuum created by the rapidly departing Irish.

This shift would become increasingly apparent in the quasi-sectarian school system now firmly in place twenty years after

[22] *MacNaughton* p. 227.

the 1875 Compromise. The Catholic schools were staffed by a corps of dedicated nuns who gradually would be replaced by more and more French-speaking lay teachers. For Acadian cultural leaders of the 1890s and early twentieth century, the school system was the number one target.

# NINE

# COPING WITH INDUSTRIALIZATION AND WAR: 1880-1918

To Frederictonians, Alphée Belliveau must have seemed the comic stereotype of the Frenchman. For forty-eight years, from 1879-1927, Professor Belliveau taught French at the Normal School. Each and every Sunday, he and Mrs. Belliveau and their seven children attended St. Dunstan's Roman Catholic Church. Dressed always in a black Prince Albert frock-coat reaching almost to his knees, a beaver top hat perched firmly on his head, his right hand holding a gold-handled ebony walking stick, le professeur on this Sunday promenade presented a memorable sight.[1]

He was much more. Alphée Belliveau maintained an Acadian bridgehead in the English and Protestant world of Fredericton. He forebade his children to speak a word of English in their home. And that home was a "sanctuary" for Acadian politicians.

As they grew to maturity, the Belliveau children followed a familiar Acadian pattern. Three migrated to the United States; one entered the priesthood; another became a nun. Somehow on his miserly salary, Belliveau found the means to send all seven to post-secondary schools. The sons attended Collège Saint-Joseph in Memramcook; a daughter graduated from Normal School and another attended a convent in Québec.

---

[1] Alexandre- J. Savoie, *Un Siècle de revendications scolaire au Nouveau-Brunswick 1871-1971* Vol. I, p. 166; hereafter cited as *Savoie*.

Throughout their long Fredericton exile, Professor and Marie Belliveau kept close ties with the wider Acadian community. Even before their marriage in 1885, both had become active in the Acadian renaissance.

In 1881, Alphée was named a delegate to the first Acadian Congress at Memramcook, but his English superiors refused to allow him the time off. In 1885, shortly before her marriage to Alphée, Marie Babineau, who had been teaching at the parish school in her home village of Saint-Louis, proudly agreed to a request from her priest, Father Marcel-François Richard, to sew together the first Acadian flag. A few weeks later, it was waving before the cheering delegates at the Miscouche Congress.[2]

Despite Alphée Belliveau's dedication to the Acadian cause, he faced great odds in maintaining French enrolment at Normal School. In 1889, his department had 29 students; by 1895 it had only 21 before climbing to a record of 50 in 1900.[3] Whatever the French enrolment at the province's only teacher training institution, it was never enough to service the burgeoning school population in the French districts.

In his report for 1894, the Chief Superintendent of Education, J.A. Inch, revealed that nearly half the schools in Madawaska were still taught by untrained teachers. But this problem was not confined to French districts. The inspector for Victoria noted that despite "the increased output of teachers from the Provincial Normal School, it is still impossible to secure trained teachers for several districts in the Danish Colony."

George Mersereau's 1894 report for Beresford parish just north of Bathurst suggested the problem was both linguistic and economic. "Some speak only English; some only French, when they start." Also, each term brought a different group of students: "graded in the summer, ungraded in the winter."

Under provincial regulations, each school district was required to hold its annual meeting in October. In many districts of Gloucester, this was impossible "as the Ratepayers are always absent at that time engaged in fishing."

[2] *Savoie*, p. 163.
[3] *MacNaughton*, p. 234.

Reading these informative and sympathetic reports by dedicated inspectors like Mersereau emphasizes the huge task of operating a successful school system in one language, let alone two. That system's objectives, textbooks and teacher-training were overwhelmingly urban. Often the people it was trying to educate were predominantly rural. In this era before rapid transportation and electronic communications, rural life followed an oral tradition.

For example, when a dairy expert from Québec addressed a gathering in Petit Rocher, Gloucester County, on the best ways to produce quality butter and cheese, his audience understood. For years afterwards, their products earned prizes at local and provincial agricultural fairs. Their task was made easier because they worked in their own language. Not so their children.

"Most of the Acadian teachers in Restigouche," noted Inspector Mersereau in his 1895 report, find much difficulty in teaching their pupils oral lessons based on a text book which is entirely in English and every word has to be translated. Others have found the better way [is] to speak English with the pupils every day, in addition to reading and composition in that language so that by grade III the child is quite fluent." [4]

Social and economic conditions in many remote French districts unwittingly slowed down this assimilation process. Visiting a Tracadie school during his rounds in 1896, Mersereau discovered the principal, W.L. Allain, was absent. He was suffering from typhoid fever.

In an adjoining district, Mersereau reported on "a peculiar state of affairs." He found that most pupils "attend each session only long enough to recite their reading lesson. Often one of the parents awaits at the door till this scholastic duty is performed, and then accompanies the pupil home, to engage him or her in manual labour for the rest of the day." Mersereau also noted that these parents "will not procure other than reading books for their children. Reading is all they require of the schools; all else partakes of vanity."

[4] *Journals of the Legislative Assembly of New Brunswick,* " Report of the Chief Superintendent of Education," December 31, 1894, p. 21.

This astute public servant also had a comment on the aftermath of the Bathurst school affair. "The teachers in both town and village are all doing their duty faithfully under trying circumstances, and hoping earnestly for the time when all the wealth and energies of heart and brain now squandered on legal contests shall be directed ... to the schools."

This doughty inspector, who travelled twice a year by carriage and sleigh, over the entire northeastern counties, had the Victorian age's appreciation for words. Modern scholars trying to fathom New Brunswick's social history should look closely at the careers and reports of Mersereau and Alphée Belliveau.

Both of these men worked in a state education system that was English in tone and direction. Neither probably expected any major changes but Acadian politicians kept pressing. In 1900, the veteran MLA from Kent, Urbain Johnson, requested more bilingual inspectors for predominantly French districts. It mattered not to him whether the person was French, English or Scot, so long as he could speak both languages. His plea was ignored.

Johnson made the same request the next year. He was supported by Joseph Poirier of Gloucester who asked that French students be given "a series of French school books on the same footing as the English."

No English-dominated government would go that far in 1901 but a short time later, it increased the number of school inspectors from six to eight. The new appointments included J.F. Doucet of Gloucester, whose territory included all French schools in the province.[5]

During the 1900 legislative session, Fred LaForest, a new member from Edmundston who had recently crossed the floor to join the Opposition, raised some awkward questions. How did it happen that for the first time in twenty-five years, the cabinet had just one Roman Catholic? LaForest thought it "most extraordinary" that the mostly French and Catholic county of Gloucester had chosen John Young, a Protestant, to represent them in a

[5] *MacNaughton*, p. 235.

recent by-election.[6] Was this not proof that the French political influence was declining?

The lone Catholic referred to was the veteran member from Campbellton, Charles LaBillois, Commissioner of Agriculture. He replied that Young had "large interests in the country", no doubt a reference to his family's extensive fish and merchandizing business. In choosing him "in preference to one of their own nationality" LaBillois thought Gloucester voters had shown "a spirit of liberality which could not fail to win approval." He promised that the Liberal administration of Premier Emmerson would "look after the French and Catholic" constituents.

LaForest's later remarks revealed his anger at being ousted as Madawaska's chief patronage dispenser. His continued criticisms uncovered other facets of the Liberal support system. His charge that the government planned to revive the defunct Bathurst *Courrier* with new grants for carrying translations of the legislative debates brought an admission from Labillois: similar grants had been given in the past to *Le Courrier* as well as *Le Moniteur Acadien* and *L'Évangéline*.

*Le Moniteur*, a long-time Conservative supporter, had lost this patronage plum when it published the Opposition members' remarks in full, but had failed, in the Liberals' judgment, to give equal coverage to the government. LaBillois thought *Le Courrier* had been fair to both sides.

Whatever LaForest's motives for raising this cultural issue, he had touched a sensitive nerve. Every speaker following him in the lengthy budget debate mentioned his charges and tried to refute them. What they could not overlook was the lack of French and Catholic representation in the Liberal cabinet.

With the Bathurst and Manitoba schools issues so recently laid to rest, few besides LaForest were anxious to re-open old wounds. Instead, they seemed to welcome the chance to talk about anything else.

All participants in this debate mentioned the Boer War and all, including LaForest, fervently supported the British cause. Other topics included the overspending for roads and bridges because

[6] *Debates*, February 16, 1900, p. 23.

of the need to replace structures washed away in a disastrous fall flood; the smallpox epidemic that swept through lumber camps in Gloucester, Kent and Westmorland; the possible development of Grand Falls' hydro-electric potential to meet the needs of pulp and paper mills expected to set up in the province; and as always, more railroads.

Items contained in the 1901 budget estimates reveal the priorities of that day. On March 20, the following expenditures were approved in quick succession:

— $40,000 for the Lunatic Asylum in Saint John, for 534 patients, including "some old people of weak mind who should be in the alms house";

— $300 for the dependents of about 40 Acadian fishermen drowned when a terrible storm swept across lower Gloucester during the previous September;

— $500 for transporting New Brunswick's display of stuffed birds to an exhibition at the Imperial Institute in London.[7]

As the new century got underway, so too did the bandwagon for industrial development. Public leaders, notably politicians, carefully avoided anything that smacked of old 19th century taboos like religion and cultural diversity and division. Yet these divisions did not vanish; rather they seemed to grow along with the pulp mills, with a little encouragement from religious bigots like Louis Joseph King, who might best be described as a renegade Acadian.

Born into a family that traced its ancestry back to the early Acadians who founded French Village above Fredericton, King left his Catholic faith to pursue a long and stormy career as a Protestant evangelist and fierce anti-Catholic polemicist both in the Maritimes and in the United States.

His *Scarlet Mother on the Tiber* first appeared in 1908 and reflected a point of view found widely among Protestant com-

[7] *Debates,* March 20, 1901, p. 108.

munities along the lower Saint John river valley, an area still known in some circles as New Brunswick's "Bible Belt".[8]

King chose his title from his version of religious history "reaching from the Twentieth Century back to the Inquisition." According to King, "the Protestant need not expect mercy from The Scarlet Beast on the Tiber."

Along with his accounts of hair-raising escapes from Catholic mobs trying to disrupt his evangelical meetings, King has some pithy descriptions of Saint John valley communities he knew as a young man. At St. Ann's Catholic Church at French Village, where his parents attended, "the worshippers were divided into three classes or castes or nationalities. The Indians held the left, the French the right side and the Irish occupied the gallery."[9] King saw Fredericton "as a beautiful place ... composed of a proud, aristocratic people, with no salvation."

Alexander Gibson, the creator of Marysville, "was a kind of Protestant Pope, as he owned the entire village, built a sixty-thousand dollar church, hired his own preacher and dictated to him what should and what should not be preached ... But how like the modern pulpits of today? The man of thousands generally carries the modern preacher in his vest pocket."

King's diatribes were aimed at English-speaking Catholics — mostly Irish, judging by the fierce responses he often got when angry crowds tried to break up his rallies. Except for a vivid account of the St. Bartholemew's Day Massacre, French Catholics were ignored by "ex-Romanist" King (as he described himself in his many books). But his bigotry must have helped keep alive the cultural animosities separating New Brunswick's two linquistic communities.

During the first fourteen years of the new century, when French representation in the Legislature nearly vanished, the English politicians acted in much the same way and with the

---

[8] Louis J. King, *The Scarlet Mother on the Tiber,* (St. Louis Missouri/L.L. Queensbury, York Co., N.B.). I am indebted to Dr. D.M. Young of the University of New Brunswick for bringing this remarkable volume to my attention and for providing a copy for examination.

[9] King, p. 8-9.

same priority as their predecessors. They wanted and got more railroads.

Through the persistent efforts of Dr. William Pugsley, Saint John became the eastern winter terminal for the C.P.R. and had its port facilities greatly expanded. The National Transcontinental from Moncton through the forest wilderness to Edmundston was completed in 1914. The International or Restigouche and Western was finished in 1910, linking Campbellton with St. Leonard.

The notorious Saint John and Québec line, known as the Valley Railroad, ran from Woodstock to Westfield near Saint John. Before it was finally completed in 1919, it had sunk the career of Premier James Kidd Flemming in the worst kickback scandal of the age. The details of that affair were slowly revealed to the House by Auguste Dugal, who along with J.H. Pelletier from Madawaska, formed the entire Opposition after the 1912 election.[10]

One of the few Acadians on the Government side of the House in these years was Dr. D.V. Landry, a medical doctor from Buctouche. First elected in 1908, he was the last of the old-line Conservative Acadians to be in the Cabinet. From 1912 to 1917, he was Provincial Secretary. This was an awkward post for an Acadian to hold in these years when the English were so completely in control and the main political thrust was big business. From his vantage point, Dr. Landry had to watch a sad process that had begun much earlier: the steady exodus of young New Brunswickers from rural areas.

If his English businessmen-colleagues had given the same priority to land settlement, agriculture and teachers' salaries as they did to railways, hydro projects and pulp mills, they might have stemmed New Brunswick's population loss.

Some idea of the state of affairs in education can be seen by the level of teachers' salaries. A New Brunswick male teacher

---

[10] For a detailed account of the Valley Railroad scandal, see Arthur T. Doyle, *Front Benches and Back Rooms* (Toronto, 1976), pp. 139-174.

with first class qualifications earned $520 a year; the few women in this top category received $312. No wonder so many were leaving for the booming prairies, a point raised by many inspectors in their 1906 reports.[11]

Professor Alphée Belliveau noted that his French department at the Normal School had attracted 34 French student teachers (23 in the first term, 11 in the second). He regretted "that our French people do not, in their own interest, take more advantage of the opportunities which this Department offers, by sending larger numbers, as many at least as will fairly meet the requirements of the Acadian schools."[12] Acadian students probably avoided Fredericton and Normal School for two reasons: they lacked the money and could not speak enough English to get along in anglo Fredericton.

In his 1906 report, Chief Superintendent James Inch referred particularly to the "poor districts." This was an official designation for those parts of rural New Brunswick with assessed evaluations under $12, 000. They received from 25 to 33 1/3 percent in additional grants. In this year, this came to $11,967 for the entire province. And there were many "poor districts." In 1906, Kent County had seventy, the most in the province.

By contrast, the International Railway had received in 1906 a total of $30,000 under the provincial Railway Subsidy Act for the 27 miles completed that year betwen Campbellton and St. Leonard. The project's main promoter was Charles Riordon, an Ontario pulp and paper manufacturer. Shortly after its completion, this line was sold to the federal government for $2.7 millions.[13]

Faithful public servant that he was, Chief Superintendent Inch was not about to challenge this gross imbalance in public expenditures. Neither did he ever comment on the fact that most of these "poor districts" were in French areas. Inch did comment in

---

[11] *Journals of the Legislative Assembly of New Brunswick 1907* Appendix B. Hereafter *Journals*.
[12] *Journals*, Report of Normal School, pp. 9-10.
[13] *Public Archives of New Brunswick*, Railway Files; International Railway, correspondence for August 1914.

this 1906 annual report about a possible remedy for a system that more or less forced property owners to keep their property assessments as low as possible in order to qualify for "poor district" grants.

Noting that there had never been a case where a district had been removed from the "poor district" list with the consent of its rate-payers, Superintendendent Inch saw one way out: a uniform taxation rate for all property in the province.

If this included railway and timber property, it would have transformed New Brunswick's fiscal policies. This was not going to happen. When major tax reform finally came with the 1963 Royal Commisson on Finance and Municipal Taxation, it was almost too late. By then, some counties, notably Gloucester, teetered on the edge of bankruptcy.

Instead of reform, New Brunswick's political leaders adopted a policy of drift ... allowing more and more young citizens, French and English, to leave the province, never to return. Those remaining, especially in the villages and rural countryside, continued to receive minimal schooling. Boys usually left before the legal age of fourteen to work as pulp cutters or fishermen; the girls joined their mothers and older sisters in the new textile mills and fish plants. Meanwhile, their patrimony shifted more and more to foreigners.

In September, 1907, the International Paper Company of New York purchased 250,000 acres of New Brunswick forest land for a dollar an acre.[14] The largest lots were in Gloucester County. The firm's president stated that it was a case of getting raw materials or closing his mills, most of them located in the United States.

This kind of timber purchase brought growing cries of protest — not from the inhabitants of the "poor districts" most directly affected — but from New Brunswick mill owners. H.W. Schofield of the Partington Pulp and Paper Company in Saint John

---

[14] *Journals of the Legislative Assembly 1908*, Report of the Commissioner of Crown Lands, xvii.

and W.B. Snowball of the J.B. Snowball Company in Chatham demanded export duties on wood pulp.[15]

Opposing such legislation were forest land owners on the Miramichi who could profit from sky-rocketing demands (and prices) for pulp in the United States. True to New Brunswick's established political tradition, Saint John voices proved stronger: the province soon followed Ontario and Québec's example and banned the export of raw wood pulp.

A new chapter in New Brunswick's economic and social history began to unfold as new, foreign-owned, pulp companies began to set up in Bathurst, Dalhousie and Newcastle. It would mean big salaries for the English hired to manage the new plants. It would tie much of the province's timber resources to twenty-five and thirty-year leases. As a result, huge areas of the province became virtual fiefdoms for absentee corporate directors.

From now on, ordinary New Brunswickers reluctant to trespass on leased land could best view their province from the windows of railway cars or as pulp cutters hired out to local contractors at starvation wages.

Traditional hunting and fishing privileges were gradually restricted as the provincial government, locked into long-term financial arrangements giving the better deal to private corporations, looked for new revenue sources. It leased out prime fishing and hunting areas to rich tourists, often the same Montréal and New York executives who owned the pulp mills and forest leases.

French New Brunswickers were among the most affected by these corporate intrusions and privileges. By 1900, their communities on the fringes of the pulp company's vast cutting empires were providing much of the cheap labour demanded by this new economy.

Little new land was now available for settlers, whether French or English. An exception was the Blue Bell Tract, a 50,000-acre stretch in Victoria County purchased by the government in 1906 from the New Brunswick Railway Company. Smaller sections around Arthurette, near Perth and others in the interior of

---

[15] Castell Hopkins (ed.), *The Canadian Annual Review 1907*, p. 228.

Gloucester, Restigouche and Madawaska Counties along new rail lines were also serviced.

The going rate was a dollar an acre — a bargain in today's terms but not eighty years ago when hard cash and/or easy credit were rare commodities for ordinary citizens. Hundreds moved onto these tracts as squatters, hoping that Fredericton politicians would relent and give them legal title if they stayed.

Many did, especially in the Blue Bell tract, but the efforts by the provincial government to encourage British farmers to buy abandoned farms points to a familiar story. People moved in to cut the most accessible timber and then moved away.

Besides trying to lure mature British farmers, New Brunswick entered into an agreement with the Middlemore Home Corporation "for the settlement annually in our Province of some hundreds of boys and girls, principally with the farmers." [16] The province paid them $3 for each child placed in their care and the federal government returned eighty cents a head as part of an annual subsidy.

These children, as the Crown Lands Report for 1907 frankly admitted, were to make up for "the scarcity of men and high rates of wages ... seriously felt by many of our farmers who required such help." A similar arrangement had been made with the Salvation Army which in addition to receiving the same rates per child also got $500 a year "for advertising the Province."

From time to time, Opposition members in the Legislature complained that similar help should be extended "to our people." On an even rarer occasion, French members noted that too much was being done to maintain and strengthen English New Brunswick.

This new industrial age, with its foreign-owned pulp mills, seemed to be helping the English at the expense of the French. One exception or challenge to this world was La Société Mutuelle l'Assomption. By 1907, it had a New Brunswick charter and twenty-one branches. Except for those in Rogersville

---

[16] *Journals of the Legislative Assembly 1908*, Report of the Commissioner of Crown Lands, xxvi.

and Caraquet, all were located in Westmorland and Kent Counties.

Eventually, this organization would become prosperous enough to finance major real estate and other ventures, but during the first two decades of this century it confined its lobbying to French education. Three of its executive members had played key roles, along with two French school inspectors, in getting a French version of a Canadian history text for elementary grades.[17] Because it had chosen Moncton as its headquarters, much of the Society's earlier activities at the grass roots level remained concentrated in southeastern New Brunswick. Yet, others continued to work farther north, notably in Caraquet.

An energetic priest, Father Théophile Allard, was largely responsible for the Congrégation des Eudistes, a wealthy teaching order, to establish a boy's college in Caraquet, where Allard had set up a small school.[18] In March, 1900, Joseph Poirier, the MLA for Grand Anse, introduced a bill to incorporate the Caraquet's Collège de Sacré Coeur. He informed the House it now had four ecclesiastical and two lay teachers and forty-five students. Instruction was in "both English and French" and covered "all branches of education." [19]

Over the next ten years, this Caraquet institution flourished — in sharp contrast to the under-financed and often poorly-attended public schools scattered through Gloucester County. A visitor to this remote fishing village might have wondered how it found the resources to support two school systems. The answer lay in the wealth of the Eudistes Order and the means of some of its members. They had contributed to the cost of a magnificent chapel, whose tall carved pillars and high vaulted dome quickly became a source of local pride. One Eudistes, Father Pujos, had donated the chapel's Casavent organ.

---

[17] *Savoie*, Vol. I, p. 189.
[18] Marcel Tremblay, *50 Ans d'éducation catholique et française en Acadie* (Bathurst, 1949), pp. 38-42. Hereafter *Tremblay*.
[19] *Debates*, March 20, 1900, p. 176.

In 1910, the new college dormitory and the "grande salle de récréation" were quickly transformed into an emergency hospital when a typhoid epidemic struck down hundreds of citizens. Father Pujos later gave generously so Caraquet could improve its water system, a move that prevented later outbreaks.[20]

Five years later, a more familiar scourge, fire, destroyed the magnificent main convent structure. Only the graceful chapel was spared. Two choices faced the Eudistes: rebuild on the same location or follow the suggestion of Archbishop LeBlanc of Saint John and find another community. Near the end of January, 1916, the National Council of the Eudistes, meeting in Bathurst, decided to locate in that centre. Caraquet was too remote and its rail link unreliable. Bathurst was on the main Intercolonial line, making easier access to more students, especially from the rapidly expanding Madawaska area.

Bathurst was also better located to challenge a rival Irish school at Chatham. It had been revived as St. Michael's College by the Basilian Order. In a letter to Bishop Barry, the college rector, Father W.J. Roach thought "a college in Bathurst, would to a large extent, cut off from us the best territory in the Diocese in Chatham, since our record shows that the majority of our boarders from this diocese come to us by way of Bathurst." [21] The old tug of war between French and Irish was still alive!

The Eudistes already had a Bathurst base. In 1915 they had purchased property to house novitiates destined for the Seminary in Halifax. It was here that Bishop Barry granted them permission to set up a temporary college so long as "no work of a definite character calculated to make it in any way necessary institution to remain in Bathurst be undertaken ... until a definite decision was made after consulting with Rome."[22]

The boys had scarcely resumed their classes in this Bathurst location when another fire struck. In the fall of 1917, the Eudistes reached an agreement with Bishop Barry for a permanent struc-

---

[20] *Tremblay* p. 157, 162.
[21] *Tremblay* p. 181.
[22] *Tremblay p. 186*.

ture. It seemed the francophone Eudistes had more influence at the Vatican than the anglophone Irish.

The Collège de Sacré-Coeur remained a vital cultural force in Bathurst for the next sixty years. Throughout that period, Sacré-Coeur became the inspiration and training ground for hundreds of young Acadians and francophones rapidly reaching numerical supremacy in the northern counties.

The annual reports of county school inspectors gives proof of this population shift. P.G. McFarlane, in his 1916 report, noted that Restigouche's school population had doubled in the last three years "owing to the influx of large numbers of French families from the Province of Québec and elsewhere." They had "taken up homesteads to engage in pioneer work in the northern wilds of New Brunswick." [23]

The Ontario editor of an annual review, Castel Hopkins, as a super patriot and Imperialist, suggested another reason for this migration. The French were hiding to avoid "possible compulsion to serve overseas." His description in the 1917 edition of *The Canadian Annual Review* described "the exodus of young men from Québec to the States" and referred to similar movements along the Ontario and New Brunswick frontiers.

Two years earlier, Hopkins reported that New Brunswick "was enlisting men at the rate of a battalion a month" or roughly 500 recruits. At the end of 1915, an Acadian battalion was created under the command of L.C. Daigle in an apparent attempt to shore up the already sagging recruiting campaign among New Brunswick's French-speaking citizens. By September 1916, *L'Évangéline* noted that it still needed 200 men.[24]

In March 1916, the New Brunswick Legislature gave an enthusiastic welcome to wounded war hero, Lt. Col. Percy Guthrie, MLA for York. He made a strong appeal for conscription and later led a recruiting drive for the New Brunswick 236th Battalion.

---

[23] Castell Hopkins (ed.), *The Canadian Annual Review 1916*, p. 635.
[24] Philippe Doucet, "La Politique et les Acadiens" in *Les Acadiens des Maritimes* (Moncton, 1980), p. 276 Hereafter *Doucet.*

"Beacon fires were lit in every county," editor Hopkins later reported. "A fiery cross of St. Andrews was passed from meeting to meeting in the old Highland tradition." It was carried by car, bicycle, horse and pedestrian for a total of 1500 miles.

"In Saint John on September 25," wrote Hopkins, "it was a most spectacular sight with great crowds, torchlight processions, eloquent speeches — only four young men reported."

Gung-ho imperialists like Hopkins would never admit it, but toward the end of 1916, Canada's supposedly inexhaustible supply of "cannon fodder" had been used up. Young native-born Canadians were showing a marked reluctance to follow the earlier example of recent immigrants from the "Old Country" to serve overseas.

Among the leading opponents to conscription were the Irish. The Easter Sunday outbreaks in Dublin in March of 1916 had killed any spark of sympathy they had for the English cause. In many parts of far-away Canada, it was never strong although Canada's linquistic struggles left many Anglos with the erroneous impression that only the French opposed conscription. In June, 1917, the Military Service Bill was passed in a badly-divided House of Commons. Among the yea-votes was that of F. Robidoux, MP for Kent in the heart of Acadian New Brunswick.[25] Other members of the French establishment, including Bishop LeBlanc of Saint John, counselled adherence to the new law.

For New Brunswickers, conscription was just one more issue separating French and English. Prohibition was another. *Le Moniteur Acadien* continued to support the Conservative cause and the more aggressive *L'Évangéline* was even more strongly Liberal.

During the winter election campaign called by the provincial Tories in 1917, the growing French presence was the big issue, according to some Conservative newspapers. The shady deals of former Tory premier James Kidd Flemming, the potatoes-for-victory scandal, blatant patronage in running the Farm Settle-

---

[25] *Doucet*, p. 275. Also *Canada, House of Commons Debates*, June 26, 1917, p. 2703

ment Board — these issues were ignored by militant Tory editors like James Crocket.

His Fredericton *Gleaner* stated repeatedly during the campaign that the French had taken over while brave English New Brunswickers were dying for democracy in France. The day after one of Crocket's anti-French editorial diatribes, a young Acadian arrived home from the front. His right leg was missing. He was the son of Auguste Dugal, Liberal MLA for Madawaska. The *Gleaner* did not mention his home-coming.[26]

Crocket and other die-hard English Tories could only see the furious electioneering of Acadian Peter Veniot. He had been working at it for five years and this February 1917 election finally brought the desired results. More than any other Liberal, Peter Veniot was credited with "delivering" the Acadian vote. Whether he did or not, the French made the difference and gave the Liberals the victory. A modern Fredericton historian has summed up the election this way:

> The five Liberal victories in Saint John, Sunbury and Queens were by less than one hundred votes; in two cases, by the turn-around of single parishes. Every other Liberal seat was won because of overwhelming Acadian support. In the "mixed constituencies," pockets of English-speaking voters supported the government, only to be buried by the Acadian-Liberal vote surrounding them. It was unprecedented that a government winning handily almost everywhere in southern New Brunswick was defeated simply because of complete rejection by the Acadians. Now it seemed that the Liberal Party was the Acadian party, and it was "they" who were going to govern New Brunswick ... To thousands of English-speaking New Brunswickers, it was a terrifying prospect — a diabolical plot.[27]

---

[26] *Doyle*, p. 134. See also M.S. Spigelman article in *Société historique acadienne*, Cahier viii, 1977, pp. 5-22.
[27] *Doyle*, p. 131.

English Liberal newspapers like the Moncton *Daily Transcript* rushed to the defence of Acadian voters. After all, said an editorial in the *Transcript*, it was the Tories who had failed to elect a single Acadian or even a Roman Catholic. By contrast, several predominantly Acadian ridings had elected several English-speaking Protestants.

The English backlash had one immediate result: Peter Veniot, the one man who delivered the Liberal victory, could not be the next premier. This would only embarrass and perhaps anger English Liberals and support Tory contentions that Acadians were in command. The job went to the lacklustre Saint John businessman, Walter Foster. Veniot was given the next most important post — Minister of Public Works. The only other Acadian in the new cabinet, Auguste Dugal, received no portfolio.

The dust had hardly settled from the wholesale dismissals of Tory appointments by the revengeful Grits than another devisive election campaign swept over New Brunswick. This time, the government of Conservative Prime Minister Sir Robert Borden was asking Canadians to support its new conscription policy. Once again, Peter Veniot marshalled the Acadians to support Laurier's anti-conscription stand. Once again, he succeeded. Voting with them were Irish New Brunswickers as well as many English Protestants from rural areas.

For the next two generations, the Acadians and the Liberal party were inseparable. The fact that they were not always in power during those years points to the complexity of New Brunswick politics. Maintaining power took more than the Acadians' growing numbers. It involved economic power, which the Acadians lacked. If they could have produced an Acadian K.C. Irving, their march toward equality would have been faster and shorter.

# TEN

# P.J. VENIOT, PROHIBITION AND PULP MILLS: 1919-1929

Politics has long been New Brunswickers' favourite backroom sport. After the 1917 provincial election, Acadians had a more active part to play in that game. French power was now a vital part of the new Liberal government. No one symbolized Acadian political hopes more than Peter Veniot, the Minister of Public Works and the key figure in the cabinet of Premier Walter Foster.

The English in Saint John and Fredericton continued to dominate much of the Liberal party organization but Veniot held the most influential cabinet post and used it to build "an elaborate patronage machine."[1] It would cement the northern French-speaking counties to the Liberal cause for most of the twentieth century.

P.J. — as he was known far and wide — was never one to leave political allegiance to chance. As a veteran of the political wars since his early apprenticeship to the arch-Liberal John Hawkes, the fiery publisher of the Moncton *Daily Transcript*, P.J. had organized Gloucester county's first Liberal convention. During the 1890's he emerged as the political spokesman for the Acadian area stretching from Moncton north to Campbellton and over to Edmundston.[2]

---

[1] Arthur Doyle, *Front Benches & Back Rooms* (Toronto 1976) p. 176. Hereafter *Doyle*.
[2] *Doyle*, p. 30.

Born in Richibucto in 1863, he was raised in Nova Scotia and could not speak a word of French when he graduated from Pictou Academy. He learned the language when he fell in love and married an Acadian girl from Scoudouc, near Moncton. At the tender age of 24, he moved his family to Bathurst where he became editor of the French weekly, *Courrier des Provinces Maritimes*. He bought it in 1892 but eight years later he had a bad accident which led to a serious illness and then to financial problems.

Veniot was forced to fold his newspaper, resign his seat in the legislature and accept a sinecure as Collector of Customs for Bathurst so he could provide for his wife and six children. He remained an active Liberal and lost his federal job when the Borden-led Conservatives gained power in 1911.

Failing to be re-elected to the provincial legislature the following year, Veniot was hired by the New Brunswick Liberal party as one of their two full-time organizers. During the bitter 1917 election campaign, he proved to one and all how well he knew the local and especially the French political scene.

As the new minister of public works, Veniot played the old game of ins and outs with a vengeance. He ordered the firing of hundreds of Tory-appointed roads and bridge inspectors. Even some Liberals who owed their jobs to Conservative politicians got the axe. Veniot replaced them all with Liberals of proven loyalty. Many of these new "civil servants" were Acadians.

Veniot's power increased even more after 1919 when the federal government agreed to contribute forty percent of the cost to up-grade provincial highways so Canada could cope with the burgeoning automobile explosion. This deal gave New Brunswick an additional $230,000 a year and provided the energetic Veniot with the collateral to borrow large sums to improve ordinary and semi-trunk roads.[3]

His Conservative opponents, especially those from the Saint John River Valley, accused him of "spending more attention" (and presumably more money) on the northern and predominant-

---

[3] *Synoptic Reports of the Legislative Assembly 1920*, p. 169 Hereafter *Debates*.

ly French counties. One Tory newspaper thought the reason for this was that "Veniot was a Frenchman."

Answering this charge on the floor of the legislature, Veniot cited figures showing that $200,000 more had been spent on the Saint John river counties than all the rest combined. His department's spending policies faced renewed criticism during the 1920 general election campaign. Its road-building program was described as "reckless and extravagant" and intended for "the idle rich." The idea was to spend millions "on tourist roads for idlers, speedways for sports to race the railway trains." It was all at the expense of cross-country roads vital to farm production. But far worse criticism came as the campaign reached its final days.

On October 8, 1920, the day before the polls opened, the Saint John *Daily Mail*, a Liberal supporter, claimed that a Fredericton women's committee had been making "a house-to-house canvass ... trying to influence voters by raising the race and religion cry." One woman was told that if the Foster Government was returned to power, "there would be a civil war between Catholics and Protestants in New Brunswick within the year."[4]

If this was a Conservative campaign scheme, it backfired. The Conservatives lost six seats to a bloc of United Farmers candidates in southern constituencies, while Veniot once more delivered the French vote. The Liberals were returned with 24 seats. Another four were added after Veniot paid a hurried visit to gain the support of four farm-labour members elected on the Miramichi.[5]

After the 1920 election, the French members increasingly spoke up. In 1922, while seconding the Throne Speech, Seraphin Léger from Caraquet thanked the government for helping to reduce the post-war slump in the lumbering industry "by the adoption of regulations in the interests of new settlers on Crown lands."[6]

---

[4] Saint John *Standard,* October 8, 1920, cited in *Doyle,* p. 214.
[5] *Doyle,* p. 216.
[6] *Debates*, March 2, 1922, p. 26.

Léger also appreciated the introduction of short agricultural courses in French and hoped this would become a permanent policy. He stressed the need for more help "to settle the large new population on farms in the north where the population was increasing so rapidly."

Another new member in that 1922 House was Henry Diotte, a Conservative from Restigouche who had gained his seat after a court decree was required to settle disputed results. Like other French speakers before him, Diotte apologized "for having to address the members in a language not his own." Describing himself as a "poor lumberjack and farmer," he reported that Restigouche had been spared the ravages of the spruce budworm that had eaten through thousands of acres of New Brunswick forest land. Earlier, the House had been told that the insect had destroyed four billion cubic feet valued at over $19 millions. The experts believed "the problem would occur in a cycle of years."

The next speaker, John Robichaud, Liberal member from Shippagan, made no apologies about his language. Speaking English, he blamed the current business slump on federal freight rates and a banking system that was reluctant to invest in New Brunswick, especially in its fishing fleet. The banks "eagerly took all the money they could get at 3 percent interest and loaned it in the Canadian west at 7 percent to develop wheat farming." He urged the government "to get Ottawa to establish a separate fisheries department. In fish culture, New Brunswick was fifty years behind the times." He suggested sending young men to Seattle to learn new methods.

Turning to the most controversial issue of the day, prohibition, Robichaud acknowledged the obvious: it was not working. He thought New Brunswick "should have a better grasp on the sale of liquor. Medical prescriptions were only fakes. Out of 100 bottles of liquor sold by prescription, 99 were sold contrary to the law." It was probably correct to say that prohibition had closed the bar rooms, "but many secret bar rooms had been established in their place. What went on [there] was not to be told in the House."

Few New Brunswickers had to be told. Prohibition was the poor man's joke and often his profit. The federal law had been pushed through in 1916 as a wartime measure and election ploy. Its continuance after the war was subject to a plebiscite in each of the provinces. The New Brunswick vote on July 10, 1920 was won by the "drys," but as elsewhere in Canada, it was an impossible law to enforce.

The whole idea had been promoted by a well-organized and articulate minority, many of them middle-class women trying to win the right to vote. Using the emotional cover of the war, this largely English and Protestant group was able to ignore the deeply-held beliefs of the "silent majority" that drinking alcohol was a personal decision, beyond the jurisdiction of any government. In short, prohibition was a bad law because it lacked popular support. The "silent majority" did not believe in it, so they either ignored or worked around it.

With its lumbering and sea-faring traditions, New Brunswick was the least likely "dry" province. Its numerous coastal communities; its principal seaport of Saint John dominated by an Irish population which looked upon the city's numerous taverns as their "inner sanctum"; its long undefended and undefendable border with the United States — all these factors made effective enforcement impossible.

Prohibition meant the chance for easy money at a time when a post-war depression held New Brunswick in its grip from 1919 to the early 1930s. And hard-up New Brunswickers were not alone in taking advantage of this "bonanza." The provincial government did too.

By 1922, the government's revenues from the liquor exporters' tax and the Board of Liquor Commissioners amounted to over $525,000 out of a total revenue of $3.1 millions.[7] No comparable figures are available for the bootleggers' and rumrunners' returns for that year — or any other.

When mass circulation American magazines like *Ladies Home Journal* could quote P.J. Veniot that "We all know that the border warehouses are for shoving booze across the border" —

[7] *Debates*, Budget Address, March 23, 1923, pp. 70-72

it was clear to everyone that New Brunswick's illegal liquor trade was an open secret.[8]

In the same article, an unidentified Saint John resident told of seeing a vessel loaded with liquor at the government-bonded warehouse sail out at dusk. The official destination was Bermuda, but later that same night, this ship returned to unload at another wharf. The cargo was then trucked to a drugstore "owned by the son of a city detective." The rest went into boxcars and trucks for distribution in Maine, Québec and Ontario.

In Victoria County, everyone knew about Joe Walnut and his gang of sixteen "of the toughest lumberjacks or sailors that could be gathered together." Joe owned the Arrow Hotel in St. Leonard which also served as his bootlegging warehouse.

In the hotel basement was an open bar where "police and revenue officers were seen drinking with well-known bootleggers and smugglers." According to an article from a Toronto newspaper reprinted in the *Carleton Sentinel* of Woodstock, "probably nowhere along the international border from the Atlantic to the Pacific is booze-running so rampant and so open as it is from New Brunswick into Maine."[9]

During the Throne Speech debate in March 1924, P.J. Veniot had considerable difficulty denying opposition charges that the enforcement of the provincial Prohibition Act had become "a sham, a farce and a public scandal." He reminded the House of his earlier warning that "rum-row would be established off the coast of New Brunswick." He added that his forecast "was not as bad as the actual resulting conditions."[10]

Enforcement was the big problem, P.J. admitted. The municipal authorities were getting no cooperation from the police, many of whom were acting under "special orders" from town councils to ignore the liquor laws.

John Peck, the Conservative member for Albert, reported seeing "a tremendous quantity of de Kuyper gin" coming in by

[8] Cited in *Doyle*, p. 235.
[9] *Doyle*, p. 237.
[10] *Debates*, March 7, 1924, p. 26.

express. According to the shipping invoices, this was for medicinal purposes and Peck asked the Minister of Health what gin would cure. "It is said to be good for kidney trouble," was Dr. William Robert's tongue-in-cheek reply.[11]

People living through this colourful era had their favourite prohibition stories. Even bootleggers passed on some to eager journalists. The biggest and most accessible supply of "booze" was on the French islands of St. Pierre and Miquelon, just off the south coast of Newfoundland.

"I've seen so much liquor in cases stacked in the open air on Miquelon," a Saint John liquor dealer told one American reporter, "that it was like a town with streets through piles of boxes." He added that shipments were picked up by New Brunswick bootleggers "operating from Shediac, Buctouche, Richibucto, Shippagan and Caraquet."[12]

According to a report carried in the Charlottetown *Guardian* the fishermen in these villages received from $100 to $120 a month and the captain about $500 to transport this Miquelon contraband to within twelve miles of the United States coast. Here it was picked up by American smugglers.

This lucrative business continued until 1933, when the new Roosevelt administration, with the cooperation of state legislatures, cancelled their country's prohibition laws. Until that happened, many New Brunswickers, including hundreds of Acadians, coasted through the early depression years on a fairly steady and tax-free income.

Meanwhile, their political champion, P.J. Veniot, continued his march toward the peak of power. He reached it on March 13, 1923 when he rose in the legislature to take part in the Throne Speech as Premier Veniot. A few weeks earlier, Walter Foster told a party caucus meeting in Saint John's Cliff Club that he was stepping down "in the interests of his personal affairs." He asked his fellow Liberals to support Peter Veniot as his successor and they quickly agreed.

---

[11] *Debates*, March 7, 1924, p. 41.
[12] Cited in *Doyle*, p. 237.

In his inaugural adress to the legislature as the first Acadian to achieve New Brunswick's highest political office, Premier Veniot thanked "the English-speaking fellow citizens on their recognition of such a measure of toleration." It would bring more closely together "the two great races who inhabited New Brunswick."[13] Actually, his new position was more a tribute to a gifted and partisan politician than to the steadily-increasing Acadian population.

Unlike the events and the thrust associated with the second Acadian-led government in the 1960s, the Veniot administration made no abrupt shift in policy. Instead, it dealt with the issues of the day. A major one was whether the proposed giant power development at Grand Falls should be in private or public hands. Another was the growing public debt, a perennial issue made more acute because of expenditures needed to repair the enormous damage caused by a terrible freshet occurring in May, a few weeks after P.J. took over as Premier. The worst single result was the partial destruction of the new earthen dam at Musquash near Saint John.

The only election P.J. Veniot fought as Premier was a classic struggle. Like previous New Brunswick elections, it was a complex affair involving prohibition, government extravagance, record-high freight rates and cutthroat competition from Quebec lumber mills. The unpopularity of the national Liberal leader, Prime Minister Mackenzie King, was a significant factor. The election that P.J. called for August 10, 1925, in the final year of his legal mandate, had two other elements: pressures from large forest-based companies, and religious bigotry.

This 1925 election was the first one where a large American-owned pulp and paper mill — International Paper — had a critical role. It led the fight for a privately-controlled development of Grand Falls Power. This was also the first election where the American-style anti-Catholic element appeared in the form of the odious Ku Klux Klan.

---

[13] *Debates*, March 23, 1923, p. 29.

Premier Veniot fought a bitter battle — and lost. Some of the details of that conflict came out during the campaign; others surfaced during post-election speeches in the legislature.

The president of Bathurst Paper Company, Angus McLean, played a confusing but crucial role in the election's final outcome. In February, 1925, he had openly supported Premier Veniot's plans for a government development of Grand Falls. His name was the first on the nominating papers of Ivan C. Rand, the successful contender in a Gloucester by-election. In April, Rand introduced the Grand Falls Hydro Bill authorizing the New Brunswick Power Commission to borrow more money for an immediate start on the huge development. At the same time, McLean assured Premier Veniot that his mill would buy up to 15,000 horsepower of power when the dam was finished, so long as the cost would make Bathurst Paper competitive with Québec mills.

McLean did not reveal that he was encouraging J.B.M. Baxter, Conservative Member of Parliament for Saint John, to leave Ottawa and become provincial Tory leader. He was also helping to prepare a brief for the New Brunswick Lumbermen's Association demanding major cuts in stumpage fees.[14]

In July, Premier Veniot met with the lumbermen and granted them a general reduction. It was not enough and McLean told his old friend that he and his associates would oppose the government in the election campaign. When it got underway, P. J., making his first political appearance in Saint John, told how McLean had supported Rand in the by-election. "I trusted him as I would my most intimate friend. I have been deceived ... He still continued to urge me up to two weeks ago to rush the work" on the Grand Falls project.[15]

The most remarkable platform show of the entire campaign was delivered by Ivan Rand before 1500 people jammed into Saint John's Imperial Theatre. The outspoken young Moncton lawyer accused John Baxter and the Conservatives of being associated with the Ku Klux Klan.

[14] *Doyle*, pp. 245-246.
[15] *Doyle*, p. 250.

He also got into a shouting match with Donald Fraser, the teetotaller president of Fraser Companies and a fellow Liberal.

"This man," Rand declared as he pointed his finger at the startled Fraser, was not interested in the province's welfare. "But he's gravely concerned about its soul. He has been strongly advocating temperance and preaching it throughout the province, even in districts where the inhabitants were going around in rags and poverty and on the verge of starvation."[16]

It was a memorable evening, but it probably indicated how desperately Rand, Veniot and other Liberals were fighting against the big forest interests. Once again, the big forces won.

P.J. was returned, but Rand and most other English Liberal candidates were defeated. From a healthy majority of 29, the Veniot-led forces were reduced to eleven, mostly from French constituencies. Was it another example of an English backlash? It would seem so.

The new legislature heard more details of this bitter campaign when P.J. spoke in the 1926 Throne Speech.[17] He said he was reluctant to refer to the "racial and religious" slurs he had endured. He pointed no accusing fingers at the members of the new Conservative government but noted that the cry of "French domination was actively used in some of the more Protestant counties."

Veniot read into the legislative records a letter dated July 29, 1925 written by a Tory organizer in Queens County, Alvin Clark, to two of his constituents. "As you know, the Premier we have today is a Roman Catholic and a Frenchman at that and we as Protestants want to put them out."

P.J. next referred to "another and more despicable method." Thousands of copies of "the Oath of a Fourth Degree Knight of Columbus" were distributed throughout the predominantly English counties of Carleton, Queens, Sunbury, York, Kings, Saint John and Charlotte. They were printed in Flint, Michigan and were sent "at first to separate members of the Orange Lodges and after the election was well underway, thousands were pur-

---

[16] *Doyle*, p. 252.
[17] *Debates*, March 16, 1926, pp. 24-26.

chased for use in this province at forty cents per hundred." He continued: "According to this bogus oath, a Knight of Columbus binds himself to recognize only the will of the Church of Rome in matters political or of state, and shall have no opinion of his own in such matters. He further binds himself to extirpate Protestants from the face of the earth, and to use for such purposes the poisonous cup, the strangulation cord, the steel of the poignard or the leaden bullet."

On many of these circulars, the following was printed in red: "Premier Veniot is a fourth degree Knight of Columbus. This is what he subscribes to. Can any Protestant vote for his government?"

P.J. had more to tell his legislative colleagues. Pamphlets delivered to Fredericton householders proclaimed: "A vote for Veniot is a vote for the Pope of Rome. If Veniot is returned to power he will introduce a system of Catholic separate schools ... No Protestant will be allowed to enter the Department buildings without having first learned to make the sign of the cross."

The former premier paid tribute to "certain broad-minded ministers of the gospel" who warned "their flock against the influence of such degrading methods." He also "would not accuse any member of the Legislature of having participated in this nefarious work, yet ... they must have been very blind or extremely deaf if they knew nothing of the doings of their over-zealous followers."

Then there was the Ku Klux Klan. Veniot described how "certain persons" organized lodges of the Klan in some areas. "A number of American Klansmen, under the guise of tourists, whose expenses were paid by the New York organization, were persistent in using the whispering campaign against the government because its leader was a Frenchman."

He referred to a post-election speech made in Ontario by the Imperial Kliegle of the Klan, when he acknowledged the organization took an active part in politics. "Look what we did in New Brunswick," he was said to have told his Ontario audience.

P.J. Veniot did not directly accuse the Conservatives of introducing the Klan to the province, but he said bluntly, "There was one thing they could not get away from: no matter who was responsible for introducing this method of political warfare in this province, it was not the Veniot government which benefitted."

In an attempt to set the record straight, Veniot read the exact wording of the pledge taken by all members of the fourth degree of the order of the Knights of Columbus. It bore no resemblance to the biased version used during the campaign. Neither did it suggest any conflict between a member's duty to his Church and to his country.

"There must always be a difference of opinion in the political sphere," Veniot concluded, "but surely we could meet on the ground of politics and judgement, not by their race and creed but by their deeds."

The next day, the first government speaker to resume the Throne Speech debate, L.P.D. Tilley of Saint John, carefully avoided replying to Veniot's charges. Instead, he talked about the hydro and prohibition issues.

The new premier, J.B.M. Baxter, later dismissed the anti-French and anti-Catholic charges by pointing to his front benches. One was occupied by Antoine J. Léger of Moncton, provincial secretary-treasurer in the Tory cabinet, a position he would hold throughout Baxter's premiership.

Léger may have represented tokenism: he was the only French cabinet minister. He proved to be a capable one, introducing many budgets and administering his department with ease. The only other new face was the Liberal member from Edmundston, J.E. Michaud, destined for a distinguished federal cabinet career with Mackenzie King.

Veniot's spectacular revelations of blatant anti-French biases did not inhibit him from raising the French fact one more time. During the 1926 Budget debate, he noted that as premier he had sent a man to the United States to persuade former New Brunswickers to return. He especially wanted them to take up land between Campbellton and St. Leonard, where a new highway was being built. He deplored proposed budget cuts to this project. The road would pass through "some of the most fertile land in the province." And he added: "If the English-speaking people would not go back to the land, the French-speaking people would." They already were, judging by the reports of French school inspectors.

This was P.J. Veniot's last major speech in the legislature. By the next session, he had resigned to become Postmaster General in the federal cabinet of Mackenzie King. He became the Member for Gloucester — a constituency he would represent in Ottawa until his death in 1936.

His departure from the provincial scene left a void. Had P.J. been driven out of Fredericton because of an anti-French climate? Probably not. He had been around New Brunswick politics too long to be surprised or miffed at that kind of mudslinging. Far more significant was the loss of business support the Liberal party had suffered under Veniot's leadership. Perhaps the most glaring proof was the turnabout of his one-time friend, neighbour and business partner, Angus McLean.

In 1920, P.J. Veniot and McLean spearheaded a group that had purchased the Bathurst Electric and Water Power Company from J.P. Léger. Five years later, the same McLean had played a key role in marshalling opposition to Veniot's plan to develop Grand Falls power under public rather than private control. This must have been quite a knock for a politician then at the peak of his career.

P.J.'s departure to the safer political world of Ottawa probably had many English New Brunswickers looking over their shoulders for an Acadian successor. He was nowhere in sight. New Brunswick's Acadian community was too diverse and too poor to produce another P.J. Veniot in 1926.

Many English New Brunswickers were also suffering from inadequate schools and abysmal wages, but they seemed more willing than Acadians to pick up and leave for greener fields. Their exodus quickly resumed flood-like proportions during the Maritimes' prolonged post-war slump of the 1920s. They left behind a steadily-increasing number of French citizens who were easy prey for the expanding pulp and paper industry.

They formed the bulk of the army of underpaid wood-cutters hired out to private contractors gathering pulp for the new mills. It was ironic: young Acadians were leaving school in a semiliterate state so they could cut down trees that eventually became the pages of mass-circulation newspapers which they would never read.

What was equally tragic, mill towns like Bathurst, Dalhousie and Edmundston, run by councils dominated by mill managers, granted the companies major tax concessions. As a result, the towns' meagre revenues were never enough to meet the growing needs of locally-run hospitals and schools. In each of these three northern communities, the English minority ran the show.

The real power was in the hands of the directors of two giant firms which by 1930 controlled most of the forest acreage in the northern half of New Brunswick. The two firms were International Paper Limited of New York and Fraser Companies of Plaster Rock.[18]

International — or IP — was the key player. Its owners had New Brunswick in its corporate sights as far back as 1905. In that year it had purchased 256 square miles of timber limits from the William Richards Company of Chatham. It gobbled up another 700 square miles of rich forest land in 1908 when it bought out the E. Hutchinson Company. Later that same year, IP acquired the assets of Dalhousie Lumber Company, which owned a mill and 550 square miles of timber leases.

By 1927, IP's New Brunswick operation controlled 2362 square miles of forest land, but to achieve its larger goals it needed more. In February 1928, Bathurst Company Limited became the Bathurst Power and Paper Company; few New Brunswickers knew that IP had fifty percent interest in this new firm.[19]

[18] This and the information following on New Brunswick's expanding pulp and paper industry were taken from a paper prepared by Burton Glendenning for a history graduate class taught by the author at Concordia University in Montréal. The paper was presented April 18, 1974. Mr. Glendenning is now a senior staff member at the Public Archives of New Brunswick in Fredericton. [Hereafter cited as *Glendenning*.]

[19] *Pulp and Paper Magazine*, Vol. 26, no. 6, February 9, 1928, cited in *Glendenning*.

The stage was now set for IP to establish a modern pulp mill. Dalhousie's elected council was quick to oblige. It approved long-term financing of $335,000 to provide the additional services required by IP. It also gave IP a fixed property evaluation for the next fifty years.[20] This meant that regardless of what was added to the new Dalhousie mill, its tax rate would remain the same from 1927 to 1977.

Who made up the difference? Dalhousie's other property owners. Individual families were assessed about 70 percent of the value of their homes, while IP paid as little as 5 percent. Small wonder that Dalhousie's schools, hospitals, water works, streets and fire fighting facilities were starved for money.

Power for IP's new Dalhousie mill came from Grand Falls, which IP developed jointly with Fraser Companies. The long-discussed hydro development was built by the St. John River Power Company, a subsidiary of Gatineau Power Company, in turn controlled by Canadian Hydro-Electric Power Corporation, a wholly owned subsidiary of IP.

Fraser Companies, the other partner in this corporate squeeze-play to control northern New Brunswick, was also busy in these years. Besides a pulp mill at Edmundston, a large lumber mill at Plaster Rock and a small coal-mine operation at Minto, Fraser owned the Dominion Pulp Company at Chatham and by 1925 held 2400 square miles of Miramichi timber limits.

Anticipating the new source of cheap Grand Falls power, Fraser expanded rapidly even while this giant project was under construction. It built a mill to make fine paper at Madawaska, Maine, just across the river from Edmundston. In 1926, Fraser purchased the Sinclair Lumber Company at Newcastle along with its 219 square miles of timber leases. Another 350 square miles were bought from two other Miramichi firms.

Fraser established a presence in the Campbellton area in 1926 by buying the Richard Manufacturing company and its 291 square miles of leases. Later that same year, it announced plans

---

[20] *Royal Commission on Finance and Municipal Taxation in New Brunswick*, Fredericton, 1963, Appendix N7.

to build a mill at Atholville near Campbellton and another on the Miramichi.

Only once in these years of steady expansion was Fraser challenged. In 1919, a group of Edmundston citizens, led by a young medical doctor, Albert Sormany, objected that Fraser was not paying its fair share of taxes, especially for schools. Hiring Max D. Cormier as their lawyer, the citizens won their case. It was a lesson Fraser directors remembered.

When the time came for Fraser to negotiate tax arrangements in Restigouche County, it got a "sweetheart deal." Effective January 1, 1929, Fraser would pay no property taxes for the next fifteen years and from 1944 to 1959 its maximum tax rate would be two percent of a fixed assessment of $200,000.[21] For the last twenty years of the fifty-year agreement, the rate was to be no more than three percent of a $300,000 evaluation. School taxes were separate but fixed at the same low rates.

Such arrangements had long been accepted in other parts of Canada, notably Ontario and Québec. These much larger and vastly more wealthy provinces could and did call on other financial sources to meet the growing needs of their social sector. It was a different story in New Brunswick, especially in new communities like Atholville. In 1921, it had fewer than 500 citizens, most of them with young families. They did not have the money to fund the schools and hospitals they required. And this was long before anyone thought of asking the provincial or federal governments to make direct contributions to the local coffers.

With the advantages of hindsight, we know now that company towns like Dalhousie and Atholville were sitting on social time bombs. By 1968, the awful results were plainly visible. During the federal election campaign of that year, the citizens of Atholville took Pierre Trudeau on a guided tour of a slum community just outside of the town. Meanwhile, two generations of New Brunswickers, most of them French, had suffered in silence.

---

[21] *Pulp and Paper Magazine* Vol. 27, No. 7, February 14, 1929, cited in *Glendenning*, p. 35-36.

Some outside observers knew what was going on, but their comments did not get out to the general public. According to a writer in the *Pulp and Paper Magazine*, a Montreal trade publication, New Brunswick in 1929 "was the private preserve of Fraser Companies of Plaster Rock ... and International Paper of New York."[22]

He could have added that they conducted their affairs like Siamese twins. Fraser sold timber leases to IP and transmitted the power for its Atholville mill over lines shared jointly with IP. The citizens in Dalhousie and Atholville also used Grand Falls power, but they paid much higher rates than the mills did.

The social costs, especially for French New Brunswickers, were enormous. No one was more aware of these costs than French teachers, doctors, and nurses. People like Dr. Albert Sormany had no access to corporate board rooms. Schools were easier targets for Dr. Sormany and what would soon become his small band of Acadian activists.

---

[22] Cited in *Glendenning*, p. 44.

# ELEVEN

## THE SORMANY-SAVOIE EDUCATION LOBBY: 1922-1939

"The French don't care what they do actually as long as they pronounce it properly." So declares the biased Professor Higgins in the musical "My Fair Lady," the popular version of Shaw's *Pygmalion*. In it Shaw argued that our social and economic status depends on the way we speak.

More recently, some scholars have taken up where Shaw left off. They see a close relationship between economic status and literacy. The late Newfoundland economic historian, David Alexander, noted that Newfoundland's unusually high illiteracy rate (32 percent in 1891 compared to 13 percent for the Maritimes) may be linked with that colony's poor economic growth.[1]

New Brunswick's French traditionally occupied the lowest rungs of New Brunswick's economic ladder; until very recently they have also been the province's most illiterate group. If research supports Alexander's thesis, it will also give credibility to the great efforts by a small group of educated French citizens to provide their people with a French school system. Eventually, this was achieved, at about the same time as they greatly improved their economic status.

[1] David Alexander, "Literary and Economic Development in Nineteenth Century Newfoundland," in *Acadiensis*, Vol. I, No. 1, Autumn, 1980, pp. 3-34.

If we look at P.J. Veniot's political defeat in 1925 in the light of this educational/economic thesis, it could be argued that the lumber barons who deserted him did so for more reasons than their desire for cheap hydro power. It could be they saw this French politician as a threat to their cheap labour.

By 1925, semi-illiterate French New Brunswickers formed the bulk of the huge force of pulp cutters providing the new and expanding paper mills with their basic resource. If they got more political power, with their own premier, they might become better schooled and less inclined to toil in the woods for paupers' wages. This actually did take place during the 1960s under the Program of Equal Opportunity's impact.

The tremendous gains French New Brunswickers made in that later era could not have been achieved without the efforts of two people who began their cultural fight in Edmundston in the early 1920s.

Dr. Albert Sormany established his medical practice in Edmundston in 1910, a year before the Fraser Company erected its mill in that community. Seven years later, Calixte Savoie arrived in town as principal of L'École Supérieure, where Dr. Sormany served as a member of the school board. Their close friendship and lobbying activities over the next three decades coincided with the birth and steady growth of several key organizations that spearheaded a twentieth-century cultural drive for French New Brunswickers. Sormany and Savoie were the heart and soul of that movement.

As early as the mid 1920s, this duo knew all the key figures involved in the broader tide of French Canadian nationalism that was building both in Québec and eastern Ontario. Largely through Sormany and Savoie, this central Canadian phenomenon moved into New Brunswick.

They began getting "their act together" in the autumn of 1922 when Calixte Savoie was adjusting to his new responsibilities as a school administrator. At Sormany's suggestion, they formed a weekly study group to discuss ways to improve the school system for Acadians. They called their group "La Petite Boutique" and enlisted the following to join them: Gaspard Boucher, owner and editor of *Le Madawaska* ; Edgar Poirier, director of

L'École Commerciale; Alphonse Chiasson, an employee at *Le Madawaska* ; and Léon Gagnon, a CNR office worker. Later, a newly-ordained priest, Father Aurèle Godbout and Hypolite Richard, the only blue-collar worker among them, also attended weekly sessions held in each other's homes.[2]

At the group's suggestion, Savoie's school began its own little newspaper, *Le Madawaskaien*. It was published in English and French and was strongly supported by at least two English-speaking teachers. Both students and teachers contributed articles which usually stressed how badly the public school system was serving French New Brunswickers. Before long, some of these articles were being reprinted in *Le Madawaska* as well as *L'Évangéline* in Moncton.

In 1924, members of La Petite Boutique broadened their efforts with a series of educational articles for *Le Madawaska*. Intended as a build-up for Madawaska County's first teachers'conference slated for December of that year, its main theme was "the teaching of French in our schools." No doubt encouraged by the newspaper articles, the delegates to the December gathering unanimously resolved that the provincial school system should take measures to meet the urgent needs of French students attending both the regular schools and the Normal School in Fredericton. Copies of these resolutions went to educational officials as well as members of the government. Perhaps not coincidentally, another provincial election was due.[3]

Meanwhile, La Petite Boutique's carefully-orchestrated campaign shifted back to the school journal *Le Madawaskaien*. In February, 1925, it printed a hard-hitting editorial arguing that in New Brunswick schools, French should be on an equal footing with English. The French language was a bulwark against the

---

[2] Calixte Savoie, *Mémoires d'un nationaliste acadien* (Moncton 1979), p. 79. [Hereafter cited as *Mémoires*.] See also Alexandre-J. Savoie, *Un Demi-siècle d'histoire acadienne* (Montréal 1976) p. 109. Hereafter *Savoie, 1976*.

[3] Alexandre-J. Savoie, *Un Siècle de revendications scolaires au Nouveau-Brunswick 1871-1971* (Edmundston 1978) Vol.1, pp. 195-196. Hereafter *Savoie, 1978 Vol.I*.

heretical and materialist infiltration of a foreign tongue. Judging by the attention he gave it in his memoirs, Calixte Savoie wrote the editorial. It claimed that Acadians were being asked not to raise this delicate issue until after the provincial election. Surely this was more important than the fate of a political party! The children were "demanding these language rights."[4]

Regardless of its authorship, this editorial touched a sensitive nerve. Local politicians were furious. So were the English bosses at the Fraser mill, still smarting over losing their school tax court case. Together they urged the school board to silence *Le Madawaskaien* and the man behind it, Calixte Savoie. By June, 1925, the little school journal was no more. Its supporters fought back in the school board elections the following April, but their candidate was defeated. At the end of the 1926 school term, five teachers, including Savoie and his two anglophone colleagues, resigned in protest. The old guard had won this battle but the war had just begun.

The scene shifted to Fredericton and the annual teachers' convention. Its chairman, Chief Superintendent Dr. W.S. Carter, obviously concerned about the recent events in Edmundston, seemed to go out of his way to placate the teachers in French schools. "If in the past they have been blamed for New Brunswick's high illiteracy rate, we are proud to say that it is not the case today."

The unemployed Calixte Savoie was one of the convention's main speakers. He called for a bilingual programme — a suggestion that received strong support from his mostly English audience.[5] This proved to be Savoie's last public appearance as a teacher. In desperation, he had taken the first position offered: regional sales manager in Moncton for *World Book Encyclopedia*, an English publication. He and his young family were no sooner settled in Moncton when a more appropriate position appeared: general manager and secretary-treasurer of La Société l'Assomption.

4 *Mémoires*, p.90.
5 *La Madawaska*, July 8, 1926, cited in Memoires, p. 213

Thus began an association that would carry Calixte Savoie all through his working years, and beyond. He immediately launched a membership drive to boost the fortunes of this languishing organization. Aided by his former Edmundston associates Dr Sormony, Gaspard Boucher and others, he soon signed up 1755 new members.

That number had not been chosen out of a hat: it was the date of the Acadian Expulsion. By February, 1927, the campaign had brought in 2463 members and $698,250 in new insurance. A target of 10,000 members was easily reached in time for the Society's tenth convention held in Moncton in August, 1927.

At that gathering, Dr. Sormony was named president, a postion he would hold until 1951. The Society, working closely with Le Comité Langue et éducation (formed back in 1890 but all but dead until revived by La Petite Boutique and others in the 1920s) began lobbying in Fredericton for more French in Acadian schools. These pressure tactics paid off to the extent that in the autumn of 1929, Savoie and representatives from Collège Saint-Joseph in Memramcook and Collège Sacré-Coeur in Bathurst earned a meeting with educational officials in Fredericton. For the better part of an afternoon, they talked about a new curriculum.

The English were not sympathetic and a discouraged Savoie returned to his hotel room. Suddenly, as he recalled later, he overheard a lively discussion in the next room among several cabinet ministers and two members of the education department. Why was the government always turning a deaf ear to a just cause, refusing to grant this one thing Acadians needed to escape from their ignorance? Savoie thought he recognized the educational official who offered this explanation: "It is by keeping them ignorant that we are best able to dominate them. Allow them to teach themselves and you place in their hands the most powerful weapon to wean themselves from their cultural and economic poverty."[6]

Autobiographer Savoie, writing about this event half a century later, could be excused for engaging in some poetic license.

6 *Mémoires*, p.145.

Nevertheless, it is a fact that within a year the Tory government of J.B.M. Baxter authorized the adoption of Regulation 32 recognizing the bilingual nature of New Brunswick's school population.

The Normal School would set examinations for bilingual teachers, enabling them to teach in French in the first three grades. Effective July 1, 1929, this bilingual program would be adopted in all predominantly French school districts at the discretion of the local boards. Teachers would have five years to earn their bilingual certificates. In effect, only those with a working knowledge of French could teach in Acadia-area schools.

Savoie, Sormony and other Acadian leaders were ecstatic. They should have known better. They should have known Regulation 32 would prompt a back-lash from the Orange Order. The Grand Master quickly issued an angry letter to provincial lodges in December, 1928, when the *Educational Review*, the official publication of the New Brunswick Teachers' Association, carried details of the proposed changes. The Grand Master warned that it posed a great menace to the English population. New Brunswick was not a bilingual province! There would be no "Frenchifying" of the school system.[7] The wave of English pressure grew as another general election neared.

Premier Baxter realized his mistake. Caving in to the English protests, he rescinded Regulation 32. After winning the 1930 election, and shortly before being named to the provincial Supreme Court, Baxter took the safe route and appointed a Royal Commission on Education. Its chairman would be Dr. A.S. MacFarlane, Chief Superintendent of Education. Among the twenty other members were just four French-speaking citizens: Calixte Savoie, two Acadian school inspectors and Rev. H.A. Vanier, rector of l'Université Saint-Joseph, as the Memramcook institution was now called.[8]

---

[7] This letter was translated and carried in *L'Évangéline* and later cited by Savoie in his *Mémoires*, pp.157-8. See also *Savoie*, Vol.I, pp.209-210.
[8] *Mémoires*, pp.172-3.

The commission's terms of reference contained no mention of bilingual schools or a curriculum for New Brunswick's growing number of French-speaking students. As Savoie later wrote, the commission probably was meant to end debate on Regulation 32. He and his French colleagues tried unsuccessfully to have the bilingual question added to the study. When faced with a filibuster from the Acadian commissioners, Chairman Mac-Farlane, who had been Savoie's professor at Normal School, was adamant. The issue was finally referred to the new premier, C.D. Richards. He suggested that the commission accept their recommendations for Acadian schools.

The Acadians again would be disappointed. When the final report was tabled before the 1932 legislature, nothing happened. The Richards administration "needed time to prepare the legislation." It gave the same excuse in 1933 and again in 1934. By then, the continuing economic depression provided the excuse.

Sweeping changes in the education system would cost money. Premier Richards repeated this excuse in a letter to La Société l'Assomption, sent after he had departed for Europe. Savoie was probably correct in assuming that Richards did not want to antagonize members of the Orange Lodge.

Determined to pursue their goal, the Acadian lobby changed tactics by turning to central Canada for their models. One was l'Ordre de Jacques Cartier; the other was l'Association Catholique de la Jeunesse Canadienne (ACJC). Both organizations were in the vanguard of militant Catholicism in Québec and Franco-Ontario.[9]

Working closely with existing Acadian organizations and the two Acadian bishops in Chatham and Saint John, these two central Canadian groups began to send offshoots into French

---

[9] Alexandre-J.Savoie, *Un Siècle de revendications scolaires au Nouveau-Brunswick 1871-1971: les commandeurs de l'Ordre à l'oeuvre 1934-1939*, pp. 19-26. Hereafter *l'Ordre*. [Savoie drew his material on the founding of the order from an article appearing in *La Presse*, October 28, 1976. An earlier general description can be found in Mason Wade, *The French Canadians* (Toronto 1955), pp. 998-1002.]

New Brunswick. While nameless Acadians were using their axes and their wits to survive during the depths of the Great Depression, their more affluent and better-schooled leaders were preparing the next stage of a cultural war of independence.

L'Ordre de Jacques Cartier began in Ottawa in 1926 when several disgruntled French civil servants on the lower end of the ladder decided to try and overcome what they regarded as job discrimination. They blamed their lowly state on English Protestant bosses with close connections to the Order of Freemasons or the Orange Lodge. If that was how to get promoted, why not form a similar Catholic group?

A few of these minor civil servants met in the presbytery of Father F-X. Barrette, an Ottawa parish priest and so l'Ordre de Jacques Cartier was born. The first group received its charter in October, 1927, one week after the Order received official Church sanction. The motto would be *Dieu et Patrie*. The goal was to win tangible recognition of the French fact in Canada.

The founding members, chosen mostly from professional classes and those regarded as natural leaders, pledged themselves to secrecy, following the tradition of the Masonic Order. The organization, like the Masons, would be military in tone, with a headquarters in Ottawa having supreme authority over regional committees and local commands. Franco-Ontario took to the Order with enthusiasm, creating nine of the first twelve local groups. It was not until 1933, after repeated delays to implement requested reforms in the French schools, that the order established its first New Brunswick branch.[10]

Medical doctors played key roles, probably reflecting the powerful influence of Dr. Albert Sormany. By this time, the order's centralized administration had perfected ways to set up new branches. The officers of one branch would seek out a likely group of new members in a neighbouring community, hold an initial meeting, distribute literature on the rules of the order, and elect the officers.

---

[10] *Savoie*, Vol. II p. 57. Chapter 1 details the early organizational efforts in New Brunswick.

On November 17, 1933, Elzéar Coté of Rimouski arranged such a meeting in Campbellton. Dr. Félix Dumont was named grand commander and three other physicians and a dentist were among the twelve officers chosen to lead New Brunswick's first commanderie of l'Ordre de Jacques Cartier. It would be called the Noël-Broussard Commanderie after a legendary Acadian sea captain who escaped his English captors during the 1755 Expulsion and later transported scores of his compatriots safely back to their Acadian homeland.

This same folk hero later gave his name to a talented and successful group of young Acadian musicians, *Beausoleil-Broussard*. He also figures prominently in Antonine Maillet's novel *Pélagie La Charrette*, the story of how some Acadians went overland from Louisiana and returned to New Brunswick after years of effort. This work earned its author France's highest literary honour in 1979.

These examples emerged in the 1970s, as the modern Acadian renaissance was bursting forth in words and music. Historical themes and folk heroes have often been used to further nationalism. As l'Ordre de Jacques Cartier was emerging in central Canada in the late 1920s, Abbé Lionel Groulx from his academic base at Université de Montréal was skillfully using history as a rallying cry in an effort to create a Laurentian nation out of the old Québec.

Correctly assuming that ordinary French Canadians needed help in learning about their past, l'Ordre de Jacques Cartier, through its monthly publication, *L'Émerillon*, would carry brief biographical sketches explaining, for example, Broussard's role in early Acadian history.

Campbellton was a good choice for the order's first New Brunswick branch. In 1932, a year before its formation, it had hosted the first regional conference of l'Association Catholique de la Jeunesse Canadienne (ACJC). It brought together lay and religious leaders from northern New Brunswick as well as neighbouring Québec. Among the speakers were Mgr. Patrice-Alexandre Chiasson, Bishop of Chatham, Dr. George Dumont of Campbellton, and Dr. Sormany. A Campbellton lawyer, Benoit Michaud, read a paper on "La Question scolaire au

Nouveau-Brunswick." Clearly, the next stage of the school battle was underway.[11]

In the July 1934 issue of *L'Émerillon*, the Campbellton members got their "marching orders." They were to group themselves under the banner of La Société l'Assomption, which was described as performing the same role for Acadians as la Société Saint Jean-Baptiste did for Québécois.

Teenage Acadians should be encouraged to enrol in the ACJC and the younger ones should join the French Catholic branch of the Boy Scouts. These organizations, explained *L'Émerillon*, would help young Acadians overcome the lack of French instruction in the public schools because all their members would speak and write only in French.

The same issue urged everyone to use French when communicating with federal departments, including government railways. They should subscribe to *L'Évangéline*, buy wherever possible from Acadian or French-Canadian stores, hotels, restaurants and barbershops. They should always speak French first when asking the operator for telephone numbers. Above all, they should never distribute to the general public any circulars from these national societies. It was preferable to spread their ideas by word of mouth or by personal action.[12]

The goals were easier to achieve and maintain in French communities like Edmundston, Caraquet and Buctouche, where commanderies of the order were quickly formed. Mixed centres like Moncton could expect a strong reaction from the English.

Much later, judging from views expressed in a small monograph, some Acadians were also resentful. Médard J. Léger asked in his *Du Miel au Fiel*, published in 1970, whether exchanging English bosses for Acadians had brought any real advantage.[13] His perspective may have been coloured by the forty years he spent with the CNR, mostly in Moncton, where

---

[11] *Savoie*, 1980, Vol. II pp. 62-63.
[12] *Savoie*, 1980, Vol. II, pp. 68-69.
[13] Médard J. Léger, *Du Miel au Fiel: histoire de la Patente dans le comté de Gloucester*, (Ottawa, 1970).

the earliest and strongest English backlash to militant Acadians took place.

A concerted campaign to get bilingual services in Moncton's stores began in the spring of 1934. The initiative did not come — at least directly — from l'Ordre de Jacques Cartier, but from the two Moncton branches of La Société l'Assomption. Of course, the same people probably were involved, regardless of the organization.

Apparently, the idea to launch the campaign came from T.J. Léger, president of T & A Léger Ltée, a successful hardware store. He told a combined meeting of the two society branches that all his clerks were bilingual. He deplored the fact that most Moncton Acadians could only be served by unilingual English clerks. Before the meeting ended, a committee was formed to draft a letter to be sent to all French families in the city.

It went out on April 23, 1934 and urged Acadians to address all store clerks in French. If they could not reply, they should insist that someone be found who spoke French. If this failed, they should complain to the manager or send the details of the encounter to Le Comité de Propagande Française. Any store with French-speaking clerks should be patronized. Also, all cheques and letters should be in French.[14]

As secretary-manager of La Société l'Assomption, Calixte Savoie sent out a similar circular to all New Brunswick branches. He told the members they should not blame the English merchants if they operated only in English. They logically assumed that most Acadians could speak English. "It is we, the Acadians, who are the guilty ones."[15]

As he was also president of the Moncton diocese of the ACJC, Savoie sent this same letter to all branches of the organization. Alfred Roy, editor of *L'Évangéline*, published a lengthy article entitled "Une Campagne de Refrancisation."

In a matter of weeks, the campaign was getting results. The T. Eaton Company, the Maritimes' largest retail system, began

[14] *Mémoires*, p. 196.
[15] *Mémoires*, p. 197-8.

hiring more bilingual clerks for its large Moncton store.[16] Things were going so well that the over-worked Savoie decided on a rare holiday to Cape Breton.

He and his wife no sooner got there when they received an urgent message from the campaign committee. "The English-Speaking League" had launched a counter attack: he must return immediately. Before he could get back, his colleagues had decided to abandon their efforts.

"The English-Speaking League" had been formed to defend their linguistic group's domination of the market place. It had issued its own circular claiming that this refrancisation campaign was costing English jobs. "Can you speak French?" asked the letter appearing in the Moncton *Times* and the *Transcript*. "If you cannot, the time has arrived when you are about to get your orders to quit your job and dig elsewhere for a living."

Perhaps the most damaging blow to the Acadian cause was "The Word of Explanation" appearing in both the French and English newspapers on May 29, 1934. It was signed by Arthur T. LeBlanc, Judge of the New Brunswick Supreme Court; Antoine J. Léger, Provincial Secretary in the Conservative government; and two city aldermen, A.E. Tremblay and B.A. Bourgeois.

Claiming that "a very few members of the local council of l'Assomption Society not authorized by the Grand Council were connected with the circular letter," this foursome had conducted their own survey of Moncton's Acadians. "The vast majority" had disapproved. They said that despite his name appearing on the circular, Bishop Cormier knew nothing about it and had agreed with them that it was a bad idea.[17]

In his memoirs, Calixte Savoie argues that A.J. Léger, the legal counsel for La Société l'Assomption, not only had been aware of the original campaign: he had proposed certain amendments and later had approved the final draft of the letter. So had other members of the executive council.

---

[16] *Mémoires*, p. 199
[17] *Mémoires*, p. 207

Whatever the reasons for what may have been their second thoughts about the campaign, the foursome seemed to lack the single-minded determination of Calixte Savoie, Dr. Albert Sormany and other members of the nationalist clique. Others may have wanted to join but lacked their economic security. This was, after all, in the middle of the Great Depression.

A few paid a heavy price for their militancy. T.J. Léger, the hardware merchant who had helped launch Moncton's refrancisation drive, was forced to sell his store in January, 1935. The new owner was C.H "Ford" Blakney, mayor of Moncton and soon to be Minister of Education in the Liberal government of A.A. Dysart, elected later that year.

If Léger had been able to hang on for a few more years his store would have benefitted from the steady shift of Acadians into the surrounding area. With the creation in March 1936 of a new diocese of Moncton, plans got underway to erect a new cathedral two blocks away from the former Léger store. About ten blocks to the north, a new French-speaking elementary school had opened on Mountain Road on a large property that also contained the Hôtel Dieu Hospital. Over the next few years, this area of Moncton would become increasingly French-speaking.

English Monctonians watched this growing evidence of the French presence with some apprehension, even though their political and economic domination remained unchallenged for another generation. The mayors continued to be unilingually English, as were the managers and department heads of the CNR and the T. Eaton Company, the region's largest employers.

Throughout the early 1930's, the city council had a lone Acadian, elected from a predominantly French-speaking ward. The other eight members were English. In 1935, following the aborted refrancisation campaign, the French lost their one representative. Except when the token Acadian seat was filled again in 1940, from 1953 to 1958, no Acadian sat on the city council.[18]

To the outside world, as well as to its French citizens, Moncton's English maintained their position. They refused to

---

[18] Lloyd A. Machum, *A History of Moncton* (Moncton 1965), pp. 374-5.

recognize the growing French fact, even though the great spire of the new cathedral rose to dominate the city skyline and more French stores and elementary schools gave a truer indication of Moncton's bicultural state.

The English living near the Mountain Road school knew things were changing. The large section of Church-owned real estate now included a home for the elderly run by the Sisters of Charity, the Mountain Road school for French students, the Hôtel Dieu Hospital and a thriving tennis club run by the A.C.J.C.

One memorable Sunday, probably in the early summer of the late 1930's, Protestant families walking home from church noticed great activity in the big empty field behind Mary's Home, as the home for the elderly was called.[19] Hundreds of Acadians, many of them children dressed in white, were pouring into the field. Soon loud-speakers were being tested on a platform set up on the tennis court. By two o'clock, the field was a solid wall of people, listening and now and then responding to speakers standing before the microphones. It went on all afternoon, often in a language neither French nor English. It was Latin. The open-air mass was later followed by lengthy and often excited speeches. To English ears, it was so much Greek. Some English would have preferred that to French.

These well-staged Acadian events did not prevent many from being assimilated into the dominant English milieu. Later census statistics and studies for the Royal Commission on Biculturalism and Bilingualism indicate that Acadians quickly lost their language and other cultural elements when they moved into cities from their rural and solidly French-speaking communities.

Just what the assimilation rate was in the 1930s remains a mystery. We do know that decade saw a tremendous intrusion into Canadian society of American movies and radio programs, with their spin-offs in language, dress, music and cult heroes. In rapidly-growing centres like Moncton, organized leagues for hockey, softball and basketball sprang up like mushrooms.

---

[19] These events are part of the author's experience growing up in this neighbourhood.

Acadians usually took part as individuals rather than enter their own teams. The team language was always English.

Moncton's public school system remained the most powerful institutional assimilator. In 1935, the city built an impressive new high school. It has remained staunchly English. Lacking a high school of their own, students from the French elementary schools who decided to continue went to Moncton High School where they rapidly improved their English. The city's second high school opened in 1961. It too was unilingually English.

In Edmundston, the overwhelmingly French population faced a different school problem. The chairman of the school board, Donald Fraser of the mill-owning family, proposed in 1935 that an anglophone, David McLelland, be named principal of the largest school and supervisor for two others.

School board member Dr. Albert Sormany objected strongly. "A principal who does not speak a word of French" was "a bad policy to follow in a town like Edmundston" where ninety percent of the students were French. He expressed these views in several letters to *Le Madawaska*, pointing out that no English community and no Board of School Trustees "would even think of being party to such an absurdity as hiring a principal who could speak no English."[20] McLelland was hired. At the end of June, Dr. Sormany resigned from the board and began concentrating his efforts on the larger educational problems facing all New Brunswick French students.

He and his old friend and fellow lobbyist Calixte Savoie must have been heartened by the general election results of June 20, 1935 but the campaign itself was disgusting. It produced what one New Brunswick historian has called "the last desperate gasp of the Ku Klux Klan" in the province. During the campaign, a letter supposedly written by a KKK official was circulated, urging New Brunswickers not to vote for any Roman Catholic candidates.[21]

---

[20] *Savoie,* 1978, p. 173.
[21] Dr.D.M. Young, University of New Brunswick, to author, July, 1982; see also Hugh G. Thorburn, *Politics in New Brunswick,* (Toronto, 1961) pp. 116-117.

The Conservative premier, Leonard Tilley, accused the Liberals of trying to win the election by stirring racial hatred. Speaking in Sussex, Tilley noted that the same letter had appeared in York County and Saint John and he said they had been distributed by Liberal organizers.

A prominent Fredericton Liberal, John B. McNair, replied that he knew where the letters had been printed and who had carried them to the mail. "They were not Liberals." His threat to publish the name of the man "who, while in the pay of the Tilley Government, had been guilty of such practices" brought what some took as a panic reply from Tilley.

The premier released an official letter from the Klan organization denying any responsibility. Such a reply probably convinced some voters that the Tilley government and the KKK were connected.

How many votes shifted over this emotional issue will never be known. A more decisive factor was the continuing depression and the Tilley administration's inability to cope with it. Like their counterparts in Ottawa, the New Brunswick Conservatives in 1935 went down to a crushing defeat. The entire cabinet was turned out. The party elected only five members, compared to 43 Liberals led by A.A. Dysart, an Irish Catholic lawyer from Buctouche, Kent County.

The return to power of this pro-Acadian party seemed to spur the various branches of l'Ordre de Jacques Cartier. At their monthly meetings throughout 1935 and 1936, they took up the cause of education. On March 30, 1936, they selected delegates to arrange a meeting in Fredericton with Premier Dysart and his French colleagues. He would be asked to act on his election promise to name a second French cabinet minister and broaden Acadian educational opportunities within the public school system. When nothing happened, the regional commanders of the Order met in July to apply pressure on the lone Acadian cabinet minister, Clovis T. Richard, the provincial secretary-treasurer.

The prospects for a meeting with the premier did not look promising. Dysart had already promised citizens in Hartland that he would not increase the number of French-speaking cabinet ministers. He must have been keenly aware that the English in

Moncton were angry over the refrancisation campaign. For this reason, he was not keen to meet with the Acadian lobby.

Rebuffed but not discouraged, the New Brunswick commanders of the order gathered on October 18, 1936 at the mother house of Des Filles de Marie-de-l'Assomption outside Campbellton.[22] They decided to form another lobbying organization, l'Association Acadienne d'Éducation. It would study the necessary steps to achieve the educational changes that had almost been won with Regulation 32 five years earlier.

The two Acadian bishops in New Brunswick would be honourary presidents. In fact, Mgr. Chiasson, Bishop of Chatham, was present for this Campbellton meeting. The active president was the indispensable Dr. Albert Sormany, the lynchpin for all Acadian lobbying groups in the province. His new executive included three vice-presidents: his brother Alphonse from Shédiac; Benoît Michaud, commander of the Campbellton branch of the Order; and Hédard Robichaud, a young Shippagan lawyer, destined to be a federal cabinet minister and New Brunswick's first Acadian lieutenant-governor.

No Acadian organization could do without the services of Calixte Savoie, or so it seemed. He, along with two Campbellton doctors, Charles Dumont and Théophile Godin, served as directors. Dr. Honoré Cyr of Saint-Basile near Edmundston was named treasurer and Amédée Blanchard of Edmundston secretary. As the slate suggests, l'Association Acadienne d'Éducation began as an Edmundston-centred lobby with Dr. Sormany in charge. He and the other members of the Edmundston branch of l'Ordre de Jacques Cartier were to prepare for the new group's first conference. They immediately contacted l'Association canadienne française d'éducation d'Ontario, informing it that they were also working closely with La Société l'Assomption, another Sormany-led group.[23]

Loading all these offices on the shoulders of one man probably simplified inter-group communications. If they had been spread around to other New Brunswick leaders, some ordinary Acadians

[22] *l'Ordre*, p. 149ff.
[23] *Savoie,* 1976, pp. 171-172.

would have found it easier to get rid of the notion that a small clique had perhaps too tight a control of Acadian cultural affairs.

In any case, the strategy of this latest group was to keep its existence secret until a big "coming-out party" could be arranged in the form of a conference. It had been originally slated for Bathurst in 1937, but was postponed a year until the various branches of the Order recruited other influential Acadians. Also, two other francophone conferences were to be held in 1937: one in Québec city on the state of the French language in Canada and the other in Memramcook to mark the tenth national Acadian congress.

The extra time enabled the Edmundston group to launch a publicity campaign identical to the one Dr. Sormany, Calixte Savoie and other members of La Petite Boutique had conducted ten years earlier on the eve of Madawaska's first French teachers' convention.

The new effort involved the entire province: editorials in *Le Madawaska* and *L'Évangéline*, speeches by members of the order to their various professional organizations, and countless meetings, some as far away as Montréal. The theme was always the same: Acadian education.

In January, 1937, four commanders of the Order, serving as delegates to a Moncton meeting of the New Brunswick Association of Farmers and Dairymen, got this group to endorse a resolution calling for a reform of the school system. A week later in Fredericton, a conference of educators decided in favour of secondary schools for New Brunswick's rural areas and a revision of the entire school program. Among the participants was a professor of French at Fredericton's Normal School and three French school inspectors — all members of the Order.[24]

Three weeks later, the Throne Speech opening the 1937 Legislative session announced plans to modernize teaching. In moving the Address in Reply, the new Liberal member from Madawaska, Dr. P. H. Laporte urged that for the wider recognition of French, MLAs should speak to the House in their own language. Dr. Laporte and Gaspard Boucher, editor of *Le*

---

[24] See *Savoie*, 1980, pp. 171-172.

*Madawaska,* spoke a few days later over Fredericton radio station CFNB to mark Education Week. Boucher later printed his speech in his newspaper to start off a hard-hitting series on the sad state of education among New Brunswick's French schools.

Eventually, this careful and persistent lobby began to get results. Still, it took the direct intervention of Dr. Clarence Veniot, Member of Parliament for Gloucester and son of the former premier, to arrange a meeting with Premier Dysart.[25] Veniot reminded the new Liberal leader that Ontario, "perhaps the most British province of the Dominion," had recognized its "past errors" by providing French textbooks and methods for its francophone minority. He also noted that Québec had always given its English minority "the greatest facilities for the education of their children."

Dr. Veniot's letter passed on a comment by Dr. William Roberts, New Brunswick's first health minister. He had been informed by Premier Veniot that French students were "compelled to study the important principles of hygiene from English textbooks." When Veniot had asked him what he would do if English students faced this situation, Roberts is said to have replied: "I wouldn't stand for it."

The Sormany group's session with Premier Dysart and his cabinet did little more than inform them of the existence of l'Association Acadienne d'Éducation and its goal to improve Acadian school standards.

A more direct and public lobbying effort showed up in the February 5, 1938 issue of the Saint John *Telegraph-Journal* with a long letter from J.T. Lejeune, a Gloucester County school inspector. It obviously was meant to inform English readers about the poor deal being given French students.

Lejeune's remedies were almost identical to those made by a predecessor, George Mersereau, a generation earlier. Give Acadians a solid education in their own language first. Provide

---

[25] *Savoie,* 1980, p. 186.

better training in Fredericton for francophone teachers. Find better French textbooks.[26]

The letter brought a reply from a Saint John teacher, William M. Campbell, who reminded Lejeune (and the newspaper's English readers) that New Brunswick was officially a unilingual English-speaking province. He agreed with Lejeune that the high illiteracy and drop-out rate among Acadian students was unacceptable and required a closer look at the entire school system.

Now it was Calixte Savoie's turn. The former teacher's letter published a short time later in the *Telegraph-Journal* referred to the same Ontario report cited by Campbell. It had been based on a two-year inquiry from 1925-1927 that caused the Ontario legislature to abolish the notorious Regulaton 17, passed amid fierce French opposition in 1912. Ontario now had opted for radical changes giving its growing francophone population more freedom to have their children taught in French. If this was what Campbell had in mind for New Brunswick's Acadians, Savoie was all in favour.[27]

A few weeks after this exchange, the Acadian position on educational reform was outlined to the legislature by Gaspard Boucher and Dr. P. H. Laporte. At the same time, other members of l'Ordre de Jacques-Cartier wrote a series of 22 articles on education for the French press. These appeared every week from April 14 to August 25, a week before the educational conference at Université Sacré-Coeur in Bathurst. As an example of sustained lobbying, this effort had few parallels.[28]

When the big day finally dawned August 30, 1938, five hundred delegates, including a large number of clerics, were on hand for what would be the Acadians' most important educational gathering. It was also an unofficial coming-out party for the five-year-old Ordre de Jacques-Cartier, whose *raison d'être* in New Brunswick was to get a French educational system.

---

[26] *Mémoires*, p. 236.
[27] *Mémoires*, pp. 241-245.
[28] *Savoie*, 1980, pp. 192-195.

The list of participants and special guests at the two-day affair indicated how far the Acadian community had progressed since the days when it was challenging the Irish bishops and when a handful of deputies in Fredericton had to seek permission to say anything in French.

The high mass opening the ceremonies was conducted by Mgr. P-A Chiasson, Bishop of Chatham, and the new archbishop of Moncton, Mgr. L.J.A. Melanson, delivered the sermon.

Among the speakers at the public session the first evening were J.E. Michaud of Edmundston, the federal Minister of Fisheries; Dr. Clarence Veniot, MP for Gloucester, Senator Antoine Léger, C.T. Richard, the provincial secretary-treasurer, and Dr. P. H. Laporte, minister of health and labour.[29]

At the first study session, Calixte Savoie delivered a paper he called "Notre Système d'Éducation: ses défauts, ses remèdes." The product of two weeks of vacation-time work, it showed once again that this full-time administrator at heart was still a teacher.

In his welcoming speech, Dr. Albert Sormany expressed what would become the motto for l'Associaton Acadienne d'Éducation: "Soyons sur la brêche. Demandons, réclamons ce qu'il nous faut. Présentons un front uni."

The fifteen resolutions, passed unanimously, summed up what in effect was the educational "Magna Carta" for New Brunswick's Acadians: Here were the key ones:
- The public school system should recognize the bicultural and bilingual nature of New Brunswick's school population.
- French districts should have their own Home and School groups.
- The teaching of English to French students should be improved.
- All texts should be in French except those for English classes.

---

[29] *Savoie*, 1980, p. 205. This volume contains a copy of the entire program. After the conference, the proceedings were described in a 114-page booklet published by *Le Madawaska*.

- In Acadian districts, the first two years of schooling should be entirely in French, with oral English instruction to start in grade three.
- A bilingual Normal School should be established in a French district.
- Primary schools should have appropriate instruction in agriculture (that is, in French as well as English).

One of the most controversial and current educational issues did not surface in any of these resolutions. This was the question of summer school training for teachers. In 1937, Dr. Fletcher Peacock, the deputy minister of education, authorized such a program and 350 teachers took part in sessions held in Saint John. Everything was conducted in English.[30]

This situation spurred Calixte Savoie to action. He set in motion a plan providing French-speaking teachers with their own summer school. In the spring of 1938, he received a visit from Père Joyal of l'Association Canadienne-Française d'Éducation de l'Ontario. Their discussions on how to launch a French summer school were resumed when Père Joyal attended the A.A.E. convention in Bathurst the following August.

At the request of Archbishop Melanson, Savoie led a delegation to Fredericton to ask Peacock to authorize a French teachers' summer program. He refused. When he was informed of this decision, Archbishop Melanson decided to get Savoie to organize one anyway.

Faced with a challenge so close to his heart, the energetic Savoie wrote to members of the Acadian elite as well as to Père Joyal and Mgr. Camille Roy, rector of Université Laval to obtain Québécois teaching staff.

Dr. Sormany was not sure such a school was a good idea. Was there a danger, he wrote to Savoie, that a summer school at Memramcook, the designated locale, would weaken support for the one recently established by the Eudistes in Bathurst? If a professor from Université de Ottawa, for instance, were hired, would this not upset the educational authorities in Fredericton?

---

[30] *Savoie*, 1980, p. 215.

Savoie could see no conflict with the Bathurst summer school program. It was aimed at helping Acadian teachers get academic courses towards their arts degrees. At Memramcook, the emphasis would be on teaching English and French "à nos petits Acadiens." He had already discussed the matter with the director of Collège Sacré-Coeur and had received his strong approval. Savoie added that his recent trip to Fredericton had convinced him they had nothing to lose and everything to gain by pushing ahead.[31]

As Deputy-Minister Peacock probably suspected, the Acadian request could lead to the establishment of a French Normal School or Teachers' College. His fears would be justified.

The first summer school at Memramcook began in July, 1938 under Brother Léopold Taillon. He became a tower a strength and a much-needed ally for the overworked Savoie. During the next few years, Brother Léopold emerged as a key figure in the long-range plans to expand the influence of the Memramcook establishment and hasten its metamorphosis into l'Université de Moncton. The Memramcook summer program was another step towards making the Moncton area the cultural and institutional hub for New Brunswick's Acadians.

A report tabled in the legislature by A.P. Paterson in March 1939 indicated that Acadian education still had a long way to go towards fair recognition by Dr. Peacock and his English-directed department. The report was the work of a committee Peacock had set up in 1937 to examine the curriculum and textbooks for the first six grades. Not surprisingly, this committee was essentially anglophone.

The only French members were school inspector J.T. Lejeune, Martin Thériault, vice-president of the N.B. Teachers' Association and the Rev. Dr. LePalme, Director of Studies at Université Saint-Joseph, who also chaired the special sub-committee on the French curriculum.

Paterson told his political colleagues that "an outstanding expert in the field" had been brought in to the 1938 summer school that had been held in Saint John. "A beginning was made

---

[31] *Mémoires*, pp. 262-263.

in the introduction of the modern method of handling classes where two languages were concerned."

This seemed to be Peacock's answer to the Acadians' request for major improvements in the French sector. It was an answer they were unlikely to accept, since their goal was a totally French school system. For now, they had to settle for small gains, like the situation at the Normal School.

Fifty-three Acadians were enrolled in a completely French program under their own professor. Two of the graduates of this first class, Alexandre Savoie and Léandre LeGresley, began a French student journal. Both would become important leaders in the cause of Acadian education. Savoie later became president of the A.A.E. and after retiring from teaching and school administration, he wrote several pioneer studies in Acadian history.[32]

One Acadian MLA not satisfied with the 1939 Curriculum Report was André Doucet, the Liberal member from Paquetville.[33] He told the House he could see few problems in the urban school, but the rural areas, where "we have a large proportion of French-speaking children," needed "the greatest attention ... ." They required the kind of treatment Ontario was giving to its francophone students.

Doucet congratulated Horace Porter, the member from Saint John, for wanting all children to learn French, but he could not accept his view that New Brunswick could never have unity "unless there is a common English language." After all, Switzerland was united even though it had three official languages.

Furthermore, Porter "should not place the French-speaking population of this Province in the same position as that of a few immigrants who come to this land." The Acadians now formed one third of the province and if they wanted to give up their language, they would have done so long ago. Any delay in the progress of the Acadian child, "whether by unqualified teachers, improper methods or the lack of proper curriculum would also

---

[32] As the foregoing account and references indicate, the author made extensive use of the late Dr. Savoie's scholarly efforts.
[33] *Debates,* March 14, 1939, p. 173.

cause delay in the general progress of our Province." By way of softening his criticisms, Doucet indicated his pleasure "that the Department of Education is alive to this very important question." Another Gloucester County Liberal and a former teacher, W.A. Losier, agreed with Doucet that the Normal School had made some progress toward recognizing the needs of French students.[34] He noted, however, that French-speaking students writing high school entrance examinations often could not answer the questions on history, because they were written in English. He urged the department to heed the requests of Gloucester county teachers to correct these "unsatisfactory conditions."

In the general election that everyone expected and which took place November 20, 1939, Losier, Doucet and a solid bloc of Acadian members greatly aided in the re-election of the Dysart administration. No doubt mindful of this significant Acadian support, Dysart knew he could not delay much longer the growing demands for educational reform being pressed by the A.A.E. and l'Ordre de Jacques Cartier.

Dysart's problem was a delicate one. What could he do to appease the Acadians without raising the fears of the English, who still controlled the Liberal party? As history would show, the issue could only be resolved to the Acadians' satisfaction when they had a government led by one of their own, who had a cabinet containing more than a token French representation.

In 1939, few Acadians, including the determined and single-minded team of Calixte Savoie and Dr. Albert Sormany, could imagine such a government in their lifetime. Yet, both would live to see it appear in 1960 with the election of Louis J. Robichaud as Liberal premier. In the interval, much political spadework remained to be done.

[34] *Debates* April 5, 1939, p. 272.

An Acadian Goelette (Fishing Schooner) off Caraquet, circa 1925.

Hemlock Bark Awaiting Rail Shipment — Kent Co., circa 1885.

Harvesting Cod Flakes — Caraquet, circa 1900.

Monument to Mgr. Marcel-François Richard, St-Louis-de-Kent, N.B.

Dignitaries celebrating 200th Anniversary of Acadian Expulsion, Grand-Pré, N.S. Calixte Savoie standing left of umbrella.

Crowds attending Congrès Marial, Buctouche, 1947.

Premier Louis Robichaud inaugurating New Brunswick Flag, Fredericton, March 25, 1965.

Premier Richard Hatfield with student protesters, Moncton, September 1971.

# TWELVE

## WAITING FOR P'TIT LOUIS: 1939-1952

The coming of the second world war ushered in the McNair era of New Brunswick politics. John B. McNair, a dour Presbyterian who became a successful lawyer before entering the legislature in 1935, failed to be elected in the 1939 contest. A seat was quickly found for him in his native Victoria County and he soon replaced the ailing Dysart as Liberal leader and premier.

His new cabinet included Gaspard Boucher, the former Deputy Speaker who was named chairman of the New Brunswick Electric Power Commission. Another was the former Speaker, C. Hanford Blakney, a Moncton hardware merchant who was given the education portfolio.

The new Conservative leader was Hugh Mackay, a wealthy bond dealer from Rothesay. Like his predecessors, he was acutely aware of his party's failure to have even one French member. In his maiden speech during the 1940 Throne Speech Debate, Mackay thought the recent election had seen "too much discussion of religion" and "religious and racial prejudices." In an obvious appeal to French New Brunswickers, Mackay urged the establishment of a French agricultural school at the University Saint-Joseph "or one of the other French-speaking colleges." He said he had gotten to know the French-Canadian community while he resided in Montréal as president of the Rolland Paper Company.[1]

Gaspard Boucher replied that the absence of Acadian Tories was explained by the fact that "our people are not plungers, politically speaking and will rather follow good paved roads."

W.A. Losier of Tracadie noted that all four Conservative candidates in Gloucester had lost their deposits. He blamed this poor showing on the fact that few francophones had received civil service jobs promised during the last Tory government. Losier noted that the increase had been slight since then and he wanted more. This could have been a broad hint to Boucher who had just informed the House that the Power Commission had a total of 79 workers.

Problems of political patronage were simple compared to a deeper malaise apparent in the northern counties. Stated simply, they lacked the money to finance adequate educational and basic services. Worst off were single-industry towns like Dalhousie and Edmundston. They were locked into financial strait-jackets caused by long-term fixed assessments and hence low tax rates given to the big paper companies.

Such issues rarely were discussed on the floor of the legislature. Instead, they came up in the corporation committee chambers, where private member bills were studied by high-priced lawyers sent by large firms to protect their interests. Their knowledge and influence usually overwhelmed any objections coming from members of local school boards or MLAs.

April 25, 1940 was a typical day for the corporation committee. Its members, plus several outside lawyers, debated a bill authorizing the municipalities of Restigouche and the surrounding school districts to assess and tax all the property of New Brunswick International Paper Company and its subsidiary, Gatineau Power Corporation. If passed, this big firm's tax bill would take a hefty jump.

The bill was supported by H.F.G. Bridges, the former Liberal member for Restigouche. He had resigned as Speaker during the

---

[1] *Debates,* April 17, 1940.

previous session because he had not received a cabinet post he felt was due his constituency.

Bridges wanted to end the fixed assessment rates granted to the companies when they established the paper mill at Dalhousie in 1926. "If this bill remains unchanged," he warned, "it will mean that forever these companies will not have to pay any taxes on their properties outside the limits of the Town of Dalhousie." He noted the company's good financial position compared to that of the county, which now owned 15 farms taken over for non-payment of taxes.[2]

The bill was referred to a private session and as later events showed, the final result did not help Restigouche County. Nine years later, the municipalities committee learned from Jean D'Astous, the Liberal member from Dalhousie, that his town had one school of 13 rooms to serve a population of 5,000. Additional rooms had to be rented from the local convent; classes were also held in church basements and halls.[3]

In December, 1948, International Paper had offered to pay taxes on fixed assessments of $5 million, even though the original mill had cost six times that and was now worth over $60 million. According to D'Astous, the company proposal would give Dalhousie $52,000, compared to the $43,000 it was collecting from the rest of its tax-payers. At current education costs, D'Astous argued, Dalhousie should have a school budget of $140,000 compared to the actual figure of $77,000.

The paper company's lawyer, C.F. Inches of Saint John, probably New Brunswick's most prestigious and highest-priced, successfully protected his client's interest. The bill introduced on behalf of the town, which would have raised the paper company's taxes, was withdrawn. Later, the legislative committee was told the two sides had reached "a satisfactory agreement."

International Paper would pay on an assessment of $5.5 millions for the current year and up to $7 millions for the period

---

[2] *Debates*, April 25, 1940, Appendix, Committee Hearings, p. 9.
[3] *Debates*, Appendix, Committee Hearings, April 6, 1949, p. 23.

ending in 1970. It was a profitable way to run a paper mill, but for Dalhousie it meant social and economic stagnation.

In Madawaska, the Edmundston school board faced the same situation: inadequate tax revenues because Fraser Companies' assessments were so low. In May, 1940, county officials opposed a bill making valid an agreement between the company and the town of Edmundston. It would replace the current agreement, due to end in 1943, and increase the company's evaluation from $100,000 to $4,250,000. Frasers would also give $50,000 to the town's sinking fund, presently about $200,000 in arrears.

The bill would help Edmundston's finances, but not the county's. Despite protests raised by the county's lawyer, J.J.F. Winslow of Woodstock, the bill was passed with few changes, leaving those living outside Edmundston to cope with their tax problems as best they could.

Two weeks before the corporations committee debated the Edmundston tax bill, it had discussed the fixed tax rates of Gorton-Pew Ltd., an American-owned fish-packing plant being built at Caraquet with grants from both the provincial and federal governments. The company was represented by C.F. Inches, whose opponent was Fred Young, the Liberal member from Caraquet and a fish-packer himself.

Noting that his district had faced great problems finding enough money to pay its teachers, Young wanted to know what would become of "our schools if we are to disregard their interests for any business that wants to come in." Competitors of the Gorton-Pew firm, with plants worth far less, paid several times the taxes this new firm was willing to pay.

Young was supported by his colleague from Victoria County, Fred Pirie, Minister of Lands and Mines and a wealthy potato grower. He thought the proposed taxes were insufficient to carry on school work in the Caraquet district. Pirie suggested the firm should pay $300 for the first three years instead of the proposed $150 and $400 rather than $200 for the two years after that.

Pirie noted that Gorton-Pew Ltd. was paying only 25 percent of the new plant's construction costs, while the federal government was providing $75,000. New Brunswick would also be contributing, but the amount would not be known until the plant was completed.

The corporations committee agreed to Pirie's changes. A few hours after its decision, Young died of a heart attack. His place in the legislature was filled by Joseph E. Connolly, the mayor of Bathurst and a prominent lumberman.

While these northern and predominantly French-speaking communities were struggling against what would later be called the "corporate welfare system," the McNair government was piling up bigger and bigger wartime surpluses. During the 1942 budget debate, Connolly said he was "singularly elated at the balanced budget and the largest surplus in the history of New Brunswick." He did not comment on the continued signs of financial hardship being experienced by some counties, including his own.

A week later, the minister of education, C.H. Blakney, outlined details of agreements the government had made with the counties of Kent, Northumberland, Gloucester and Restigouche. All were having great difficulty balancing their budgets. The government would allow them to reduce their contributions to the Provincial Hospital in Saint John, the Jordon Tuberculosis Sanitorium and the Boys' Industrial Home.

Northumberland owed a total of $186,541, Restigouche $73,959, Gloucester $168,622 and Kent $155,541. To help them, the government agreed to pay each county an advance on the revenues they would get from the 1943 tobacco tax.

McNair seemed reluctant to make any basic changes in New Brunswick's antiquated financial system. Yet he had to do something. It was during his speech ending the 1943 Throne debate that he revealed his reform program. It would zero in on education.

New legislation would establish the county unit as the basis of financial administration for rural schools. The province would assume ten percent of the operating costs of local school boards, and the entire "cost of bringing all rural schools up to minimum standards essential for their proper operation." The government would establish a Million Dollar Fund to construct and equip several rural composite high schools and new elementary schools.

A few days later, J.K. McKee, the Liberal member for Kent, used Department of Education figures to show that, in his county, the average grade one attendance was 1263, compared to 668 for grade two. Only 24 Kent County students were enrolled in grade eleven, the final school year, in 1941. McKee said figures indicated that 47 percent of Kent County children never got beyond grade two.

A Northumberland Liberal, H. Savoie, gave additional proof of the state of rural schools. "We have districts which have not had a regular teacher in four years. Some of our schools with 50 children have desk room for only 25."

When the education minister, Blakney, announced the details of the new rural education program, he said fifty new high schools would be built. No mention was made of the specific and obviously special needs of French school districts. A short time later, Blakney told the third convention of the l'Association Acadienne d'Éducation, that the present education system was "anti-democratic, anti-pedagogical and disastrous for the French element of the province." No education minister had ever made such a public admission.[4]

Within a year, Blakney named J.H. Lejeune as assistant chief superintendent of education, the highest post ever held by a francophone in that department. In this same year, 1944, a school of agriculture for French students was opened in Edmundston. Two years later, the new bishop of Edmundston, Mgr. M.A. Roy, announced the establishment of Collège Saint-Louis, to be run by the Eudistes fathers.

These additions to Madawaska's educational facilities no doubt pleased parents who could afford the extra costs. They did little to improve the public sector, still under-financed and often staffed by inadequately-trained teachers.

A special study released in 1944 revealed the terrible state of the provincial education system. The New Brunswick Commit-

---

[4] Cited in Alexandre-J. Savoie, "L'Enseignment 1604-1970" in *Les Acadiens des Maritimes,* Moncton, 1980, p. 454.

tee on Reconstruction, created in the wake of a similar one set up by the federal government, was chaired by Dr. N.A.M. Mackenzie, president of the University of New Brunswick. The other members included Gaspard Boucher, chairman of the Hydro Commission.

They met in the larger centres from September 21 to November 26, 1943, and presented a short report the following year. It contained few surprises and its most valuable part was an extensive economic appendix prepared by J.R. Petrie, a UNB economics professor.

Most towns and boards of trade had submitted briefs, but the report's index contained no references to any from Acadian groups. In a recent analysis of the reconstruction committee, it was found that "Acadians spoke infrequently, and were not formally represented by their defensive organizations, the co-operatives, caisses populaires and *l'Assomption* — " although committee chairman MacKenzie likely met church leaders.[5]

This response, or the lack of it, is surprising considering the number of Acadian lobby groups and their great activity, verbally and in writing, that came through with every issue of *L'Évangéline*. Calixte Savoie, in particular had a wealth of statistics and very strong views on Acadian aims and how to achieve them. Yet he joined the wall of silence formed by less-articulate and less-schooled fishermen, farmers and woodcutters.

Even so, the message Savoie and such groups as l'Association Acadienne d'Éducation had been voicing for years came from "practically every organization and individual making submissions ... the need for better education facilities."[6]

New Brunswick had the highest illiteracy rate for any province — 6.9 percent of its population ten years or over. Next came Québec with 4.76 percent. New Brunswick's teachers' salaries

---

[5] R.A. Young, "and the people will sink into despair: Reconstruction in New Brunswick, 1942-52" in *Canadian Historical Review*, LXIX, 2, 1988, p. 138. Hereafter, Young

[6] *Report of the New Brunswick Committee on Reconstruction* (Fredericton, 1944), p. 58

were the lowest of any of the eight provinces for which figures were available.

Those who laboured on the fishing grounds or in the forests fared no better. New Brunswick's agricultural and forestry industries, which provided 75 percent of the province's net primary output, paid average wages lower than any province except Prince Edward Island.

The war had shown what could be done in primary farm production, noted Prof. Petrie, the committee's secretary, in a lengthy appendix on New Brunswick's economy. Yet, he thought it "incongruous that such quantities of canned vegetables should be imported from other provinces."

As for New Brunswick's fishing industry, Petrie said it "seemed fantastic that in a region so close to fishing waters unexcelled anywhere, the 1941 landed value of fish was only $3,619,000." And he noted, almost scornfully, "no steam trawlers or draggers operated out of New Brunswick ports."[7]

In the best of all possible worlds — and New Brunswick in 1943 was not one of them — the most logical solution to such a sorry mess represented by illiteracy rates, abject poverty and inadequate schools would be a massive attempt to shift the economic balance of power. Rather than invite huge corporations to pillage crown lands for its pulp, while they paid ridiculously low taxes, rather than help foreign firms build fish plants in Caraquet while they held local fishermen in bondage, rather than allow central Canadian food firms to ship their products in over state-subsidized rail routes, and thus squeeze out local farmers — why not aid all these primary producers and ordinary New Brunswickers by helping them increase the prices they got for their hard-earned product?

This obvious solution had not escaped the notice of briefs from a number of county councils. "The most striking point of consensus", notes this recent examination of the reconstruction committee, "was the need for orderly marketing of crops, fish,

---

[7] *Report of the New Brunswick Committee on Reconstruction, Appendix A, by J.R. Petrie,* "The Regional Economy of New Brunswick", p. 465

and to a lesser extent, forest products."[8] County councils called for government guarantees to primary producers of "at least the cost of production together with a reasonable profit, all supportered by adequate organizations."

These pleas came from both English and French counties. In Charlotte and Kent, "local agricultural officials indentified improved marketing as their crucial need." More specifically, they called for government help to build quick-freezing plants, cold storage units in fishing villages, warehouses and abattoirs. With these things in place, farmers and fishermen could receive immediate cash and probably higher prices, because such storage facilities would help prevent the price slide inevitable when produce and catches hit the market at harvest time.

Rural dwellers throughout both French and English New Brunswick required electrification; only one farm in five had power in 1941. Not only would access to cheap electric power improve rural living standards; it would also reduce their costs as primary producers, and hence move them up the income ladder.

Reading between the lines of the Petrie economic appendix, one fact was clear: the French communities lagged behind the English. Far more Acadians along the Northumberland Strait and facing into the Gulf of St. Lawrence were held in bondage to inshore fishing interests than was the case with the English. Perhaps the only example where the English were worse off was in the company town of Black's Harbour, where one family ruled like medieval barons.

English woodsmen were equally exploited by local pulp buyers but in 1945 the major pulp and paper outlets were located in Dalhousie, Edmundston, and Bathurst — communities close to or in the heart of French New Brunswick. A closer look at New Brunswick's illiteracy picture would reveal that Restigouche, Kent and Gloucester — predominantly French — had the dubious distinction of being at the top.

The politicians knew these facts but they were not about to draw attention to them and possibly risk renewing the sectarian

---

[8] *Young*, p. 138.

wars of Herman Pitts' day. Premier McNair knew better than to jeopardize the faithful support he could count on from French constituencies. Neither was he about to alter the lop-sided tax arrangements enjoyed by the pulp and paper mill owners in New York and Montréal.

In proposing a plan for "permanent economic rehabilitation", the committee adopted the suggestions put forth by the pulp and paper lobby and their supporters in government and the provincial university: go for industrial development.

The McNair government complied by establishing the Resources Development Board in April, 1944, and by naming people with great technical expertise and close contacts with the forest industry.

Its chairman, Dr. H.J. Rowley, was formerly director of research for Abitibi Power & Paper; Dr. J.S. Bates, a native New Brunswicker, had been an executive of Price & Pierce, another forestry firm, while K.B. Brown, deputy minister of Lands and Mines, was also a professional forester with strong technical background. Another key member was Percy Burchill, the Miramichi's most prominent native mill-owner, who was a long-time Liberal.[9]

Instead of helping primary producers get more money for their product, the McNair government handed over the initiative for the province's economic development to big business. A new Department of Industry and Reconstruction was created, but instead of helping fishermen get more for their fish, it helped them increase production by loaning them money to build bigger boats. As one scholar notes, "many fishermen became tied to particular factories, rather like share-croppers, and had little bargaining power."[10] Shades of Robert Young and his stranglehold on 19th-century Caraquet.

In agriculture, marketing was neglected in favour of ways to increase productivity, although after federal constitutional problems were resolved in 1949, marketing boards were set up

[9] *Young*, p. 148.
[10] *Young*, p. 153.

for potatoes and hogs. As was the case with the fishery, "the main thrust of postwar agricultural policy was to increase productivity and output."[11] No wonder the days of the family-owned farm were numbered.

The overall result, in demographic terms, depended on which community was being examined. The English tended to move away from their farms and depressed fishing villages and leave the province entirely. The young in rural French areas were more likely to head for the nearest larger town, be it Bathurst or Moncton. The different response might be explained by their greater poverty and their stronger family ties. Moncton was much closer to the folks in St. Norbert than Montréal; young English people often preferred to distance themselves from their kinfolk. Whatever the reason, the result was an increase in the French-to-English ratio.

The McNair government's responses to the demands for a post-war reconstructon policy clearly favoured big business, but the wily McNair was too good a politician to ignore vote-getting measures. Providing rural electrification was a sure winner; so was a massive public works program, especially on roads and bridges. And then there was that great motherhood issue, education.

The McNair government established a Million Dollar Fund to build rural high schools, and in the words of C.H. Blakney, to provide "for equal education opportunity." With the help of increased federal grants, the government passed on some of this largess to local school boards to help them replace one-room schools and to increase teachers' minimum wages.

Considering the huge increase in provincial revenues pouring in as the result of the war-time economic boom, this spending spree made sense. And all the money coming into Fredericton had not come from Ottawa. In 1943, the provincial budget surplus broke all records: $1,742,950. No wonder they came up with ways to spend some of it — like the Million Dollar Fund. Premier McNair was fortunate — or so it seemed at the time — in having the energetic "Ford" Blakney as his education minister.

[11] *Young*, p. 153.

As a successful and self-made businessman and owner of a thriving hardware chain and building supply firm, Blakney was a confident and cocky politician. Many of his Moncton constituents regarded him as a turn-coat. He had defied family traditions and staid provincial conventions by switching to the Liberals. His Tory opponents in the House often teased him about his new allegiance, but Blakney was undeterred. He had the portfolio he wanted. Fond of books and widely read as he was, his well-articulated speeches often had quotations from the classics and usually ended with a poem.

His speech ending the 1945 Throne Debate was vintage Blakney. Concentrating on educational finances, he said the adoption of the county unit for taxation purposes had revealed "many glaring inequities." Blakney sensed "a growing and insistent demand for uniformity of assessment within the county." He was not voicing government policy but in his opinion, "the entire cost of education in New Brunswick should be borne by the Province" which "should levy and collect the taxes for educational purposes ... Not until this is done can we finally have equal educational opportunity."[12]

Many of his colleagues knew how radical a change this would be. A uniform school assessment for the entire province would end the present policy where people got the education they could afford or were willing to pay for. Citizens in English-speaking cities like Saint John and Fredericton had modern schools and the best-paid teachers. Blakney's constituency of Moncton had a superior school system — for English-speaking students. In the rural communities and in one-industry towns like Dalhousie, it was a different and dismal story.

Blakney's speech went well beyond reform of educational finances. Looking over his political shoulder to the social reform program being promoted by the CCF in preparation for the expected federal election (it took place three months later), he declared that "no man, woman or child should be denied the right to medical treatment or hospitalization and some practical means must be found to ensure this God-given right."

[12] *Debates*, March 2, 1945, p. 75.

Turning next to the recent federal-provincial agreement establishing family allowances, Blakney cited figures to show what New Brunswickers would receive once this historic act went into effect in July.

Gloucester topped the list: its monthly family allowances would total $131,000; Westmorland was next with $122,000 while Saint John was third with $108,000. Blakney also outlined the details of the forthcoming federal-provincial conference and urged the need for "formalizing the present catch-as-catch-can system of federal aid. It may be," he concluded, "that the attitude of provincialism should not be maintained in the light of vast changes which the national structure ... is undergoing."

The long-term financial and social implications of family allowance benefits for French New Brunswickers, with their traditionally larger families, were obvious. For the first time, many wives could look forward to monthly cheques to supplement the often low cash returns the men earned from long hours in the woods or out on the cold waters of the Gulf.

The Conservatives were aware that the French sectors receiving the lion's share of these hand-outs would give credit to the two levels of Liberal governments. After their latest drubbing at the polls, the Tories probably were asking themselves if they would ever gain a toehold in French constituencies, which were growing faster in terms of population than anywhere else.

These population trends were translated into political seats in March, 1946 when Premier McNair introduced a redistribution bill raising membership in the legislature from 48 to 52. Moncton, Madawaska, Restigouche and Gloucester each would receive an additional member.

Based on voting trends over the past four decades, this meant three more French MLAs, raising the number to ten — all of them Liberals, including three cabinet ministers. The implications for the Tories, without one French-speaking member, were ominous. Compounding the problem was the apparent anti-French stance of Hugh Mackay.

During the 1945 session, the Opposition Leader rose on a question of privilege to reply to an editorial in the Sackville *Tribune*, a strong Liberal supporter. It had claimed that "Bracken [the federal Conservative leader] and his side-partner, Mr. Mackay, seem to have a spite at the French people, whether or not they live in Québec, in New Brunswick or elsewhere." Mackay was blamed "rightly or wrongly ...for sneering at the rapid increase in population of the northern counties.... Certainly he holds out no olive branch to the Acadians of the province."

Accusing the *Tribune* of being "the great mouthpiece of the Liberal Party," Mackay paid tribute to the Acadians' war effort and denied his party had caused "the delicate situation which admittedly exists today." He defended the federal Tories' conscription policy and accused the Liberals of refusing to register the soldiers at Camp Utopia so they could vote in the provincial election. He concluded with a quotation attributed to Father Sabourin, who had accompanied Canadian troops in the Dieppe raid.

"We landed on the shores of Dieppe, not thinking of our faith, our tongue nor of tradition; we went there thinking of Canada, our country."

During the next session, Hugh John Flemming, a rising figure for the Opposition and the son of a former Conservative premier, made a frank appeal for more French members. "Speaking with the knowledge and consent of my leader, I say to the French people of the Province, in the interests of unity and in the interests of New Brunswick, give us some representatives."[13]

"This seems to be the last prayer in the agony of the Progressive Conservative Party," quipped André Doucet of Gloucester when he rose to reply two days later. Citing the Liberal party's democratic principles as one reason for the massive French support, Doucet accused the Tories of not fulfilling its promises of 1925 and 1930 — probably a reference to their failure to put through promised education reforms demanded by the Acadians.

André Doucet had recently been appointed minister of the new department of industry and reconstruction. Among other things he was responsible for the Fisheries Loan Board, which was created in 1946 as part of the government's response to the committee on reconstruction.

[13] *Debates*, April 2, 1946, p. 222.

Even as the bill setting up the board was being piloted through the House, applications were coming in from Gloucester, probably at Doucet's urging or at the suggestion of Hédard J. Robichaud, a young Shippagan lawyer selected as the board's first secretary.

Within months, a new wooden boat-building industry, run by staunch Liberals, began operating at Caraquet. Over the next few years, the bulk of the Gloucester fishing fleet was transformed from sail to diesel. No longer would the enterprising Acadian have to build his own *goélette,* the stout two-masted schooner that could be manned and maintained by his family and local resources.

These new government-financed vessels, built in shipyards largely created from government funds, would be more efficient and could catch more fish. They also were costly and needed more sophisticated haul-outs, which in turn required government help.

The larger catches would give higher profits to the fish plants, most of them owned by Americans or English-Canadians. They also meant more money for Acadian fishermen. At long last, after two centuries of poverty and perpetual indebtedness to fish merchants like Robert Young and his decendants, the rapidly expanding Acadian communities would start inching their way towards prosperity. Thanks to modern equipment, government loans and monthly family allowance cheques, Acadians began to close the economic gap separating them from *les anglais.*

Further proof of this social and economic transformation was the sharp increase in the number of cooperatives and *caisses populaires,* as the Acadians called their credit unions. In 1944, André Doucet told the House that Gloucester county had 18 percent of the 116 credit unions and a quarter of the 23, 446 members. Twenty cooperatives were operating throughout the provinces, seven of them in Gloucester. "There appears to be a tendancy at present in certain quarters," said Doucet, "to expand cooperatives of consumption to the detriment of the cooperatives of production."[14]

[14] *Debates,* March 17, 1944, p. 221.

Doucet was referring to a basic weakness of the cooperative movement, particularly its Acadian sector. A few centres like Lamèque and Richibucto had established fishing co-ops and Moncton was the headquarters for a large farmers' cooperative serving the three Maritime provinces. Most of the co-op activity, however, was in consumer cooperatives and *caisses populaires*.

This meant that over the long run, Acadians were preparing themselves to take advantage of the post-war consumer boom. Had they been as enthusiastic to establish and support producer co-operatives in forestry and fishing, they would have strengthened their position in the economy. To confront the foreign pulp mill owners, for instance, they would have needed mountains of ready cash and intricate lines of credit. The only New Brunswicker achieving this economic power was K.C. Irving.

By 1946, the Kent County native and rising industrialist was firmly established in Saint John. The Tory financial critic, Hugh John Flemming, a lumbermill operator, raised the issue of Irving's expanding forest holdings on April 9 when he introduced a resolution calling on the government to insist that when a large tract of forest land changed hands, the new owner should make available at reasonable rates whatever stumpage was necessary to keep small mills operating. Flemming was referring to Irving's purchase of large blocks of timberland long held by the New Brunswick Railway Company. He told the House that on May 19, 1943, 210,000 acres in the Restigouche region had been sold to Irving interests while another 713,000 had gone to Fraser Companies. Elaborating on his motion later in the session, Flemming quoted a more recent report in the Saint John *Telegraph-Journal* that Irving had acquired the remaining 700,000 acres formerly owned by the N.B. Railway Company. (Flemming and other New Brunswickers were unaware that Irving had just bought the *Telegraph Journal* as well!)

Flemming was not suggesting expropriation, but he thought Irving should be made to deal with small firms. "Do we, as members, stand for the maintenance of small industries or the further creation of a large monopoly?"

Premier McNair replied that Flemming's own firm, Flemming-Gibson Ltd. had been operating on these same NB Railway lands and had even purchased 2,000 acres in 1943. He implied that Flemming could have done the same as Irving. This was not likely, considering the vast sums Irving now had at his disposal as a result of wartime profits he gained from Canada Veneers. It produced much of the plywood used to build the Mosquito bomber.

These profits provided Irving's rapid series of expansions.

His forest land acquisitions were followed by purchase of the Port Royal Pulp and Paper Company in Saint John. It would be transformed into New Brunswick's newest paper mill. Acadians as well as other New Brunswickers would be profoundly affected over the next two decades by Irving's ever-expanding empire.

Besides revealing his political skill, Premier McNair's handling of Flemming's motion indicated his reluctance to move against the newest generation of timber barons. The Irving companies and their competitors convinced local municipalities to shoulder what would be for many an impossible tax burden to provide social services. Meanwhile, some families of pulp cutters were starving.

That was the claim of a report in the Bathurst *Northern Light* in January, 1950 and cited April 26 in the budget debate by Herb Woods, a Conservative member from Sackville.

André Doucet admitted that some reports were saying that 40 families in the snow-blocked parishes of St. Sauveur and Allardville in the interior of Gloucester had faced starvation in January. His informants said that ten families "were in dire need" out of 200 families in the area. Most were surviving with the help of social security pensions. Allardville East was getting $4500 a month from this source.

Doucet revealed that the Canadian Red Cross had sent in emergency supplies and the government had purchased firewood and had provided casual work by buying up pulpwood. He also said some companies were "taking advantage of a period of readjustment to cut pulp prices to a level ... much too low to provide decent wages to producers." Noting that in the southern counties, pulp cutters were getting $10 a cord compared to $6 -

7 in Gloucester, Doucet wondered why there should be this difference. One answer seemed obvious: starving people work for less.

A few weeks before this exchange, the Liberal member for Restigouche, Louis Lebel, charged that the lumber companies had responded to the new provincial minimum wage by cutting wages 25 to 50 percent. He noted that hardest hit was the unorganized lumberjack.[15]

Even as it fought rising costs of social services, the McNair government continued to cast a blind eye on a possible solution: higher taxes from the big forest-based companies. War-time financial agreements with the federal government had given the New Brunswick government more revenue through transfer payments, but by 1950 even this new source was not enough.

In that year, the McNair government introduced a four percent social and education tax. According to Gaspard Boucher, now provincial Secretary-Treasurer, who steered the bill through the house, it would "help the struggling municipalities and school boards." His colleague, Dr. Frank McGrand, the Minister of Health, said the new tax would redress the balance "where richer urban centres with higher tax returns can and do provide better schools."

Subsequent amendments introduced by Boucher during the second reading of the sales tax bill exempted "plant machinery and equipment of a capital nature used in production of goods for sale." Thus, the big paper companies would escape much of the tax as would religious institutions selling items at church bazaars and rummage sales.

The first year's revenue figures from this new tax source, tabled in 1952 just before the general election, bore out Dr. McGrand's predictions. The larger urban centres took the brunt of this new assault on individuals' wallets. Out of a total of $2.8 million collected, Saint John citizens paid out nearly $600,000. Westmorland, including the city of Moncton paid $622,434 while York and the city of Fredericton contributed $493,577.

[15] *Debates*, March 16, 1950, p. 68.

By contrast, Gloucester, Madawaska and Northumberland averaged about $90,000 each, while Restigouche citizens paid $74,511. The population was greater in the south, but proportionately, the people of the northern communities paid more into this new tax.[16]

The new Conservative leader, Hugh John Flemming, stressed the hardships posed by the sales tax in his successful bid in 1952 to unseat the McNair administration. Tory candidates left the impression that the tax was intended to make the wealthier English communities in the south support the poorer French ones in the north. A Conservative government would end this odious sales tax.

The strategy worked. The Flemming-led Tories gained enough support in the south to win the 1952 election, but another goal remained. Acadians continued to vote Liberal.

Once in office and faced with the same revenue problems that had plagued McNair, Flemming kept the tax. Ordinary New Brunswickers would continue to pay while the big corporations, especially the paper mills, had the best of both worlds: low fixed assessments, cheap labour and easy access to crown timber resources. Sales taxes were an easy target during election campaigns.

Religious teaching in the schools was another issue politicians knew enough to avoid. But not C.H. "Ford" Blakney. During the 1947 Budget debate, after giving his usual glowing account of progress in the education department, Blakney praised the government decision to merge 1200 "financially weak little school districts into fourteen county school finance boards under the Rural School Finance Act." He also urged the creation of a University of the Maritimes, similar to those at Toronto, Oxford and Cambridge.

Then the Minister abruptly switched to talk about the forbidden subject. "God and the Divine Creation of the world finds little plan or no place in our present school curriculum," said Blakney to a startled House. "Neither is there an assigned place

[16] This information came in response to an inquiry from H.J.Flemming; see *Debates*, 1952, Appendix, p. 42.

in the school hours for the teaching of the Scriptures ...A non-sectarian school system does not mean the negation of God."

"Hear, hear!" interjected Gaspard Boucher.[17]

"Since our entire social system and conception of true civilization is based on Christian principles," Blakney continued, "it is highly important that the youth of this country should have a working knowledge and understanding of the truth taught by the Book of Law.

"If Canada is not to become a Godless nation, to go the way of the German doctrine, to go the way of Russia, then the teaching of Christianity should find a place in the public school system." Furthermore, the Minister thought recognition "should be made of the subject in our educational and economic systems." Blakney informed his intensely interested colleagues that "both the Roman Catholics and Protestants are agreed that religious education should be introduced into the public schools and both have made formal requests that this be done." He stressed that in implementing such a plan, "there must be no element of coercion. The rights of the individual must be scrupulously observed." The minister concluded with news that his department was "exploring the possibility of having God restored in the educational system of the Province."

When the Opposition resumed the Budget Debate, its chief spokesman and one-time House leader, Fred Squires of Carleton, might have been expected to comment on Blakney's revelations. As a former teacher, Squires had often discussed education in the House. This time, he carefully avoided the subject.

So did French members, although a few made some general comments during the dying days of this 1947 session. It was not until the following March, during the Throne debate, that Hervé Proulx, the Liberal member for Madawaska, became the first one to congratulate Blakney for "his timely address last year."

"I wish to tell him that the population of this Province expects that his program will be soon be made public...That religious

---

[17] *Debates*, April 10, 1947, p. 60.

education should have priority over any program of physical fitness nobody will deny."[18]

A few days later, André Doucet repeated Blakney's promise and hoped that "this condition will be corrected soon." Then he went on to deny that the family allowance payments had any political bias.

Premier McNair ignored Blakney's remarks and promises. He talked instead about such issues as the decision by the federal Board of Transport Commissioners to authorize a 21-percent increase in freight rates. Secretly, McNair must have been furious: Blakney was a liability.[19] When McNair set June 28, 1948 as election day, the Liberal candidates for Moncton City did not include C.H. Blakney. He failed to get renominated and was replaced by E.A. Fryers, a prominent grocery store owner. In the Liberal sweep (they won 47 seats to the Tories' 5) Fryers was an easy winner. He became a backbencher and politically was a nonentity.

Premier McNair gave the education portfolio to J.W. Brittain, a Saint John steamship agent and broker. Brittain knew how to handle several queries from French members about Blakney's promise to introduce religious teaching: he ignored them.

The Liberals won all the French ridings in that 1948 sweep. Rather than take this support for granted, McNair acknowledged it by adding a third francophone minister, Isaac Melanson of Westmorland. And for the first time, Roman Catholics numbered the same as Protestants in a provincial cabinet.

Under Gaspard Boucher's direction, rural electrification expanded steadily into French as well as English counties. André Doucet, as fisheries minister, saw to it that Gloucester County's Acadian fishermen got the lion's share from the Fisheries Loan Board. A flood of private member bills in 1947 and 1948 suggested that the Acadian elite was carrying out its own gameplan. On March 20, 1947, Gaspard Boucher sponsored Bill 44 to incorporate Collège Saint-Louis at Edmundston. He explained that it would be run by the same order presently in charge

[18] *Debates*, March 9, 1948, p. 60.
[19] *Debates*, May 3, 1948, p. 368.

of Collège Sacré-Coeur in Bathurst, which now had 105 students.

A week later, Bill 56 was presented to incorporate a French nursing order, giving it broader powers to administer Hôtel-Dieu hospitals at St. Basile, Edmundston, Tracadie, Campbellton, Bathurst and Dalhousie.

In March, 1948, Claudius Léger, one of Moncton's two Liberal MLAs, sponsored a bill on behalf of Les Religieuses Notre Dame du Sacré-Coeur. They were completing a large convent near Moncton's Hôtel-Dieu Hospital. A week later, four other bills were introduced in the interests of various religious orders wishing to expand their educational and health facilities.

Another that got more than the usual perfunctory attention was one incorporating la Société d'Assurance des Caisses Populaires Acadiennes, based in Caraquet. It was establishing a mutual insurance company that would offer Acadians loan protection insurance and a life-savings plan. This was another indication of the growing affluence of this once-remote and impoverished Acadian peninsula.

In this same year, 1949, *L'Évangéline* became a daily publication in a bid to reach a growing number of urban Acadians. Its survival in recent years owed much to the support of la Société l'Assomption and the tireless efforts of Calixte Savoie. In 1942, as *L'Évangéline*'s managing director, Savoie worked hard to find new investors and subscribers. Despite this support, the newspaper had more than its share of bad luck. Perhaps its worst moment came on July 17, 1943, when its assistant editor, Thomas LeBlanc, died suddenly. The editor, Alfred Roy, returned to the office that evening to write a tribute and he too suffered a fatal seizure.[20]

Good editors are scarce at the best of times. In the middle of a war, they are even scarcer...especially French ones. A recent graduate of the French programme at the Teachers' College and the co-founder of a French student publication, Léandre LeGresley was asked to fill the breach. *L'Évangéline* survived, becoming a bi-weekly in 1947 and a tri-weekly the next year.

[20] Lloyd Machum, *A History of Moncton* Moncton 1965, p. 365.

A new era began for the newspaper in 1950 with the arrival from Québec of Jean Hubert. During his thirteen years as editor, he tried, with some success, to convince Acadians they were "an integral part of the great world of French civilization."[21]

The time was fast approaching when Acadian demands could best be articulated and achieved in the political arena. In 1952, a young Kent County lawyer, Louis J. Robichaud, was first elected to the legislature. At twenty-six, he was the youngest ever Acadian MLA.

Over the next eight years of Conservative rule, "Little Louis" or "P'tit Louis" quickly moved to the front benches of Her Majesty's Loyal Opposition. He entered the House as a brash, inexperienced lawyer. He cut his political teeth in an arena that for the first time in New Brunswick's long history, was often dominated by French voices and French views. By 1960, Louis Robichaud was the obvious choice to lead French New Brunswickers toward equality with *les anglais*.

---

[21] George F.G.Stanley, "The Flowering of the Acadian Renaissance", in Bercusson and Buckner, *Eastern and Western Perspectives,* Toronto 1981, p. 37.

# THIRTEEN

## APPRENTICING FOR POWER: 1952-1960

The 1952 general election was a watershed for French-speaking New Brunswickers. For the first time in the 20th century, they had a significant representation in a Conservative government.

The two northern counties of Restigouche and Madawaska both went Tory and consequently were rewarded portfolios in the new cabinet of Hugh John Flemming. Edgar Fournier of Edmundston became chairman of the New Brunswick Hydro Commission, the same post occupied in the McNair administration by his fellow townsman Gaspard Boucher. Roger Pichette of Campbellton — like Fournier and Boucher, Québec-born — took over André Doucet's Department of Industry along with the Fisheries Loan Board.[1]

The City of Moncton had also gone Tory, electing Joseph Bourgeois and Babbitt Parlee, who became president of the executive council. Other freshman back-benchers on the government side included Lucien Fortin of Edmundston and William Bird, a bilingual anglophone from St. Leonard. Of these new French-speaking Conservative members, only Bourgeois was Acadian.

---

[1] After being defeated by Fournier in the 1952 election, Boucher turned to the federal scene, winning the Restigouche-Madawaska seat in 1953. He died a few months later.

Premier Flemming, the only member of his party who had held a seat in the previous house, took his place at the opening session in February, 1953, and looked across at sixteen of Her Majesty's Loyal Opposition. Ten of them were Acadians.

The new Liberal leader was Austen Taylor, former agriculture minister in the McNair government. He became party leader when McNair was named to the Bench after his personal defeat in 1952. The Acadian group contained the oldest and the youngest members in the House: Gloucester County's André Doucet and the new member for Kent, twenty-six-year-old Louis J. Robichaud.

Almost from the moment that Taylor took the unusual step and waived the debate in reply to the Speech from the Throne, a pattern was established that would remain throughout Flemming's tenure as premier. The French-speaking members on *both* sides of the House carried the debate. Most of them did it *en anglais* but now and then the old chambers echoed with heated words *en français*. Repeatedly it was a clash between the Acadian Liberals and the two Québec-born ministers, Fournier and Pichette.

One francophone stood out. At times, W.J. "Tony" Gallant of Rogersville dominated the entire proceedings. Forever on his feet with points of order and questions of privilege, Tony Gallant, more than any other MLA, was responsible for extending the debates and for prompting some of the wittiest, the angriest and at times the most unparliamentary exchanges ever recorded.

After the mid-1950s, every speech, every aside, was preserved as the court reporters turned to tape-recorders to cope with the mounting torrent of words.

Gallant's special target, at least in the early years, was Roger Pichette, "that Québécois from Cross Point" (across the river from Campbellton) who had "invaded New Brunswick" according to Gallant, "just in time to qualify as a New Brunswick Tory." Gallant called him "Baby-Face" and at one point presented Pichette with a baby's rattle.

At first such antics delighted Gallant's fellow Liberals. Press reporters, eager for "colour" material, were fascinated. As the decade went on and the debates seemed never-ending — due largely to Gallant's frequent interjections — patience on both sides of the House wore thin.

Tony Gallant sometimes departed from his self-appointed role as "court jester". A long-time director of the New Brunswick Union of Municipalities, he was a knowledgeable and often critical member of the House municipalities committee.On March 24, 1954, for example, Gallant challenged the proposed four-year tax concession to Brunswick Mines, one of the major firms involved in the extensive base metal activity in Gloucester and Northumberland counties.

He argued that Brunswick Mines, controlled by St. Joseph's Lead Company, "the largest mining company in the world," was wealthy enough to pay taxes even though it was planning a four-year halt to its New Brunswick operations. Gallant charged that St. Joseph's was "lobbying to prevent the United States from importing lead and zinc," which would leave the Gloucester mine "in the sleeping stage."

Like a handful of earlier New Brunswickers who had dared to criticize special considerations for big business, Gallant's protest got nowhere. The tax concessions were approved, not only by the Conservative committee members, but by Joseph Connolly, the Opposition financial critic. Undeterred, Gallant, along with other back-benchers from both parties, continued to stress the desperate plight of county councils trying to maintain services with inadequate revenues.

Having such a "grandstand" performer as Tony Gallant as a colleague, it was not surprising that freshman member Louis Robichaud was upstaged — at first. His maiden speech on February 27, 1953, was a low-keyed effort. The young Richibucto lawyer praised recent Liberal efforts to improve educational standards but he stressed the need for more qualified teachers in Kent, where 30 percent lacked basic qualifications.

Concluding with the traditional message *en français*, Robichaud declared it an honour to participate not only as a junior member but as *the* junior member. He noted Prime Minister St. Laurent's visit the previous spring to Université Saint-Joseph, adding that New Brunswick was like a small Canada: "Let us always be united."

Contrasting sharply with these cautious tones were the remarks that another freshman member, William Bird, delivered a few days later. He concentrated on the activities of the Irving interests and what they were doing with their New Brunswick Railway acreage south of Edmundston, acquired a few years before. Noting that this area was populated mostly by French citizens "dependent on lumbering, pulping and farming," Bird informed the House that the Irvings were "now fencing and padlocking the roads" preventing anyone from hunting or fishing in the area.

He urged the government to get these lands opened again. A year later, Bird had changed his tune. He singled out the Irvings for praise because their Madawaska operations were giving "a great deal of employment."

It was Louis Robichaud who first raised a topic dear to the hearts of the Acadian elite, especially Calixte Savoie and Dr. Albert Sormany. This was the 200th anniversary of the Acadian Expulsion in 1755. In fact, Savoie had been named a year earlier to chair the celebration's organizing committee. Closing off his contribution to the Throne debate, Robichaud, speaking in French, suggested that New Brunswick issue a formal invitation to the President of France, or a "distinguished personality from England"; even "the Queen herself." He thought their presence would show the world "that racial groups are living in harmony when they have faith in their respective good-will."

André Doucet, the senior Acadian spokesman in the House, said the celebrations would not concentrate on the dispersion "but rather the triumph of the Acadian race in the conservation of its religion, its language and its ancestral virtues."[2]

How well New Brunswick's French citizens were doing was the theme taken up by Joseph LeBlanc, who was also the mayor of Shediac. He told the House that according to the 1951 census, they numbered 197,611 or forty percent of New Brunswick's total. He also listed four French universities, including St. Joseph's, now based in Moncton. In reality, they were all more similar to Québec's classical colleges than full-blown post-

---

[2] *Debates,* March 16, 1954, p. 187.

secondary institutions such as the universities of Mount Allison or New Brunswick. LeBlanc observed that Acadians were numerous everywhere except in the civil service in Fredericton, where French-speaking officials were a rare commodity. In what was probably an attempt to placate his English colleagues, LeBlanc congratulated four of them who had attempted to speak French in the debates.

They included Gordon Fairweather, a young Rothesay lawyer who had "deplored the gap in our educational system which results in English-speaking children being seldom able to speak or write French upon leaving school." His promised support for a program where French would be taught "in the very first grade" received loud applause from the Liberal benches. Unfortunately, this issue had not been included in the terms of reference of a current educational study: a Royal Commission on School Financing, chaired by Dr. W.H. Mackenzie, the Superintendent of Schools for Saint John.

On April 8, 1954, the minister of education, Claude Taylor, told the House that this three-member commission had completed its hearings. While he could not comment on its findings, he more or less responded to Fairweather's earlier reference to French in the schools by admitting that in the past there had been "too little emphasis on the bilingual nature of our teacher-training program." Taylor did say that for the first time in its history, the Teachers' College in Fredericton was providing "a strong course in the French language and literature" which was taught by a bilingual instructress. Furthermore, practice teaching was being given in French schools in Westmorland, under the direction of a French-speaking instructress from the college. She remained un-named but was probably Marguerite Michaud, who was rapidly becoming a more visible figure in Fredericton's predominantly English education scene.

It was Louis Robichaud, during his first speech in the 1955 session, who raised the most controversial educational issue. It was one "always close" to his heart: "the need for religion in our public schools. I have been taught and I believe that church and state are not separate and distinct entities. On the contrary they should operate in conjunction for the same purpose — the well-being of all citizens, but one should not be subservient to the other."

He left it at that, going on to praise the efforts to celebrate the bicentennial of the Expulsion. It would be safe to guess that his unsolicited endorsement of the restoration of religion in the public school system had been prompted by members of l'Ordre de Jacques Cartier. Later events would seem to point to that lobbying group's continuing efforts in that direction.

Lucien Fortin, one of the three Conservatives from Madawaska, also referred to this touchy and almost unmentionable subject. "What the French want," he informed the House, "were means and ways required to keep their cultural and religious heritage." French Canadians "object steadfastly to assimilation." Quoting the Quebéc patriot Henri Bourassa, who had died just three years earlier, in 1952, Fortin said that mutual agreement between English and French, "to be complete and perfect, must include official recognition of the mother tongue of both ... and a proportional participation in public offices."

Turning to what he called this "ticklish subject, religion in the schools," Fortin noted that an "interdenominational group committee representing 93.6 percent of the population has requested the Minister to introduce religious teaching." He also cited a report from the Director of Public School Services claiming that after seven years of religious teaching in Ontario, "there was a general feeling of satisfaction."

With an obvious reference to the Cold War hysteria currently gripping North America (the McCarthy hearings were underway in Washington), Fortin concluded that "the difficult age in which we live calls for this official recognition."[3]

Premier Flemming was too seasoned a politician to step into this potential quagmire. When he rose, he talked instead about the progress of the Beechwood power dam being erected across the Saint John River above Woodstock. He left his French colleagues to deal with cultural issues.

It was Edgar Fournier who announced a government grant of $20,000 towards the cost of the Bicentennial Celebrations. He

[3] *Debates*, February 18, 1955, p. 64; February 24, p. 89.

also said l'Université Saint-Joseph would receive $37,500 for the establishment of an agricultural and domestic science school. The annual grant to that institution as well as to Université Sacré-Coeur in Bathurst and Collège Saint-Louis in Edmundston would be increased fifteen percent.

These examples of the Flemming administration's recognition of the French fact were somewhat overshadowed by Fournier's opening remarks. "The Provincial Cabinet has two French-speaking members [who] during the past three years have been the principal and continual targets of attack of the French-speaking representatives of the Opposition of this House and throughout the province." He warned that "as long as the public representatives of my race will play such a game, our influence in this Province and the progress of our national institutions will only suffer greatly." After his usual descriptions of activities of the Power Commisson, Fournier returned to the topic really bothering him.

Both Tony Gallant and Louis Robichaud had been criticizing him for a truck he had bought from the commission for $100. Later, his son had traded it for $750. Explaining to the House that he had spent $1,000 repairing the vehicle, the now angry Fournier demanded that Gallant "make a public apology, resign or be subject to a motion of censure."

"Come out in the back yard now," taunted Gallant.

Fournier ignored the challenge. Later in this 1955 session, he had more verbal clashes which also involved Joe LeBlanc, Pichette and the irrrepressible Gallant.

Premier Flemming tried to smooth the ruffled feathers by referring to the great feeling of unity "between the two races." He also made a glowing tribute to the "Dean of the House," André Doucet, currently celebrating his thirty-third consecutive session.

Counter motions of censure by Gallant and Fournier were withdrawn but in the dying days of the session, Louis Robichaud returned to the attack. He obviously was annoyed at Pichette's earlier reference to his narrow win in Kent and to his inexperience. He had the same experience as Pichette; furthermore, he was a native New Brunswicker. "Such was not the case with the Honourable Minister. He arrived on the political scene in Restigouche County from Québec province, barely in time for the nomination convention in 1952."

On April 5, as the long and wordy session was ending, Fournier again referred to Gallant's criciticms. Gallant in turn told the House about a talk Fournier had made the previous December on CJEM-Edmundston, a talk that "astounded the people of Madawaska and elsewhere." Fournier had mentioned grants the government had given to Edmundston hospitals so people could be treated there rather than in Fredericton or Saint John "where there are no French doctors and our French people do not always receive the attention they deserve." Gallant also charged that Fournier had told his radio audience Gallant was "an unfit person to sit in the Legislature."

Both Hugh John Flemming and John McNair, his Liberal predecessor, knew of these two French New Brunswicks — the old Acadian community and the newer one transplanted from Québec. The senior French minister under McNair, Gaspard Boucher, had never experienced such verbal attacks as those endured by his successor at the Power Commission. Both traced their lineage from Québec and both came from Edmundston. Why did this French split appear in the 1950's?

New personalities had much to do with it. Both Robichaud and Gallant had been exposed to the new Acadian awareness promoted so persistently by members of l'Ordre de Jacques Cartier. This awareness was now firmly rooted in Acadian postsecondary institutions such as Université Sacré-Coeur, which both Robichaud and Gallant had attended.

In other respects, their backgrounds were quite different.

The son of a fairly prosperous Kent County lumber mill owner, Louis Robichaud had never known the impoverished conditions that plagued communities like Allardville, for example. Still, as one of eleven children, he had to struggle.

One of his family's first tasks, once he had completed elementary school, was to find a French high school young Louis could attend. The nearest one, in Buctouche, taught only in English, so they sent him to the academy in Bathurst. From there it was a logical step to Sacré-Coeur, where Louis edited the student newspaper in 1946-47.[4] From Bathurst, he spent two years at Laval University, where he came under the influence of Rev. Dr. Georges-Henri Lévesque, reform-minded director of the Faculty of Social Sciences.

Lacking the money to complete a university law degree program, young Robichaud returned to Bathurst and articled with a local Conservative lawyer, Albany Robichaud (no relation). It was here that he was noticed by the veteran Liberal MLA, André Doucet. No sooner had he completed writing his provincial bar examinations — in English! — than the election writs were issued. The year was 1952. Louis Robichaud had just been married and his shingle was hardly dry outside his Richibucto law office when he won the Liberal nomination for Kent.[5]

Tony Gallant, twelve years his senior, had travelled a slightly different route. He too had attended Sacré-Coeur, but then came the Second World War. After war-time service, he returned to his native Rogersville to work as a car salesman and a manufacturer's agent. Gallant earned his political spurs as a warden of the municipality of Northumberland, a vice-president of the Union of New Brunswick Municipalities and a director of Chatham's Hôtel Dieu Hospital. Along the way, he developed an intimate knowledge of and a growing concern for the problems facing municipal services.

Gallant and Robichaud, along with other younger Acadians, probably knew that the bicentennial celebrations marking the Acadian Expulsion were mere window-dressings that would do little to reduce the poverty and inequalities they could see throughout French New Brunswick. They probably agreed with Calixte Savoie and Dr. Sormany that education reform was the way to go.

During the 1956 debate on the Speech from the Throne, Lucien Fortin, the most out-spoken of the three Conservative members from Madawaska, wondered aloud when the govern-

---

[4] Marcel Tremblay, *Cinquant ans d'éducation, catholique et française en Acadie* (Bathurst, 1949), p. 288.
[5] J.E.Belliveau, *Little Louis and the Giant K.C.* (Hantsport, NS, 1980), pp. 18-19.

ment planned to implement the recommendations of the Mackenzie Commission on School Financing. It had suggested direct federal aid and district grants based on student enrolment rather than what Fortin described as the present basis of wealth and the ability of communities to pay.

According to the report, the cities had 20 percent of the students but paid only 40 percent of New Brunswick's overall education costs. By contrast, the counties had 80 percent and shouldered 60 percent of the burden.

Switching to French, Fortin hailed the Acadian celebrations which had taken place in Moncton and Memramcook the previous summer. He assured the House that the French-speaking element "has no other aim than that of getting ways and means to maintain their cultural and religious traditions." French citizens wanted only "the official recognition of their language, their share of public employment, an equitable redistribution of the seats in the House, and a bilingual normal school."

For ultra-conservative English New Brunswick MLAs on both sides of the legislature, those demands were both silly and insulting. Yet, within the lives of many of them, all but one of them would be realized. The exception was a fair share of public employment.

In 1956, most French hopes centred on educational reforms. At the start of the legislative session that year, Louis Robichaud, who seemed to be the Opposition's educational critic, expressed confidence that the Flemming government was trying. Tangible proof was a promise to have the matriculation examinations available in French.

Toward the end of the session, when it became clear that the government would not implement the main recommendations of the Mackenzie Report, Robichaud grew more critical. He pointed out that "thousands of families especially in French-speaking counties, have borne a heavy load of education costs outside their regular contributions towards financing education in their own district." Because of inadequate local high schools, "they have sent their children to colleges and convents."

André Doucet was more specific. Gloucester County was now $350,000 in arrears. Taxes were up 17 percent, making them the highest in the province. "A great many of our young men are going elsewhere, to Québec and Ontario."

Doucet noted that Gloucester County Council had petitioned the government for ten percent of the county liquor revenues.This "was a demand on the Government of the Province," he warned.

Flemming felt he could afford to ignore it. Events proved him correct. He won the 1956 general election with ease. Most of the 33 members on the Government side were the same as before, while the Liberals had a new leader. He was Joseph Connolly, the veteran member from Bathurst, who took over when Austen Taylor was named to the Senate.

Louis Robichaud had a new role: the Liberal financial critic. In his speeches, he avoided getting involved in French issues.

They were championed by Claude Savoie, a back-bencher from Gloucester, and by André Richard from Kent. Of course, the unpredictable Tony Gallant voiced his opinions on almost anything, while Lucien Fortin, nominally a Tory, became as outspoken as Gallant in matters relating to French constituencies.

Robichaud delivered a conventional speech in the budget debate, seconding Connolly's motion for a provincial-municipal conference on financial problems. It was Claude Savoie who urged the government to act on requests from l'Association Acadien d'Éducation for a bilingual teachers' college.

It was Fortin who demanded a more equitable distribution of the education costs as recommended by the Mackenzie Commission. He admitted that "a discussion of such a problem was always ticklish because it tends to involve directly or indirectly, racial matters [and] the inequalities, real or apparent, existing between " New Brunswick's two largest ethnic groups. It almost seemed that a secret plan had been worked out among certain French members from both sides of the house. Backbenchers like Fortin would raise ethnic problems while Robichaud and Connolly stayed on more pragmatic issues such as the provincial debt and the sales tax. In this way, they would avoid alienating anglophones in Saint John and the river valley.

In his first major speech in the 1958 session, Robichaud did mention the Mackenzie Report, as did Connolly, but for the most part they dwelt on things like more paper mills for the Miramichi and the ever-expanding Irving empire. "If we could establish in our province a half dozen men of Mr. Irving's calibre," Robichaud declared during the 1958 budget debate, "we would have no need of continued appeals for financial assistance from Ottawa." Such a view seemed based on an assumption that such individuals would assume a fair share of the provincial tax burden.

Again, it was Fortin who seized on a remarkable statement from the provincial president of the Imperial Order, Daughters of the Empire IODE. She wanted New Brunswick to become Canada's first bilingual province. "One could not ask for a better offer of collaboration," observed Fortin. He was probably aware that the IODE had representatives on the provincial curriculum committee. This was the body charged with authorizing all basic changes in the programs of study throughout the school system.

Fortin added that Section 133 of the British North America Act did not prevent New Brunswick from adopting bilingual road signs, especially in French areas. Neither did it prohibit departments like Agriculture, Lands and Mines as well as the Motor Vehicle Branch from publishing their communications in French.[6]

Then, as if to remind himself as well as his listeners that he was still a Progressive Conservative, he praised the Flemming government for showing "more understanding of the French than any other. Never before have we heard French spoken as often in this historic house. Never before have we seen an English Premier strive ... to familiarize himself with our language."

He might have singled out Norman Buchanan, the Minister of Lands and Mines. He had delivered his first halting French paragraph back in 1953 and had persisted so that by 1959 he made quite a lengthy statement — for an *anglais*. In it, he said his department needed bilingual employees "if we want the

---

[6] *Debates,* April 17, 1958, p. 357.

words "conservation, protection and management" better understood.

While Buchanan and Fairweather in particular tried out their French to emphasize the need for a bilingual New Brunswick, such efforts and examples went largely unheeded. The school system and the civil service remained in English hands, even as both were expanding rapidly.

Communities like Moncton and Bathurst, with more and more French citizens, stubbornly refused to provide French high school facilities. In French districts, the out-moded school taxation system remained in place, despite recommendations from the Mackenzie commission and annual briefs from the New Brunswick Teachers' Federation and l'Association Acadienne d'Éducation. Other pressures and demands for more recognition of the French fact were coming from *L'Évangéline* and programs of the CBC French radio and television stations operating in Moncton.

A Progressive Conservative government could continue to ignore these pleas "as long as the counties along the St. John River are over-represented in relation to the North Shore and Madawaska."[7] A Liberal government would do the same — until it was led by an Acadian determined to end these inequalities. That possibility moved closer in October, 1958, when a Liberal party convention elected Louis Robichaud as its leader.

The election of the 33-year old lawyer was predictable, even though Joseph Connolly made a determined bid to beat him.

Tony Gallant did not contest the leadership, probably because his legislative behaviour had been a continual embarrassment to his fellow Liberals. In March, 1958, he had to be escorted from the chambers by the Sergeant-at-Arms. Despite these antics, he would play an important support role for his new Liberal leader.

The 1959 session was just one day old when the new Opposition leader seized the initiative. With Gallant's help, he would keep it right through until Premier Flemming called the 1960 election. This early turning point came when Robichaud called for the new hospital care plan to be paid out of general revenues

[7] Hugh Thorburn, *Politics in New Brunswick,* Toronto, 1961, p. 84.

instead of the current premiums. Throughout the lengthy debate, the enthnicity issue hovered just below the surface. It came into full view when French MLAs from both sides of the House rose to speak — something they did often.

Gallant gave the longest speech — a rambling, disjointed one that dragged out over the supper recess and into the evening. Picking up on a remark by his old adversary, Pichette, that the removal of the hospital premium would benefit French counties, Gallant accused the Restigouche member of "insulting a whole ethnic group. " Acadians wanted no special favours, he told the House. "All the proud Acadians want is an equal opportunity."

Premier Flemming argued that many provincial hospital experts had been consulted before the premium plan had been started. He named Dr. Carl Trask of the Saint John General and the Rev. Mother Saint Georges, controller of Hôtel Dieu hospitals at Perth, Edmundston, Campbellton, Lamèque, Bathurst and Tracadie. Noting that the new Liberal Member of Parliament for Gloucester, Hédard Robichaud, had warned his county would not participate in the plan if it involved a premium, Flemming said his government would "not allow any municipality to interfere."

His Minister of Health, Dr. George McInerney, denied Liberal charges that many counties, especially the French, were having trouble collecting the premiums. His statistics revealed a high collection rate for southern counties, but also showed that the lowest was Gloucester. Only 60 percent had been collected there.

When the vote on the Robichaud motion was taken February 20, the government won easily: 32 to 11. Of the eleven Liberals voting in favour of abolishing the premium, seven were Acadians. Of the remaining four negatives, only two were unilingual English.

Tony Gallant confounded everyone. At the last minute he learned that the plan would mean an extra $21,000 for his Northumberland constituents so he voted with the government.[8]

The 1960 legislative session began on a sombre note. In the address in reply to the throne speech, Gallant was praised by his

[8] *Debates,* February 20, 1959, p. 159.

local political rival, J.R. Martin, the Tory member from Chatham. He described Gallant's untiring efforts on behalf of the Escuminac fishing community after the tragic events of June 19, 1959.

Thirty-five fishermen, most of them Acadians, lost their lives when a freak summer storm lashed the area. A Fishermen's Disaster Fund, established by Michael Wardell, the British-born publisher of Fredericton's *Daily Gleaner* and *Atlantic Advocate* magazine, alerted the nation to the plight of the survivors and a large sum was raised.

Another Liberal speaker in the Throne debate, Clarence Léger of Westmorland, hailed the opening of the CBC's new French television facilities in Moncton and the official opening of what he called la Cité université à Moncton by the Brothers of the Holy Cross Order. It was still a branch operation of Université Saint-Joseph, but rapidly it became the educational beachhead for Moncton's steadily-rising French citizenry.

Two days earlier, Opposition leader Robichaud had less flattering things to say about education. Noting that "education costs continue to mount," he accused the Flemming government of refusing to assume its "fair share," leaving the municipalities to "carry the load."

Michael Fournier of Gloucester said that in 1946 his county's education costs had been $111,589; in 1959 they reached over one million — " all paid by the people of the county." He also compared enrolment and other statistics of Saint John city and Gloucester and concluded: "The facts are that rich Saint John is receiving almost twice as much in educational grants as poor Gloucester." It was a familiar story — one that Flemming continued to ignore.

He could not dodge the hospital premium issue. Once again, Robichaud introduced his motion to abolish premiums. Once more, the government won, aided by Gallant. "I'm not going to run a political campaign on this hospital plan," he told the House. "I believe the people in New Brunswick and in my county have already accepted it with all its unfairness. I voted for the plan last year and was called a Judas, except by my 72 [poor]families " whose premiums were paid for by the county.

For the rest of this 1960 session, Gallant was continually on his feet, arguing points of order, making countless impromptu speeches and endless interruptions. His four-hour effort during the throne debate contained detailed criticism of the liquor laws. He cited the proliferation of private clubs and criticized the RCMP's role in enforcement. On March 10, he blocked unanimous consent to a motion calling on Ottawa to build the Chignecto Canal. It was carried a few days later during his absence.

Louis Robichaud had raised many of these same issues during the Budget debate, giving rise to speculation that he and Tony had agreed to a secret plan of action. A bitter debate in the dying days of the session dispelled this idea.

It was sparked by a patronage issue involving a former Tory member for Restigouche, Fred Somers. He had resigned in 1957 after being implicated in a kick-back scandal. Robichaud reintroduced the issue in a private members bill — a ploy he had used repeatedly in what proved to be a successful way to embarrass the Flemming government. On April 11, after some bitter exchanges between Robichaud and the normally calm premier, the Speaker, Arthur Moore, recognized Gallant as the "Independent Member from Northumberland." "Now that we have three parties in this province," he added, he would give Gallant five minutes, the same time he had allotted to Flemming and Robichaud.

Gallant took fifteen minutes to argue that Somers should not be tried a second time. Then, amid great desk-pounding from the government members, he crossed the floor to sit between "two clean men" — Robert McAllister from Simonds and Arthur Carten from Lancaster.

Robichaud quickly rose to announce that the move had the permission of the Official Opposition. Gallant had left the Liberal caucus in January, 1957, "disgruntled because he had lost his bid to get the leadership of the party." Switching again to the Somers affair, Robichaud concluded by giving the names of Liberal nominees for the coming election.

Premier Flemming's five minutes turned out to be a fierce attack on Robichaud and his "frantic" search for an issue. He accused his young opponent of making "an outrageous series of misstatements on hospital care insurance." Now he was turning "to the first love of present-day Liberalism," the smear campaign. Then, as if to calm himself, he read extensively from old speeches to show how many bridges his government had built since 1956.

If the premier had revealed a rare display of temper, it was mild compared to the next diatribe directed at the Liberal leader. Edgar Fournier accused him of being "one who pretends to be the defender of the French people. He belongs to many French and Acadian associations. He proposes to promote a higher standard for the French people of this Province." Yet he had refused "to stand behind his own people in the Bathurst raid" — a reference to a much-publicized RCMP action against a private club for alleged liquor offenses. "Today again he is trying by all devilish means to kill the reputation of one of his own ... Killing the reputation of his brother is all good and well if he can gain a few votes." [9]

It was amid this bitter mood that the 1960 legislative session drew to a close. Ironically, of the four major participants in the Somers debate, only one would return to the House after the general election, held June 22, 1960.

It would make a neat thesis to argue that the 1960 Liberal victory was due to the solid bloc of Acadians determined to elect their own government led by Louis Robichaud. New Brunswick's politics are never that simple.

Many factors were involved in the Robichaud victory of 32 seats. They were as diverse as the Liberal promise to restore moose hunting and the Tory decision to support a Belgian conglomerate wanting to build Rothesay Paper Mill over the opposition of K.C. Irving.[10]

The man most responsible for the Liberal victory was Louis Robichaud. He had begun campaigning almost from the moment his party caucus chose him leader in 1958. His youthful energy and enthusiasm, his fluency in both English and French, and his

---

[9] *Debates*, April 11, 1960, p. 934.
[10] For a more detailed account of this election by a participant, see *Belliveau*.

support staff, led by Frederictonian Charles McElman, a veteran of the McNair era, all help to explain the results.

The Robichaud-led forces won back the French counties of Restigouche and Madawaska, as well as the English counties of Charlotte and Sunbury. In each of these contests, as with most of the others, a wise choice of candidates helped spell victory. The Liberals' media campaign was ably run by Ned Belliveau, an Acadian who had left his native Moncton to carve out a successful advertising career in Toronto.

Whatever the reasons — and they tended to vary with each constituency — the result was an historic French presence in the WASP capital of Fredericton. This presence had disappeared in the late 18th century when the Loyalist troops and settlers moved up the river to occupy the remains of the old Acadian settlement of St. Anne, ravaged by Colonel Monckton in 1758.

If ever a politician had a reason for assuming the reformer's mantle, that person was Louis J. Robichaud. Reared in impoverished Kent County, nurtured on an early diet of renewed Catholicism and rekindled Acadian awareness, he was of a new generation. His mentors had been New Brunswick-born and educated priests, lay members of the *caisse populaire* movement, and leaders of l'Ordre de Jacques Cartier.

His "finishing schools" were Université Sacré-Coeur and Laval's faculty of social sciences. During two sessions in a Tory dominated legislative assembly, he gained additional evidence, if any was needed, that New Brunswick's antiquated and unequal taxation system had to go.

Backed by a cabinet containing a record-number of his fellow Acadians — seven, and with an aroused Acadian elite waiting outside, P'tit Louis had to deliver.

# FOURTEEN

## THE ROAD TOWARDS EQUAL OPPORTUNITY: 1960-1967

In 1960, the old Loyalist city of Fredericton was the physical and social embodiment of nineteenth century Britannia. Its magnificent stock of wooden houses would remain intact but its social structure was in for a rude shock. The first sign came with the arrival of seven French-speaking cabinet ministers appointed by the first Acadian ever elected to be premier.

Until the summer of 1960, one of Fredericton's few modern contacts with New Brunswick's Acadian community was the chief French instructress at the Teachers' College, Dr. Marguerite Michaud. For a decade and more, this colourful individual had become a familiar sight. Together with Dr. Gérald DeGrace, the senior French civil servant in the Department of Education, Dr. Michaud maintained the French presence in Loyalist Fredericton. Their lonely cultural vigil, which they taken over from Dr. Alphée Belliveau, was ending.

Premier Louis Robichaud and his French colleagues from the northern and eastern counties quickly settled in. So did the vanguard of a small army of French-speaking civil servants, from young secretaries to farming and fisheries experts. They were the overdue corps of intermediaries needed to link the new government with French citizens so long neglected or underserved by well-meaning but unilingual English.

Robichaud never allowed himself the time to ponder the implications of these changes. He had too much to do. On July

12, 1960 — a glorious Twelfth for New Brunswick's Acadians as well as for the fading Orange Order, Lieutenant-Governor J.Leonard O'Brien swore in Canada's youngest premier and a cabinet containing a record number of French-speaking citizens.

In terms of years, the senior member was Dr. George Dumont, 62, from Campbellton, who took over the sensitive health portfolio. André Richard, a Buctouche car dealer, assumed public works while Adrien Lévesque of Edmundston became the province's first agronomist to head up agriculture.

Michael Fournier of Gloucester took over Industry and Development and Ernest Richard of Shippagan would occupy the Speaker's chair. The mayor of Shédiac, Joseph LeBlanc, was named to municipal affairs, while the premier himself followed tradition by becoming attorney-general.

His anglophone ministers included L.G. DesBrisay of Moncton, the new secretary-treasurer. DesBrisay's father-in-law was C.H. "Ford" Blakney, who had held the education portfolio for one session a generation earlier before being blackballed for suggesting that religion should be taught in the school system.

A farmer from Middle Sackville, Donald Harper, took over as chairman of the Power Commission, and Graham Crocker of Newcastle became minister of lands and mines. Two Charlotte County members, Ken Webber and Henry Irwin, assumed the labour and education portfolios, respectively. The youngest minister, William Duffie of Oromocto, the community recently created to serve the Camp Gagetown army base, would head a new department, youth and welfare.

Conspicuously absent from this line-up was anyone from the city of Saint John. Like Fredericton, it had returned a solid block of Conservatives. Another election would be needed to fill this critical gap. In the meantime, New Brunswick's political affairs were largely in French hands for the first time.

In the political sense, New Brunswick had always been a small community. This was especially true of the French Liberal MLAs. Just how close-knit its Acadian members were was revealed in some of their maiden speeches given during the new session. It began November 17, 1960, in the first fall sitting since Confederation.

The freshman Liberal Member from Moncton, Gilbert Robichaud, informed the House that his father John, had represented Gloucester County 44 years earlier, before entering the House of Commons, where Gilbert's brother Hédard now carried on the family tradition as Gloucester's MP. [1]

Jean-Marc Michaud, one of three francophone Liberals elected from Madawaska, in moving the 1963 Address in Reply to the Speech from the Throne, noted that his father, J.E. Michaud, a long-time federal MP, had performed the same honour 45 years earlier. This time, the senior Michaud was a proud observer in the visitors' gallery. [2]

Adrien Lévesque revealed in his maiden speech that he had been persuaded by the premier to leave his Fredericton civil service job to enter politics, and he had agreed partly because of their close friendship established as students at Collège Sacré-Coeur. [3]

In an opening speech that was largely autobiographical, Dr. George Dumont said he had grown up in Rogersville next door to Fidèle Richard, the grandfather of Speaker Ernest Richard, whose mother he had cared for during her last illness. [4]

Switching to French, Dumont continued: "It is with emotion that I recall the memory of Mgr. François Marcel Richard, whose imposing stature has been present through my whole life. I was 17 years old when this man of great strength in Acadian revival, gradually weakened by illness and difficulties, was finally laid to rest." Father Richard had given Dumont "a lesson in life — that the Acadians are here to fulfill a mission in this land sanctified by the heroism of their forefathers."

Referring to his arrival in Campbellton in 1925 to begin 35 years of doctoring, Dumont said he had been "captivated, impressed and won over by another of our great Acadian leaders" without whose influence he never would have taken part in the public forum. He was Father Arthur Melanson, the one-time

[1] *Debates,* February 21, 1961, p. 184.
[2] *Debates,* February 11, 1963, p. 63.
[3] *Debates,* March 22, 1961, p. 570.
[4] *Debates,* March 3, 1961, p. 372-377.

parish priest of the town who in 1936 became the first Archbishop of Moncton.

"He made me understand that everyone has a role to play in the society in addition to the duties of his particular calling or profession. And that is why I am here today."

Louis Robichaud, Adrien Lévesque and other younger Acadians in his audience that day in the legislature were probably aware too that Dr. Dumont had helped form the first chapter of l'Ordre de Jacques Cartier in Campbellton in 1933. They knew he had been a key figure in the Acadian lobby pressing for better educational facilities. In Dumont, they recognized a colleague who was not there for the spoils of office.

The heavy burden Dumont assumed as minister of health probably shortened his life. He died in 1966. But during his brief political career, he saw a cherished Acadian dream come true. This was the birth of a French university in Moncton.

Its creation was the key recommendation of John Deutsch, appointed by the Robichaud government in 1961 to study New Brunswick's higher education facilities.

Deutsch had another recommendation which harkened back to a stormy chapter in New Brunswick's cultural history — the French-Irish antagonism. He called for the removal of St. Thomas University from Chatham to Fredericton, and in a surprisingly short time this was done.

Thus, while a new French university was rising on a Moncton hillside overlooking the marshes, an old Irish institution carefully nurtured by Bishops Rogers and Barry two generations earlier, was being dismantled from its Miramichi roots to begin a less distinctive existence under the shadow of the older, wealthier and essentially Protestant University of New Brunswick.

The cause of Irish New Brunswick had suffered another blow, one that would create stresses within the Robichaud government as the Irish element, notably in Saint John, coped with the Acadian influence within the Liberal party. For Leonard O'-Brien, as Lieutenant-Governor the most prestigious and possibly the wealthiest Irish New Brunswicker of his day, it must have been difficult to see his beloved Miramichi lose another round to the rising Acadian cause.

It was left to another Miramichi native to play a major role in the most important event of this lively decade. On March 9, 1962, Premier Robichaud announced the members of a new Royal Commission to inquire into municipal taxation. Heading the study would be Edward J. Byrne, a native of Chatham but now a Bathurst lawyer and a former mayor of that town.

Byrne had shrewdly used Gloucester County's mining boom during the 1950s to amass a fortune and gain access to the corporate boardrooms of Montreal and Toronto. Among other things, he was a director of Bathurst Pulp and Paper Company Ltd.[5]

The Byrne Commission, as it was called, included two francophones. Dr. Alexandre Boudreau was a native of the old Acadian fishing community of Cheticamp, Nova Scotia. From 1938 to 1948 he had helped organize and manage the Québec United Fishermen, a federation of cooperatives. More recently he had become director of extension and public relations for Université Saint-Joseph, now being amalgamated into Université de Moncton.[6]

The other French-speaking commissioner was Ulderic Nadeau of Baker Brook, a long-time warden of Madawaska County. He was also the owner of a large lumbering and merchandizing firm.

Rounding out the five-member commission were A.E. Andrews of St. Stephen, a one-time teacher who ran a small clothing store, and Charles Wilson, recently retired president of the Saint John Shipbuilding and Dry Dock Company. The commission secretary was James F. O'Sullivan, who had filled the same role with the Deutsch inquiry.

Together, they toured the province for two years, hearing briefs from 101 organizations and individuals. The input from French New Brunswick was rather small, considering the many French lobbies. Of the 101 briefs, 25 came from French citizens,

---

[5] Saint John *Telegraph-Journal*, March 6, 1966.
[6] *Report of the Royal Commission on Finance and Municipal Taxation in New Brunswick* (Fredericton, 1963), pp. v-vii. [Hereafter *Byrne Report*.]

organizations, municipalities and counties. Of the sixteen briefs from private companies, not one was French, while only five French citizens were among the 28 individual briefs.[7]

According to the 1961 census, about 35 percent of New Brunswick's citizens were French-speaking. The commissioners carefully avoided singling out French from the English in their final report, more or less implying that the current taxation system, out-moded though it was, was felt equally by all citizens.

The French briefs maintained this façade: New Brunswick was a single community in dire need of fiscal reform.The one exception, revealed only by a close reading of the report, was the subject of education. Citing the brief from l'Association des Instituteurs Acadiens, the commissioners noted that 83 percent of the most poorly-trained teachers, those with local permits, were to be found in Kent, Northumberland, Gloucester, Restigouche and Madawaska. No one needed to be told that these contained most of New Brunswick's French-speaking citizens.

"There seems to be a particularly acute teacher shortage," the report noted, "in the French language schools, largely because of the particularly low salaries in many of these districts." These low salaries were due "to low fiscal capacity stemming from economic retardation."[8]

Translated into plain language, these French areas were too poor to support a basic school system. The commissioners did not mention two other contributing factors to this sad state of affairs: the absence of a French teachers'college and the economic privileges enjoyed by the large pulp and paper mills.

This latter omission is not surprising considering that Commission Chairman Byrne was also general counsel to Bathurst Power and Paper Company.

Did the lone Acadian commissioner, Alexandre Boudreau, leave a recognizable imprint on the final report? Ten years after it was released to the public, both Boudreau (now back in his native Cheticamp) and the commission secretary, James O'-

---

[7] *Byrne Report*.These statistics were compiled from Appendix C.
[8] *Byrne Report*, p. 126.

Sullivan, recalled that while there was no one source for the ideas, Chairman Byrne had been the boss.

"Each person made a contribution," said O'Sullivan to a reporter doing a retrospective article. "But it was the chairman who pushed it through." Both he and Boudreau recalled one marathon three-day session that took place in Saint John's Admiral Beatty Hotel. There were "diverging opinions" on some important principles "which would lay the foundations of the report." Byrne had insisted they stay there until an agreement was reached rather than break for the weekend. He got his way as well as a unanimous agreement.[9]

Was Boudreau the odd-man out on this and other occasions? It is more than likely. He was the only commissioner without a conventional business background. Helping Québec fishermen to organize a cooperative was a long way from running the Saint John Dry Dock or a Madawaska lumber mill.

Yet Boudreau was the only commissioner to have a special place in the final report. Appendix H was the result of a trip Boudreau made to Sweden on behalf of the commission. When the author queried Byrne about this a decade later, he said, half in jest, half in earnest, "We sent him over there to get rid of him."

During that trip, Boudreau studied Sweden's cradle-to-the-grave social welfare program. He learned that it was financed solely through direct taxes on income and wealth, with the former providing the lion's share. This program was based on two principles: humanitarianism and economic progress with full employment. Swedish officials told Boudreau that for New Brunswick, with an unemployment rate of from eight to ten percent, to start a similar program would lead to economic bankruptcy.

This could have been the thorn causing the division among the five commissioners during their long session at the Admiral Beatty. We may never know. Yet this same agrument was raised repeatedly later by industrialist K.C. Irving when the Robichaud government began implementing the report's recommendations.

[9] Saint John *Telegraph-Journal,* October 11, 1975.

The Byrne Report was made public on February 4, 1964, when New Brunswickers were coping with a paralyzing snow storm. The political storm that followed in the wake of the recommendations shook New Brunswick society far more than any natural storm had ever done.

They called for sweeping changes that would centralize education, public health, social welfare and justice under provincial rather than local or county jurisdiction.

Teachers with similar qualifications would get the same pay, no matter where they worked in the province. "No longer shall children be limited to the quality of education which their own neighbourhood can afford; henceforth they will be entitled to that standard of education which the province as a whole can support."[10]

The commissioners felt that education, health, social welfare and justice were too important to be administered by government departments and presumably be subject to the patronage whims of politicians. Instead, these services should be handled by commissions or autonomous crown corporations.

To pay for these services, the current three percent sales tax should be increased to five percent and a uniform system of taxation assessments should be implemented based on a rate of 1 1/2 percent of the market value of all real estate.

"The tangle of overlapping statutes of great diversity which currently regulate the structure and taxing powers of local government should be swept away and be replaced by a single, comprehensive municipalities act." Only buildings and land would be taxed; businesses in cities and towns would pay a uniform local tax on business property, plus a uniform public schools tax.

All taxes would be collected by the provincial government.

The municipalities would be compensated by equalized unconditional grants. There would be no more need for county governments; an expanded bureaucracy in Fredericton would take over their role.

---

[10] *Telegraph-Journal,* October 11, 1964.

The commissioner stressed that these changes would not lower the high standards of service existing in some parts of the province. No specific areas were named, but the detailed charts and statistics at the end of the report made it clear that these were all located in southern New Brunswick.

Emerging into the lobby of Fredericton's Lord Beaverbrook Hotel the day after presenting the report to cabinet, Chairman Byrne was embraced by Dr. George Dumont. "I've never read anything with more enthusiasm," he told the somewhat startled Byrne.

"The reaction of the other cabinet ministers," Byrne later recalled, "was less demonstrative."[11]

Premier Robichaud undoubtedly realized that Eddy Byrne had handed him a "hot potato." Committed though he professed to be to the need for large-scale economic and social reform, the young premier hesitated before implementing the Byrne Report.

He had good reasons for delay. First, he had to find and train the administrative team needed to draft new legislation. He also knew that the powerful forest-based companies were eyeing him nervously: the Byrne Report had recommended ending the long-term tax agreements giving pulp companies fixed assessments (and hence much lower tax rates).

Restigouche county was the prime example of how such a taxation policy had undermined its ability to provide basic services. Among the fifteen counties, it was the only one that still had not adopted a county-wide finance system. As a result, many of its schools operated with unqualified teachers and of course the children bore the brunt of these inadequacies.

Many of the young men, both in Restigouche and other northern counties dominated by the forest economy, ended up as *bûcherons* or wood-cutters. They were perhaps the most exploited members of New Brunswick's labour force.

Repeatedly during the early years of the Robichaud decade, their desperate plight was revealed in the legislature by Liberal backbenchers, including three soon to become cabinet ministers.

[11] *Telegraph-Journal*, October 11, 1975.

On February 20, 1961, in his maiden speech, a young Caraquet lawyer, Bernard Jean, urged higher pulp prices for private woodlot owners.

A few days later, H.H. "Bud" Williamson, a Bathurst lumber contractor, answered recent press reports that Gloucester County wood-cutters preferred to accept unemployment insurance benefits rather than work in the woods. By including the pulpcutter's fixed costs for his chain saw, his transportation and board, Williamson estimated that the average woodsman netted from $9 to $12.50 a day. He compared this to the $16.48 paid to mill-workers who had the added bonus of being at home 16 hours a day. Williamson urged the government to find ways to ensure that woodsmen got a fair wage.[12]

Ten days later, in his maiden speech, Norbert Thériault, a general merchant from Baie Ste. Anne on the south side of the Miramichi estuary, thought an inquiry should be launched to see why woodlot owners in Newfoundland got $6 a cord compared to the New Brunswick pulp price of only $4.

Gloucester County's cabinet representative, Michael Fournier, the minister of industry and development, admitted that "there is no possible legislative excuse for such disparity." Noting that many crown forest leases would expire in 1962, Fournier said they should not be renewed unless the companies promised to sponsor new industries.

Premier Robichaud's immediate solution was a token one-man investigation which resolved nothing. His longer-term answer was more paper and plywood mills, notably South Nelson Forest Products, an Italian consortium that began operations on the Miramichi in 1963 amid unflattering rumours about a secret "sweetheart" deal.

Robichaud used this charge as an excuse to call a snap election. It netted the Liberals a few more seats, notably in the Saint John area. There, another paper mill, Rothesay-MacMillan, was now adding its sulfur stench to the air over that port city, which more accurately could be called "Irvingville."

---

[12] *Debates,* March 2, 1961, p. 296.

By now, the remarkably successful Buctouche native had his own paper mill overlooking Saint John's Reversing Falls and the Irving Refinery was becoming the linchpin in the industrialist's ever-expanding but tightly-integrated empire.

At the same time, more and more outside firms were setting up shop to profit from New Brunswick's apparently unlimited forests. Most had received healthy grants and forgiveable loans as part of a generous, almost spend-thrift policy of the federal Liberals.

Yet, as this tumultuous decade with its focus on the Byrne Commission rolled on, the lowly wood-cutters were forgotten amid all the "hype" surrounding Robichaud's widely publicized Program of Equal Opportunity.

Based on the Byrne inquiry's recommendations of 1964, this program would not appear for another two years. Robichaud and his expanding staff obviously needed time to prepare the complicated legislation, but New Brunswickers didn't seem to mind the delay.

They were too caught up with an economic boom stemming from several causes. The buoyant national economy of the mid-to-late 1960s could be felt even in the long-depressed Maritimes. Commodity prices were low; risk capital was abundant and New Brunswick's resource and industrial sectors seemed to be taking off.

Mining provided the biggest example, especially in the Bathurst area. After years of exploration and speculation, it began to assume physical shape in the form of headframes, deep underground shafts, new roads and rail lines and a fertilizer and port complex farther up the coast at Belledune.

In the public sector, a flood of federal capital grants helped create new centrallized schools to meet the needs of the post-war baby boom and to satisfy modern educationists' conviction that "bigger was better." The new federal-provincial hospitalization agreement meant new or expanded facilities. Just above Fredericton, one of the Robichaud government's pet projects was the giant Mactaquac hydro dam. Large contracting firms from central Canada tended to dominate much of the work in the industrial sector, but many New Brunswick firms, including some owned by Acadians, were among the successful bidders for the lucrative contracts to build and equip new schools, mills and hospitals.

Then there was Québec's "Quiet Revolution," and the one that was not quiet — directed by the FLQ. For many anglophone New Brunswickers, it seemed that the French were everywhere. They listened to almost daily reports from neighbouring Québec about the changes Premier Lesage was making to help his province catch up to the rest of Canada.

To many Canadians, but especially to those in such WASP strongholds as the Saint John valley, it must have seemed that the French were taking over. French speeches were commonplace in the provincial legislature. They sometimes contained pointed reminders that some French MLAs were impatient with the rate of progress.

"My rights are encroached upon," declared Phillippe Guerette, the Liberal member for Kent in March, 1964. "I can address you in French, but the British North America Act does not recognize that I have the right to speak this language." He wanted the necessary amendments immediately. "Let us not wait until a revolution faces us ... We have waited long enough." [13]

Guerette reminded the House that French New Brunswickers made up 38 percent of the population and half of the school enrolment. Francophones were getting tired of being told that a French teachers' college would come — some day. Then, with an obvious reference to the sometimes explosive Québec situation, he added: "There will never be any separation in New Brunswick. We accept our political system. But our rights as French Canadians must be respected."

One week later, Dr. Dumont picked up this theme in denying a published statement by Conservative senator Edgar Fournier of Edmundston that the French daily *L'Évangéline* and "its friends and compatriots in Moncton" were separatists.

Dumont said that for thirty years he had been a director and for many years the president of *L'Évangéline* publishing company.

[13] *Debates,* March 6, 1964, p. 161.

He was also a forty-year member of L'Assomption Society and a charter member of the l'Association Acadien d'Education. He supported Guerette's view that few if any Acadians supported a Québec separatist movement. With the establishment of Université de Moncton — "substantially supported by the provincial government," Dumont was confident the Acadians were at long last "entering a new era of prosperity." Yet he too was a little impatient. He wanted French to be recognized as an official language in New Brunswick.

"Tolerance is not enough," declared Dumont. He wanted a separate French teachers' college established on the campus of the new university in Moncton.[14]

His request was finally granted in the 1965 Throne Speech. A bilingual teachers' college would be established at l'Université de Moncton. Introducing the bill on February 19, Daniel Riley of Saint John stressed its bilingual nature.

This was not good enough for Gilbert Robichaud of Moncton. He urged the creation of a separate French institution open to both English and French students who planned to teach French.

Sensing that this was dangerous political ground, H.H. Williamson of Bathurst warned the house: "Let us not fall into this trap of hate which has been set up in the province of Québec by a small minority of rabble-rousers.... New Brunswick for the first time is on the march. Do not let the cloud of separation move in and destroy us. There is no place in New Brunswick for radical racists and separatists. We will be one people with equal rights and equal opportunity for all." [15]

Great desk-thumping and applause followed, but more prophetic words came the following day from Claude Taylor, the former Conservative education minister. He feared that with the new facilities planned for the Moncton campus, the Teachers' College in Fredericton would "deteriorate into a purely English-speaking institution for English-speaking students only. The Moncton one would become a French institution. "Then we shall

[14] *Debates*, March 12, 1964, pp. 240-248.
[15] *Debates*, February 24, 1965, p. 107.

be fostering the Two Solitudes that all of us should sincerely be trying to avoid."

Of course, this happened almost as soon as the Moncton facility began training its first students. Like the campus as a whole, it rapidly became unilingually French.

In this same speech, Taylor made another accurate prediction. "In the minds of the press and the people, this is the session of the Byrne Report."

On March 4, 1965, Premier Robichaud introduced a White Paper. The first of its kind ever tabled in the legislature, it really replaced the Throne Speech for that year. It strongly endorsed the main principles of the Byrne Report while rejecting the idea that basic services should be administered by commissions rather than departments of government.[16]

All New Brunswickers, declared Robichaud, were entitled to minimum acceptable standards of public services, regardless of the state of the financial resources of any particular community. The rich must be expected to share some of the burden to raise the standards of the poor.

The White Paper had some hard facts and figures to illustrate the gulf between rich and poor areas. Saint John county spent more on public education than any other: $312 per student. Gloucester was at the bottom with only $144. The White Paper challenged the richer regions to develop "a new awareness of an ideal as old as Christianity itself, a new conscience towards our neighbour."

Devout Christian though he was in private life, K.C. Irving was not about to play the Good Samaritan in the market place. During this same 1965 legislative session, his lawyers prepared an act incorporating Bay Steel Company, expected to be the centre piece of a new base metal complex in Gloucester County.

Irving and his partner, M.J. Boylen of Toronto, wanted the Robichaud government to guarantee $50 million worth of bonds in their new company, even though the government would get no equity in return. It also wanted to deal directly with municipal authorities to arrange tax concessions for periods of up to twenty

[16] *Debates*, March 4, 1965, p. 209.

years. The present municipal act placed a five-year limit on such arrangements.

In the spring and summer of 1965, these matters of high finance received scant notice from ordinary citizens. They were concerned with a government decision making them pay for what had long been a right: catching fish for sport. From now on, all residents would pay $2.50 for a trout license and $5 for the more exotic salmon.

As one writer to the *Telegraph-Journal* put it, "There are only two fishing holes in the Miramichi river left for the poor man. The best pools are in the hands of private leaseholders, often wealthy Americans." By November 1965, the fishing licenses had been grudgingly accepted. The same was not the case with the Program of Equal Opportunity. K.C. Irving had come out four-square against it.

After years of being a New Brunswick version of a reclusive Howard Hughes, Irving emerged from his "closet" with a vengeance. Actually, he had made his public debut, so to speak, a few years before as he shared platforms with Premier Robichaud to accept the plaudits for new joint ventures like Brunswick Mining and Smelting Company's plant near Bathurst, opened in 1963. Robichaud's decision two years later to establish a fifteen-member law amendments committee where citizens could discuss proposed legislation under the Program of Equal Opportunity, gave Irving and others an opportunity. The industrialist was quick to make use of it.

Surrounded by the best legal talent his wealth and influence could command, Irving voiced his strong opposition to any legislation that would eliminate existing tax concessions. He also appeared before a special cabinet committee, saying bluntly, "No sane people would put this through." [17]

From now on, all the weight of the Irving-owned media, mostly based in Saint John and Moncton, would be directed against the Program of Equal Opportunity. Some of the arguments were contrived but the strongest were based on economic

[17] See J.E. Belliveau, *Little Louis and the Giant K.C.* (Hantsport, N.S., 1980) pp. 74-77.

logic: New Brunswick would never be able to afford this far-reaching program.

The editorial responses of Michael Wardell's *Daily Gleaner* harkened back to the bigotted outpourings of Herman Pitts in the 1890s. Wardell had been introduced to New Brunswick in 1950 when Lord Beaverbrook bought the Fredericton paper and placed Wardell in charge.

With his black eye patch and his fervent support for a few favourite causes (especially British Royalty), the Brigadier, as he liked to be called, became a New Brunswick institution. His initiative in setting up a relief fund for the families of the Escuminac fishermen lost in a terrible storm in the 1950s had endeared him to many Acadians.

The *Daily Gleaner* also supported the Robichaud forces in the 1960 general election and when the Byrne Report was released four years later, Wardell cautiously endorsed its main recommendations. Then he seemed to sit back to await developments. He could have been waiting the lead from K.C. Irving who was in the process of absorbing the paper and making it part of a complete monopoly of English-language dailies in the province.

"Robbing Peter to Pay Pierre." That was how a well-timed anonymous letter to the *Telegraph-Journal* described the Program of Equal Opportunity as it slowly was unveiled in the fall of 1965. Like a pent-up cloud, the great debate broke into the open. The anti-French overtones of that letter unleashed a torrent of invective and resentment, mostly from residents in the Fredericton area.

Under Wardell's editorial supervision, the *Gleaner*'s cartoonist, William Werthman, a talented German, began producing a series of derogatory illustrations on the editorial page. They usually depicted Premier Robichaud as a modern version of Louis XIV, somewhat the worse for wear. His crown was askew, his eye had a wild gleam, his hand held a sword pointed at his foes, and at his feet, rats crawled out from the bottom of his tattered ermine robe.

The message was clear. Democracy was in danger. Businessmen would be ruined by the new assessment bill. The

Loyalist traditions were being shoved aside by this French up-start from impoverished Kent County.

Wardell also added his monthly magazine, *Atlantic Advocate*, to his editorial arsenal. The program, which was "frankly based on Swedish socialists," resulted from "the unbounded ambition" of Robichaud, "a little man with a violently-expressive mouth." Wardell argued that the Program of Equal Opportunity "would be disastrous to human liberties" because it would mean a provincial take-over of the tax base. Robichaud would have "arbitrary control over every branch of local affairs, and with it the exercise of patronage involving every detail of the public life of the province. No such powers have ever been held in a democracy by one man." [18]

Frederictonians took all this to their Tory hearts. Or so it seemed to outside journalists flocking into the capital in record numbers. Most expressed shock and disgust at the anti-Robichaud hysteria now apparently gripping this anglophone town.

At the University of New Brunswick, most academics kept a discreet silence while privately trading the latest stories about the premier's alleged personal indiscretions. Downtown, these stories gathered colour and venom as businessmen, led by clothing retailer and mayor William Walker and a realtor with a French name, A.J. Rioux, launched a province-wide campaign against Equal Opportunity.

Inside the legislature, some Conservative members did little to raise the level of debate. On November 16, 1965, the premier introduced a motion establishing a law amendments committee where details of the massive legislative program could be examined by the public. Both the Opposition leader, C.B. Sherwood and back-bencher Richard Hatfield expressed mild objections: they feared the public might be restricted in its rights to appear.

When Robichaud declared that their fears were groundless, that he was "in favour of democracy," the Fredericton Tory

[18] *Atlantic Advocate,* February 1966, pp. 14-16.

member Dr. Everett Chalmers made one of his frequent interjections. "Little dictator! You can't fool the people with that." [19]

Chalmers' skill and charm as a medical practioner had made him a revered figure in the area. As a legislator, he rarely displayed these positive traits. Increasingly over the next few weeks, Chalmers was among the most active Tory back-benchers in needling the government and especially Robichaud.

On December 16, he called the premier a liar. When he reluctantly withdrew this remark, he was overheard as he left the chambers: "I can't take that stuff. The biggest liar in the country." "Coward!" Robichaud shouted back.

Later that afternoon following more exchanges, the Speaker said: "There is a member in this chamber who utters all kinds of abusive language, without rising from his seat. I am expecting the whip of his party to advise him to discontinue this practice." No one needed to be told who it was.

To most observers, and New Brunswick had an unusual number during this prolonged and historic debate, it seemed as if the beleagured Acadian premier had his back to the wall to ward off reactionary and even racist English. This was not the case.

Louis Robichaud's advisory staff was mostly English. The most influential was Charles McElman, Fredericton born and bred, and of Loyalist lineage besides. The most important part of his background was that he had attended a Baptist Sunday School and was finely attuned to the susceptabilities of that distinctive segment of New Brunswick's political community. In York and Sunbury counties, one of the Liberal Party's main bases of support was among Baptists and Reformed Baptists.

In 1966, McElman was named to the Senate and his position as Robichaud's executive assistant was filled by a United Church minister from Sackville, Rev. Charles Forsyth, who had offered his services at the start of the Equal Opportunity debate. Forsyth was useless as a "weathercock" because he had no sense of the historical differences among the Protestant sects, at least in New

[19] *Debates,* November 16, 1965, p. 1041.

Brunswick. McElman knew how to manage "born-again" Christianity to party advantage.[20]

Inside the Robichaud cabinet, the only other prominent Acadian taking part in the debate beside Robichaud was Norbert Thériault, the minister of municipal affairs. The other key ministers were English: Wendall Meldrum, a Sackville lawyer who was now Minister of Education, and L.G. "Dud" DesBrisay, the minister of finance and industry.

Meanwhile, a powerful English presence was building up in the rapidly expanding bureaucracy considered necessary to launch the new program. A former deputy minister in the NDP government in Saskatchewan, Donald Tansley, was now DesBrisay's deputy minister. He was considered Fredericton's most experienced and most influential civil servant.

Fred Drummie, a scion from an old Saint John Loyalist family, filled the new post as economic advisor, while a young Frederictonian, Barry Toole, had been lured away from a CBC position in Montréal to head the Office of Government Organization, or OGO as it became known. It was intended to coordinate the new administrative apparatus.

Contrary to the impressions Wardell and the Irving-owned press were trying to convey, the Program of Equal Opportunity was anything but a French show for Pierre, at Peter's expense. Judging by the bewildering number of new government jobs, Fredericton's image as a WASP town was being strengthened.

In retrospect, while Equal Opportunity dramatically eased the tax burdens of French as well as many English property owners, it was also widening the ethnic gap already yawning like a chasm in the provincial civil service. It would be another decade before French New Brunswickers began looking more closely at the French-English ratio in the public service. They would be angered and dismayed at the continued disparity. In 1966, there were too many diversions for an easy or rational examination.

The main diversion came in the person of Charles Van Horne. The former Conservative Member of Parliament for Restigouche

---

[20] I am indebted to Dr. D.M. Young of the University of New Brunswick for this information and opinion.

reappeared on the provincial scene in the fall of 1966. Van Horne quickly stole the spotlight from Fredericton. For a time, he even eclipsed Louis Robichaud and the Program of Equal Opportunity.

New Brunswickers got their first hint of his arrival when the *Telegraph-Journal* carried a feature story in February by one of its senior editors. "Is Charlie Coming back?" he asked.[21]

Some readers saw this as proof that K.C. Irving was bringing back his former employee (Van Horne had been his executive assistant for a short time in the early 1950s) to lead the fight against Equal Opportunity. Observers reached this conclusion after Irving and Robichaud had a major disagreement over how best to proceed with the base metal developments in Gloucester County.

The fast-moving events during the winter of 1966-67 suggested a carefully conceived plan to move the colourful Van Horne to the New Brunswick political arena. The sudden resignation of C.B. Sherwood as Tory leader caught many by surprise and in the leadership race, Van Horne was the easy winner on the first ballot at a convention held in Fredericton, November 27.

For the first time in New Brunswick's history, the two parties had bilingual, Roman Catholic leaders from eastern counties. In Van Horne, the Conservatives had their first leader from the North Shore and one with strong Acadian connections.

In February, 1967, Van Horne entered the legislature after winning a free-wheeling, high-spending by-election in his home county of Restigouche. The vacancy had been created by the death of Dr. George Dumont. Over the next few months, as the gulf seemed to widen between Robichaud and Irving, Van Horne prepared for a general election. He was not disappointed: the premier called it for October 23.

"The toughest, dirtiest election in Canadian provincial politics for at least 25 years." So wrote Walter Stewart in the

---

[21] *Telegraph-Journal*, February 4, 1966. See also author's article on New Brunswick in *Canadian Annual Review of Public Affairs for 1966* (Toronto, 1967) p. 129.

Toronto *Star Weekly*, one of many central Canadian journalists to descend on the province during this colourful period.[22]

The *Globe and Mail* pontificated that Van Horne was "as close to a reincarnation of the late Huey Long of Louisiana as is likely to be inflicted on any province in Canada." A reporter for this same newpaper sent to cover the 1967 election looked past the wild posturings and promises of Van Horne to what he considered Robichaud's real adversary, K.C. Irving.

The premier tended to agree. During the last week of the campaign, Robichaud challenged the industrialist in Buctouche, his birthplace. "This man who had his home not far from here, this man wants to run the province. Well, let him, like me, present himself before the people and seek election. That's democracy."[23]

Irving continued his traditional silence while rumours flew that he was bank-rolling Van Horne's free-spending campaign. This proved to be one election money could not buy. Van Horne lost his own seat, thanks to some shrewd Liberal gerrymandering. New electoral boundaries forced him to run mostly in rural areas where the voters were less impressed with his big city style of campaigning.

In the wake of all the national media attention and its conclusions, it is tempting to assess these results in absolute terms. It was a great victory for Robichaud and his Program of Equal Opportunity, and a stunning defeat for K.C. Irving. This was not the case.

In the circus-like atmosphere of this wild election campaign, Van Horne never seriously challenged or debated the program. Neither did the Irving media. Instead, Van Horne produced an entertaining, high-budget show complete with Don Messer and his Islanders. People thronged to his rallies, but to have a good time rather than express their support for the Tories.

---

[22] Cited in Belliveau, p. 97.
[23] *Belliveau*. Belliveau was not a neutral observer, as he makes clear in his account. He directed the Robichaud goverment's public relation campaigns during the 1960's. See pp. 10-11.

The bilingual and Catholic Van Horne failed to deliver the goods so desired and expected by his backers: to win over some French constituencies. The Tories did take all four seats in anglophone Charlotte County plus another in Irving's stronghold of Saint John. This made the final results a cliff-hanger, but the evidence was plain enough: the Tories did not make a single dent in French New Brunswick.

As one veteran observer from Nova Scotia, Professor Murray Beck, wrote: "The key to the election, as in 1963, was that Robichaud took all 28 seats in which the French vote was dominant or substantial."[24] The Progressive Conservatives won 26 of the 30 predominantly English ridings.

After seven exciting years, Louis Robichaud's star still shone over the Acadian world. The Program of Equal Opportunity may have been upstaged by Charlie Van Horne, but it would be implemented. French New Brunswickers were certain of that. And P'Tit Louis was still their man.

He had delivered. L'Université de Moncton was a reality.

Its French teachers' college soon would be. Who could have guessed that in three short years, the Robichaud decade would end?

---

[24] J. Murray Beck, "Flamboyant Charlie versus Acadia's Hero" in *Commentator*, December 1967, p. 11.

# FIFTEEN

## THE NEW GENERATION AND THE ASSIMILATING SIXTIES

By 1967, Canada's centennial year, many French New Brunswickers must have been breathing easier in the majority Anglo-Saxon world. One of their own had just won his third consecutive term as premier. Université de Moncton was rapidly enveloping an old farm site on the outskirts of the city. Another dream, a French teachers' college would soon be a reality. And equally vital for their cultural survival was all that Ottawa money in the form of incentive grants, forgiveable loans, and capital grants for high schools, hospitals and highways.

The 1960s were the coming-out years for French New Brunswickers. Louis Robichaud was their political proof and he underscored the French renaissance with his Program of Equal Opportunity. Members of the Acadian élite who had led this long struggle in recent years would readily admit that Equal Opportunity could not have evolved as it did without a dramatic shift in federal policies — a shift already started before Robichaud was chosen New Brunswick Liberal leader.

In 1957, the new Diefenbaker government, with a strong nudge from New Brunswicker Dalton Camp[1] established the Atlantic Provinces Adjustment Grants — $100 million a year for five years. New Brunswick's annual share was $30 million — a

---

[1] Dalton Camp, *Gentlemen, Players and Politicians* (Toronto, 1970) pp. 329-330.

huge sum compared to much smaller annual revenues it normally had. It was like winning a giant lottery, but more — much more — was to follow.

In 1961 came ARDA — the Agricultural Rehabilitation and Development Act. This precedent-setting program would have a major impact on many areas, but especially northeastern New Brunswick and the Acadian peninsula. Considered "the outstanding example" of Alvin Hamilton's accomplishments as Diefenbaker's Minister of Agriculture, ARDA zeroed in on rural Canada. With federal financing and provincial advice, ARDA launched a massive spending program aimed at easing off the land those Canadian farmers selling less than $1200 worth of agricultural products a year.[2]

For hundreds of Acadian families who over several generations had achieved a subsistance economy based on fishing, farming and lumbering, this ARDA policy and later similar programs would exert a relentless pressure to force them into urban areas.

In the ten years following ARDA's appearance, French New Brunswickers as well as rural citizens throughout eastern Canada, found themselves being interviewed, examined and manipulated by sociologists, geographers and economists. These self-styled social planners, equipped with government cars, contracts and plastic money, would temporarily dwell among "the natives," studying their quaint customs and uneconomical (yet self-sustaining) activities. Eventually, the bureaucrats would write thick research reports describing the local poverty and recommending the best ways to move the natives into "growth centres" as the nearby towns were now called.

Typical of such studies was ARDA Project No. 15002, conducted in the summer of 1965 by a team of researchers led by Pierre-Yves Pépin, PhD, of the Institute of Town Planning at

[2] Peter C. Newman, *Renegade in Power: The Diefenbaker Years* (Toronto, 1973) p. 142.

Université de Montréal. Under the terms of his contract drawn up after talks with senior ARDA officials in Ottawa, Pépin was to search "for a true image of poverty other than that expressed by statistics and external evaluation."[3]

During July and August, 1965, Pépin and his team lived briefly in five Maritime counties, including two in New Brunswick. In their report, *Life and Poverty in the Maritimes*, their chapter on Kent County was entitled "Kent — Unproductive Setting, Unfavourable Site." Charlotte County's description was only slightly less critical: "Charlotte — Prosperous Past, Under Employed Present."

Pépin had few specific recommendations to improve the economies of these counties but noted that "the organization of the tourist industry is far from having reached its peak in areas that are generally picturesque and captivating."[4]

Even as Pépin's report was being printed in 1966, Ottawa was working on plans to create a national park in the precise area of Kent County he had so recently studied — Pointe Sapin and Claire-Fontaine. Pépin had described these particular communities as "delapidated, one-street villages" in "one of the most unproductive geographical sectors of the county." And he added: "Yet, the Acadians have settled there for a century and a half."

It is quite probable that among the Claire-Fontaine residents interviewed by Pépin was Jackie Vautour, who would lead a nineteen year struggle against being expelled from his ancestral homeland to make way for Kouchibouguac National Park.

After watching their small home being flattened by bulldozers, Vautour and his large family refused to follow their neighbours' example and submit to a modern version of the Acadian Expulsion. Rejecting Ottawa's financial settlement terms, Vautour returned to the site of his wrecked home, built a shack and moved in. During the 1970s, as Kouchibouguac Park was becoming a popular summer vacation spot, Vautour led

---

[3] Pierre-Yves Pépin, *Life and Poverty in the Maritimes*, ARDA Research Report No. RE-3, Project 15002, Ministry of Forestry and Rural Development (Ottawa, 1968) p. 1.

[4] Pépin, p. 25.

increasingly violent demonstrations against park officials and the RCMP. He soon became a national figure, thanks to frequent television exposure and court appearances. To many Canadians, the Vautours came to symbolize one poor family's stand against bureaucrats and the principle of state expropriation.

Eventually, their valiant stand forced a change in federal policy. Parks Canada no longer insists that local inhabitants vacate an area designated for park development. And in the end, which came in the dying days of the Hatfield regime in 1987, Vautour reluctantly accepted a cash settlement and another piece of Kent County land.

Kouchibouguac National Park represented one "final solution" for rural New Brunswick. A less drastic one was contained in a federal-provincial ARDA Task Force Report for northern New Brunswick, presented to the two governments in January, 1966.

ARDA workers, using techniques of "social animation" that American sociologist Saul Alinsky had developed to create social awareness among Chicago's poor, moved into northeastern New Brunswick. Moses Coady and other pioneers of the Antigonish Movement would have recognized this approach. It was exactly what they had done in the 1930s and what Alexandre Boudreau had done among the fishermen of eastern Québec.

In fact, the Acadian version of the Cooperative Movement was flourishing in lower Gloucester County even as these young ARDA social animators appeared. By 1959, La Fédération Acadienne des Caisses Populaires, based in Caraquet, had 28 members, including fishermen's cooperatives in Lamèque, Caraquet and Shippagan. They were living testimonies to the efforts of early cooperative workers like Livain Cormier, who in one month in 1936 had helped set up 200 study groups in Gloucester.[5]

---

[5] Cited in Sheila Andrew, "Spreading the Word: The Development of the Antigonish Movement in Acadian New Brunswick, 1935-1940", a graduate paper presented to History 6300, University of New Brunswick. [I am indebted to Professor D.M. Young for this reference.]

These study groups survived, largely because of the managerial skills of another of Coady's disciples, Martin Légère, a Caraquet native who had grown up in the movement and went on to become the director and guiding spirit of La Fédération Acadienne des Caisses Populaires. By 1960 Légère was probably the most influential Acadian in lower Gloucester, a fact quickly recognized by Premier Robichaud. He appointed Légère to the Industrial Development Board, where he would serve as chairman throughout the Robichaud decade.

Légère was also named a director of CRAN, le Conseil Régional d'Aménagement du Nord-Est, one of several regional groups set up by the ARDA Task Force "to develop an integrated plan of action" for this pilot area.[6] Joining Légère as CRAN directors were several other prominent Acadians, including Bernard Jean, a provincial cabinet minister and Dr. Gérard St. Cyr, principal of the Caraquet Fisheries School.

The grass-roots work was done by young field workers — the animators — who organized study groups just as Légère, Boudreau and others had done a generation earlier. This modern group was also linked with a bewildering number of federal and provincial government agencies. By 1968, CRAN workers had formed about 90 local committees in Gloucester and Restigouche Counties and scores of Acadians took part in their weekend study sessions.

Despite some similarities, CRAN was far more radical than the earlier Antigonish Movement, which had never challenged

[6] *ARDA Task Force Report for the Pilot Rural Development Area in Gloucester-Restigouche-Northumberland Counties New Brunswick*, January, 1966. [This mimeographed report was prepared by H.R. Scovil and P. L. Boisclair, co-directors, and presented to R.D. Gilbert, New Brunswick Deputy-Minister of Agriculture and Co-Chairman of the Task Force.]

the status quo represented by the capitalist system. CRAN was an Acadian version of the Company of Young Canadians, established by the Pearson government in 1966.

During its stormy five-year life, the CYC sent out young idealistic university graduates among the poor "to generate a radical change for the better in Canadian society."[7] They wanted to show "disadvantaged citizens" (the word "poor" was too explicit) "how to organize, to take power over their lives, in full cognizance of the fact that this must eventually lead to exercising political power." That was the message of the 1965 War on Poverty Conference organized in the heady early days of the Pearson years.

CRAN's young workers imbibed much of this rhetoric, but being French they were far more influenced by events in Québec. Week after week throughout the turbulent sixties, news of the Quiet Revolution — interspersed with headlines about the latest FLQ bombings — reached New Brunswick Acadians via Montréal-based TV, the only French television generally available to them.

This captive audience watched spell-bound as the long pent-up cultural explosion burst forth in neighbouring Québec. For young Acadians, this was far more exciting and meaningful than Louis Robichaud's slowly-evolving Program of Equal Opportunity. Nowhere was this Québec influence felt more keenly that at Université de Moncton.

That young institution, competing for staff with the burgeoning Québec universities, including the brand new and secular l'Université de Québec, had great difficulty finding professors. As was the case with new and/or expanding English universities, they often had to take the youngest and least experienced. One of Moncton's sources was France, currently western Europe's

---

[7] Margaret Daly, *The Revolution Game* (Toronto, 1970), cited in a review article by Gary Allen, in *The Mysterious East*, (March-April, 1971), p. 3. [The latter publication was a product of the times — a short-lived anti-establishment monthly that had a meteoric rise before the departure from Fredericton of its creative editor, Donald Cameron, at the time a University of New Brunswick English professor.]

hotbed for left-wing radicalism. Several young Frenchmen with degrees in politics and sociology, were hired by Moncton under a French government regulation allowing recent graduates to serve overseas teaching in another francophone country rather than spend three years in obligatory military service.

As well, young social science graduates from Québec took up teaching posts at Moncton, where they could continue their research into another aspect of French culture — the "quaint" Acadians. Many of these "instant" professors saw the world in stereotype — *les anglais* and *les Québécois*; the establishment and the proletariat. It was all heady stuff for many young Acadians, leaving their north shore hamlets for the first time to live in Englishdominated Moncton.

The most conspicuous example of this new Acadian generation was Michel Blanchard, a handsome Caraquet youth, the son of a local personality, union leader and aspiring Conservative politician, Mathilda Blanchard. Even while attending high school, Michel had shown his leadership potential and his anti-establishment traits by helping to lead a 1964 confrontation against clerical teachers. The students wanted lay instructors — a demand easily met after 1968 when the first graduates of École Normale began streaming out of Moncton.

Blanchard enrolled in the sociology program at Moncton in the fall of 1966 and quickly soaked up the separatist bias of some of his young professors, many just a few years his senior. The most influential were two native-born Canadians. Roger Savoie had just returned from studies in France to take up a position in the philosophy department. Camille Richard, a sociologist, later described himself as the "ideologue" of the group, the one most determined to convince his young charges of the logic and merits of separation for Québec.[8]

Earlier in this same year, 1966, Savoie and Richard, along with Harold McKernin, a bilingual member of the Secretary of State's office in Moncton, had been approached by Dr. Léon Richard, a Moncton physician and president of La Société Nationale des Acadiens. He wanted them to help the SNA to shake loose from

---

[8] Jean-Paul Hautecoeur, *L'Acadie de discours* (Laval, 1975), p. 197.

its "old guard" image by recruiting younger members. The vehicle he proposed was le Ralliement de la Jeunesse Acadienne. By now, the federal government had become a great "money tree" — an easy mark as Canada prepared for its centennial celebrations amid the separatist rumblings in Québec. The Pearson government desperately wanted young Canadians to play active roles — especially French Canadians. Professors Savoie and Richard easily convinced the Centennial Commission that Le Ralliement de la Jeunesse Acadienne should receive a grant. Their application promised to recruit English Canadians as well, and the money was soon on its way.

As Richard noted later, they made sure that only certain students with known left-wing sympathies were invited to join. The question of Canadian unity was never discussed.[9] Instead, they prepared for conferences and sent out invitations to such Québécois luminaries as Jacques-Ivan Morin, René Lévesque, Léon Dion and Claude Ryan. None of these accepted, so they settled for two left-wing intellectuals who presented papers on workers' political leadership and French Canadian minorities.

Michel Blanchard quickly emerged as Le Ralliement's most committed and most capable student leader. In 1968 he led a confrontation against Moncton's Mayor Leonard Jones over the city council's refusal to use French in its proceedings. Since Moncton was the only French television production centre in the Atlantic region, local cameramen had a field day. Their lenses zoomed in on the beleagured Jones and made his name synonymous among national television viewers — English as well as French — with the WASP mentality.

The confrontations dragged on for months, giving Moncton a bad name and infuriating older local citizens from both ethnic groups. As a result, Jones went to Ottawa as in independent M.P. in 1974 after he had been read out of the Progressive Conservative party by its leader, Robert Stanfield.

For Blanchard and his growing band of dissidents, this clash with Jones was just the beginning. In January, 1969, they organized a sit-in at the main buildings of the Moncton campus to

[9] *Hautecoeur*, p. 199.

protest the disparity in university grants their institution received compared to the University of New Brunwick.

More by shrewd planning than coincidence, a National Film Board crew from Québec that had previously interviewed Blanchard and others was on hand to film the series of clashes with university officials and local police. The film's producer, Pierre Perrault, was the subject of a two-page story in *L'Évangéline*. He predicted as inevitable a political union of French New Brunswick and Québec.[10]

Perrault's film, *L'Acadie L'Acadie*, received its première simultaneously in Moncton and Montréal in the spring of 1971 and rapidly became a hit among French students both in New Brunswick and Québec. To members of the Acadian elite, *L'Acadie L'Acadie* was further proof of how the young generation had been manipulated by separatists working within the National Film Board and Radio Canada.

Blanchard was now the *bête noire* of older Acadians but his star image among his peers got an added boost when a court injunction permanently banned him from the Moncton campus. Aided by his Québécois professors, he transferred his program to L'Université de Québec à Montréal (UQAM), a creation of the Quiet Revolution and now the intellectual centre for separatists and left-wing sympathizers.

On March 2, 1970, Blanchard showed up in Bathurst as a delegate to the annual meeting of La Société Nationale des Acadiens (SNA). Near the end of the weekend sessions, he proposed that a committee study the possibility of Québec separation and its implications for New Brunswick francophones. According to *L'Évangéline's* account, mostly students supported his motion, which was defeated 61 to 44.

Earlier, another Gloucester delegate, Euclide Chiasson, a philosophy teacher at Collège de Bathurst, presented a paper recommending that the SNA be reconstituted into a federation that would include non-Acadians, notably those with Québec roots and concentrated in Madawaska County. The SNA executive had already indicated its tentative approval for such a move,

[10] *L'Évangéline*, November 27, 1970.

which had been suggested by the recently formed l'Association des Francophones du Nord-Est, based at Collège de Bathurst. Shortly after this SNA conference, this new group occupied the Bathurst campus after its director, Rev. Léopold Lanteigne, had refused their demand to allow students to receive visitors of the opposite sex in their rooms.

Today's world would dismiss such issues as either amusing or quaint. They were neither in 1970 when students throughout the entire education system seemed determined to challenge the old order. During this same cold January, a controversy erupted in various parts of the province over a general school regulation prohibiting girls from wearing slacks. Under existing rules, they were allowed to show up in the current fashion rage, mini-skirts.

The issue received its first general publicity when a mother of sixteen children from Burnsville, Gloucester County, wrote an angry letter to *L'Évangéline*, protesting the chauvinist attitude of the male-dominated school administration. In Fredericton, the deputy minister of justice, Douglas Rouse, acting as a parent and a private citizen, publicly stated that his daughter, who had been sent home from school for wearing slacks, would not be returning unless the ban was lifted. It was, and not only in Fredericton but in a matter of days throughout the province.

To those francophones who viewed New Brunswick's schools in terms of language inequality, what girls should be wearing to their classes probably seemed of little consequence. To parents on both sides of the ethnic fence, this issue dramatized the continuing inequalities and indignities endured by women of all ages. It also gave them an excuse to join the wave of protests that symbolized the 1960s.

Two weeks after the slacks issue had been resolved, another more familiar one gripped School District No.15, which included Moncton and Westmorland County. While Michel Blanchard continued his legal battle, his former classmates, egged on by *L'Évangéline* editorials, challenged the anglophones who controlled the school administration.

On March 23, 1970, a university group interrupted a meeting of District 15 commissioners, demanding that the chairperson, the wife of a prominent Moncton lawyer, speak French.

Prominent among the protestors were two Gloucester County students, Gastien Godin and Louise Blanchard, Michel's sister, along with Roger Savoie, their political science professor. A supporting editorial in *L'Évangéline* called for a separate French school board.

The minister of education, Wendall Meldrum, quickly responded by appointing a commission of inquiry under the unilingual district school superintendent, George MacIntyre.

There was little chance that the Robichaud government would yield to these new francophone demands. It was too close to a general election and giving in to them might jeopardize support from Moncton's anglophone Liberals. The French education lobby, as represented by Professor Savoie and his students, cared little for the Liberal party's political fortunes. For them, District 15's language issue was another chance to publicize their grievances and to press for more autonomy in education.

*L'Évangéline* was all for l'Université de Moncton lobby. On April 23, noting the recent legislation creating two professional associations for New Brunswick teachers, one English and the other French, an editorial trumpeted: "The teachers have won their battle; now we parents should not let up. " On May 14, a meeting of Moncton's francophone Home and School Association endorsed a proposal for a separate school board after hearing a strong appeal from Bernard Gauvin, one of Michel Blanchard's fellow student conspirators.

English Monctonians, noting the May 18th opening in nearby Shediac of a large French high school, appropriately called L.J. Robichaud Polyvalente, must have concluded that their French neighbours were winning all their educational battles. La Société Nationale des Acadiens' strategy was to press on to new goals. In its brief to the school board commission in late June, it cited the recommendations of the Royal Commission on Bilingualism and Biculturalism urging greater French representation in New Brunswick's civil service.

The Blanchard case was an even more embarrassing pressure on the government's language policy. On May 15, 1970, Blanchard formally appealed the injunction and demanded that his proceedings be heard in French. The New Brunswick Official

Languages Act giving French equal status with English had been passed in 1969 but probably due to the shortage of bilingual facilities and personnel, had not been proclaimed and activated as law.

Judge J. Paul Barry expressed sympathy for Blanchard's request and arranged for translation services. He added: "I'm just part of the system and I have no alternative but to proceed in English."[11] On May 29, the New Brunswick Supreme Court upheld the injunction. Donning his martyr's mantle, Blanchard and his bride of a few months toured his home county of Gloucester, where several town councils and two service clubs publicly supported his request for bilingual proceedings. On October 9, on the eve of a general election campaign and amid mounting pressure from its students, Université de Moncton applied to withdraw its application to enforce Blanchard's injunction. He in turn was offered "une dernière chance" to consider the seriousness of his plight.

Blanchard's response was to return to the campus, armed with his placards. He was immediately cited for contempt and given an indefinite term in the Dorchester county jail. While some of his former professors and student friends held public demonstrations to support his demands for a French trial, Blanchard added to the performance by going on a short hunger strike. After thirty days behind bars, he made the necessary apologies and was released. It had been a well-orchestrated affair.

Meanwhile, a larger but related storm was brewing. On April 30, the day after Robert Bourassa's one-sided Liberal victory over René Lévesque's Parti Québécois, *L'Évangéline* carried a large map, covering half a page, showing northern New Brunswick as part of Québec. It was intended to illustrate points made by a Caraquet subscriber, Alexis Landry, whose lengthy letter outlined the advantages Québec separation would have for New Brunswick's northern counties.

Landry's main argument was that these French counties' best future lay with an independent Québec. He claimed that all their natural resources remained largely undeveloped because the

[11] *Telegraph-Journal*, May 15, 1970.

required money and attention were going toward making Saint John and Moncton the industrial centres of New Brunswick. Landry said that a perennial demand for a bridge to Miscou Island was ignored while Fredericton, in the heart of English New Brunswick, was about to get its second bridge. Even though the French northeast had forty-five percent of the population, many of its schools were too small and its citizens could not get French books and other materials. At the same time, they knew more about Québec politics and events because the most accessible radio and television programs originated from *la belle province*.

How much support did Landry have for making French New Brunswick part of Québec? This question was put to some of the Caraquet area's most influential citizens at a meeting to promote the creation of an Acadian historic village.[12] Most agreed that Landry's views and proposals no longer represented the radical fringe. They pointed to the impact of the media's coverage of the recent Québec election campaign. Some were clearly dissatisfied with the rate of progress of the Program of Equal Opportunity. They were not about to vote Tory but some did say that by joining their region with Québec, perhaps their Acadian culture and their standard of living would benefit.

Clearly, Louis Robichaud, still their favourite son, had some grave problems, personal as well as political. Tired from ten years of frantic activity as the leader and moving spirit for administrative reform, Robichaud was also deeply concerned about his elder son, ill with nephritis. Surrounded by the increasingly unfriendly environment of WASP-ish Fredericton, the premier resorted to an old political ploy: a commission of investigation.

He named H.L. Nutter, dean of the Anglican diocese of Fredericton and Emery LeBlanc, former editor of *L'Évangéline*, as co-chairmen of a Task Force on Social Development and

---

[12] This material came from the author's notes prepared for the CBC as part of a call-in program from Caraquet to Fredericton, May 1, 1970. The program dealt with New Brunswick francophones' reactions to the Québec election victory of Robert Bourassa.

Social Welfare. They and nine others, mostly from northern French communities, would tour the province, getting responses to the government's white paper on Social Development and Social Welfare that had been tabled March 31, 1970. The task force appointments were not made public until mid-July. Meanwhile, the director of welfare had begun a detailed survey of 700 citizens, most of them welfare recipients.

Later events suggest that the Robichaud government was trying to "spike the guns" of CRAN animators in lower Gloucester. During the early years of CRAN's existence, its paid workers had kept low profiles as they established local committees and explained various proposed projects intended to revive the area's economy.

Some communities, notably Lamèque, Tracadie and Petit-Rocher near Bathurst, welcomed CRAN workers and soon had lively committees.

Caraquet, the Liberals' power centre in the Acadian peninsula was less than enthusiastic. In fact, its ruling clique, represented by Martin Légère of la Fédération Acadienne des Caisses Populaires; Bernard Jean, now minister of justice, and Gérard St. Cyr, director of the Caraquet Fisheries School, had prevented CRAN from forming a committee in their town. They were especially leery of Roderique Pelletier, who had gained wide experience at similar work in rural Québec. St. Cyr, a CRAN director, thought Pelletier had given "too much credence to local gossip and rumour."[13] Pelletier countered this with accusations that Caraquet citizens had been threatened with loss of credit at the *Caisse Populaire* if they supported militants like Blanchard and himself.

By the spring of 1970, the older directors of CRAN — people like St.Cyr — mostly government appointees, had reached their limit. They dismissed Pelletier and recommended a drastic cut in CRAN's budget. The younger full-time workers fought back

---

[13] Gérard St. Cyr to author during an interview later used for a CBC documentary, "What Ever Happened to CRAN?", aired February 3, 1971 as part of a national network series "Rule and Revolution". See also author's artice in *The Mysterious East*, March-April, 1971.

at the annual meeting, held in Bathurst a few weeks after Pelletier was fired. By a vote of 89-20 they agreed to rehire him and then dismissed the ten directors. They were replaced by a carpenter, a peat-moss worker, a mechanic, a teacher, a secretary, an unemployed worker, two students and an electrician.

The next shot was fired from Fredericton when all provincial departments except mines and resources stopped sending information to local CRAN committees. Premier Robichaud also named three cabinet colleagues, Bernard Jean, Ernest Richard and André Richard, to an inquiry into the dispute. Avoiding any direct contact with CRAN officials, they quickly came up with one major recommendation: restructure CRAN to give it closer contact with traditional groups like local chambers of commerce and Richelieu clubs (a French version of Kiwanians).

These events were duly reported by *L'Évangéline*, with no editorial comment. It seemed that its editors and owners did not wish to emphasize this obvious generational rift. Neither did they editorialize on a letter carried in its June 10th issue.

Signed by André Dumont, calling himself a separatist from Petit-Rocher, near Bathurst, it was an open invitation for Acadians to join a new political movement, le Parti Acadien. Its aim was two-fold: to regroup Acadians by democratic elections, and then to help them establish their own constitution and territory.

Subsequent issues of *L'Évangéline* made no mention whether Dumont received any response; one can assume he did not. Probably this move to form an Acadian political party was premature. Its potential supporters — the young and especially recent graduates from Université de Moncton — were too involved trying to save CRAN.

In July, the Robichaud government withheld CRAN's quarterly budget payments. After refusing to meet personally with CRAN officials in Bathurst, the premier issued a letter confirming what many now suspected: the government was looking "for a new approach to social planning" — one involving more local participation. CRAN would be replaced with a new organization representing "traditional leadership." The old guard had won.

By the time the LeBlanc-Nutter Task Force on Social Development began its hearings in August, the replacement process was well underway. After public meetings in Edmundston on August 10, the Task Force moved into CRAN territory with well-attended meetings in Restigouche and Gloucester counties. Outside Campbellton the eleven-member task force talked with welfare recipients and visited one shack housing eleven people. They also heard sharp criticisms from civic officials about overlapping jurisdiction of various government agencies involved in welfare. In fact, they were getting the same information and seeing the same evidence of poverty that CRAN workers had been experiencing since 1964. The only difference was, this government fact-finding body received much wider media coverage.

This kind of publicity about the underside of New Brunswick's society was not welcomed by politicians gearing up for yet another election campaign. Premier Robichaud announced on September 2 that voting day would be October 26. This was also the signal for the Task Force to suspend its hearings. As its co-chairman, Emery LeBlanc put it, "We don't want to get involved in an election campaign." [14]

CRAN workers in the Bathurst area, feeling the pinch of no pay cheques, took the opposite view. Some openly campaigned for the Progressive Conservatives and in fact two CRAN directors ran as Tory candidates. They stood no chance in a Liberal bastion like Gloucester, but they reasoned — and correctly as it turned out — that a new government under Richard Hatfield might restore CRAN's budget. The defeat of the Robichaud government left many Liberals even more bitter towards CRAN: to them, it was a nest of young and left-wing traitors.

After a decade of steady progress toward cultural autonomy and financial prosperity, many French New Brunswickers naturally were disappointed that the exciting and rewarding Robichaud era had ended. Despite their anger at the election activity of some CRAN workers, few died-in-the-wool Grits really blamed them for the defeat. The final ballots showed that

[14] *Telegraph-Journal*, September 4, 1970.

the vote in the north shore and predominantly French constituencies favoured the Liberals even more than in 1967.

Obviously, the anti-establishment stance promoted by Michel Blanchard and other "young Turks" — most of them graduates of Université de Moncton — had not shaken the Liberal hold on French New Brunswick. Many Liberals probably saw another reason for the defeat of their favourite son — *les anglais* ! After a ten-year entente, enough English New Brunswickers had deserted Robichaud and the Liberal party to bring about defeat.

A closer look at the results of the 1970 election does not support this thesis. It only caused a shift of seven seats and the only riding where the "English desertion" thesis might apply was the two-member riding of Sunbury. Its solidly English electorate turned out its two Liberal members, but their majorities had been dwindling over the two previous elections.

In the overwhelmingly French riding of Edmundston, the Tories won with Jean-Maurice Simard, an accountant and president of the provincial Progressive Conservative Association. He would become minister of finance and Hatfield's "French Lieutenant." Just to the south in the ethnically-mixed county of Victoria, an anglophone Tory, Stewart Brooks, was ahead on election day but a French-speaking Liberal, Everard Daigle, won on a recount.

A detailed examination of those results might uncover some ethnic backlash, but like all New Brunswick elections, it probably was more because of very local and non-cultural issues.

The most decisive shift in the 1970 election occurred in the three-member riding of Moncton, where all three Liberals were defeated. They were replaced by three Tories with exactly the same ethnic and cultural mix: a francophone, an English Protestant and an Irish Catholic. This would suggest voters' dissatisfaction with the incumbents' performances in Fredericton.

According to material gathered for a CBC documentary on the Moncton scene both before and after the 1970 election, it would appear that the Moncton results might have reflected some English reactions to the Blanchard affair and the cultural pressures borne by Mayor Jones. There was a French backlash too — against Blanchard and other young radicals who used the new university as a vehicle to promote separatist and left-wing causes.[15]

Many older Acadian Monctonians concluded that an entente had been achieved with the English. They thought their Acadian leaders had made solid gains toward cultural recognition by the slow and low-keyed lobbying methods. Some claimed that for every Acadian supporting the aggressive stance of Blanchard and his north-shore supporters (Monctonians tended to take the familiar approach that "outsiders" were the real trouble-makers), ten *bone fide* French-speaking Monctonians believed in the live-and-let-live spirit of compromise.

For tangible examples of such progress, they would cite the new Moncton City Hall complex, already on the drawing boards before the 1970 election. It had been made possible by the support of Mayor Jones and his English followers, and the financial muscle of L'Assomption Mutuelle.

Fiercely-partisan English Monctonians — Tories as their grandparents had been — were not happy about this physical expression of the entente. They were particularly incensed at the name to be given to the new hotel in the complex: Beauséjour!

Such voters never changed their allegiance, but others obviously did — French as well as English. Their reasons were briefly but accurately explained on election night by an exhausted Louis Robichaud, on hand at Moncton's CBC-Radio Canada studios: "The people decided they wanted a change."

The most obvious change was that an English government was back in Fredericton. The Hatfield forces had elected only two francophones: Simard in Edmundston and Jean-Paul LeBlanc, Moncton's deputy-mayor, who took over at municipal affairs.

Hatfield, who had campaigned long and hard in the French areas, was understandably disappointed. He may have been consoled by the fact that it had not been a case of the French voting one way and the English the other. Even in one-sided

---

[15] This material is from recorded interviews, still in the author's possession, prepared for a CBC radio documentary series, "Soundings", aired nationally August 5, 1970, on a program entitled "Acadians at the Cross-Roads".

contests such as those in Gloucester and Kent, the eight successful Liberals included two anglophones. The fight in Bathurst also disproved the English-versus-French thesis. The anglophone winner, incumbent H.H. "Bud" Williamson, collected 4,142 votes compared to the 2,768 garnered by his Tory opponent, francophone Ernest Picard.

The most important factor in the 1970 election was the young French New Brunswicker. Many were voting for the first time, and the CRAN affair suggest they could not be relied upon to vote, robot-like, for the Liberal Party. They were the first pure products of the "television age" and, being French, that meant their first major political exposure was Québec separatism. They were also the first graduates of a largely secular education system.

By October, 1970, their student revolt was over. Their leader, Michel Blanchard, had retreated to Caraquet; most of their left-wing and separatist-minded professors in sociology and political science had lost their jobs. The next wave of students would be less militant, due in part to economic uncertainties caused by the 1973 oil crisis and its aftermath. Yet, even as they graduated to accept, in a great majority of cases, secure jobs in burgeoning government bureaucracies and service-oriented positions in the private sector, many harboured a grudge. It was directed against the older Acadian élite that proved it could change with the times. These young Acadians thought this adaptability had been at the expense of Acadian cultural as well as political goals.

The best example of the élite's adaptability was what it had done to la Société l'Assomption, a remarkably successful insurance firm and a cornerstone of the Acadian cultural establishment. In 1961, its surplus funds were funnelled into a new corporate creation, la Compagnie de Gestion Atlantique. This really was a holding company for La Compagnie d'Immeuble Bonaccord and eventually in 1965, for the firm controlling L'Évangéline.[16]

Bonaccord Finance, like the more familiar *caisses populaires* moved heavily into the consumer loan business, hoping to compete with English Canadian and American loan companies now entrenched in the expanding shopping malls. By 1968, the most important and the earliest of these Acadian businesses, La Societé l'Assomption, had changed its status from a limited fraternal society to a mutual insurance company. Its new name was Assomption Compagnie Mutelle d'Assurance-Vie. According to Dr. Jean Cadieux, soon to be head of a secular administration that would run Université de Moncton, this corporate move resulted from a loss of business caused by the new national health-care plan.[17] Also, the younger officers of this old Acadian institution "responded better to the profit motive" and felt that "exhortations to religion and race might conflict with business." The new religion spoke of computers rather than parishes. These recent graduates in economics and business administration did not wish to graft the old with the new. They probably agreed with Prof. Aurèle Young, a teacher to some of them.

In 1961, while an economist at Université Saint-Joseph, Young had told a group of Edmundston businessmen that the time had come to aim seriously at the conquest "of our economic sphere if we are not to lose the benefits of two centuries of work."[18] The new managerial class which began to emerge by the late 1960s from Université de Moncton and other French institutions in Québec and elsewhere had accepted this challenge. One wonders whether they ever considered another consequence of this new direction: by creating business institutions

---

[16] These details are discussed by Prof. Robert Young in a preface to his doctoral dissertation for Oxford University in 1975, entitled "Planning and Participation in the Northeast New Brunswick FRED Agreement", p. 54. I am indebted to Dr. Young for providing me with a draft copy of his thesis.
[17] Cited in Young thesis, p. 54, note 1.
[18] *L' Évangéline*, March 14, 1961, cited in Young, p. 53.

motivated by profit, they could be hastening the end of the old Acadian culture.

For instance, what would remain distinctively Acadian after the new version of La Société l'Assomption was housed in a high-rise office tower, complete with its own computer? Would Assomption Compagnie Mutelle d'Assurance-Vie differ significantly from the Metropolitan Life Assurance office down the street — especially when the latter was also staffed by bilingual clerks? Would it still be regarded as an Acadian institution — by the great majority of Acadians lacking university degrees?

These kinds of questions were bothering a young Acadian history professor at Université de Moncton in the early summer of 1970, before the general election. "I am sometimes pessimistic, " mused Léon Thériault. "Can we survive in fifteen years? Is Université de Moncton a force of assimilation or integration? We need more education. The university is not becoming more English but the students are coming from an English-speaking environment. What little they know of the French facts of literature and history are mostly imported from Québec and France." Thériault thought Acadians were being "subjected to intellectual imperialism from Québec."[19]

Over the next decade, this young professor would remain at his teaching post, writing extensively and passionately on Acadian historical and political themes. He would also become a strong supporter of a new political phenomenon — Le Parti Acadien.[20] The anger and militancy he saw in his students in the late 1960s would be channeled into this movement. But this too would fade into history, leaving Thériault and many others of his generation and background wondering: was Acadian culture fading too?

---

[19] See note 15 above.
[20] For an excellent and sympathetic analysis of Le Parti Acadien, see Léon Thériault, *La Question du Pouvoir en Acadie*, Moncton, 1982, pp. 95-99.

# SIXTEEN

## RICHARD HATFIELD WOOS FRENCH NEW BRUNSWICK: 1970-1974

October 12, 1982 was an historic day for New Brunswick's Progressive Conservative premier, Richard Bennett Hatfield. The 51-year-old bachelor had won his fourth consecutive election and his 39 victorious candidates included eight from predominantly French ridings. It seemed that twelve years of constant wooing of French voters had succeeded for the astute and patient Hatfield. In naming his cabinet, he gave the French community its ultimate recognition: Clarence Cormier, mayor of the Moncton suburb of Dieppe, became minister of education.

What an opportunity for *L'Évangéline* to hail the great strides French citizens had made toward cultural equality. But the long-time voice of Acadian causes would be heard no more. Three weeks before election day, its presses stopped — the victim of a crippling combination of shaky finances and an ill-timed labour dispute. Despite vague election promises from Hatfield and demands for immediate aid voiced by various segments of the French cultural lobby, *L'Évangéline* did not resume publication. New Brunswick had lost its last independent daily in either language. Nothing lasts forever, and perhaps *L'Évangéline* was no longer needed in a communication world dominated by television. With Cormier's appointment to the coveted post of education, perhaps there were no other cultural battles to win.

Many unilingual anglophones, their hopes for government jobs dashed by new bilingual requirements, might have concluded that the French had no more worlds to conquer. Nothing could shake their bitter conviction that Hatfield had given in to various French pressure groups.

Had he not named an Acadian to be Lieutenant-Governor and kept him in that prestigious post for eleven years? Had he not introduced new electoral laws giving state aid to third parties, notably the Parti Acadien? Had he not sanctioned the creation of two school systems, based on language? Had he not gone out of his way to help the French build their own cultural centre in the heart of Loyalist Fredericton? Look at the money Hatfield had poured into the French northeast — building luxurious schools and hospitals and using public funds to modernize pulp mills that employed mostly French. Look at the way Hatfield had allowed his Acadian fisheries minister to spend ninety percent of his budget on the north shore while ignoring the English fishermen on the Bay of Fundy. And let's not forget the millions he spent on that Acadian Historic Village at Caraquet.

As the inheritor of a political party that had been mired in English New Brunswick for three generations, Hatfield was more than happy to take the credit for any acts recognizing French citizens. Others who shared Hatfield's keen political sense would point out that while he had indeed done much to accommodate the French fact, he had been aided greatly by federal Liberal policies and other events beyond his control.

Early in September, 1971, Premier Hatfield called his first by-election in Kent South to fill the vacancy caused when Louis Robichaud resigned. Voting day would be October 8. Meanwhile, the Fredericton *Daily Gleaner*, not known for its pro-French views, seized on a federally-funded report alleging misuse of welfare funds in Tracadie. Implicated in the study, prepared for the Moncton office of the Secretary of State under an Opportunity for Youth grant, was Alyre Breau, father of Herb Breau who had become the Liberal MP when the incumbent, Hédard Robichaud, was named to the Senate. Brenda Robertson, minister of youth and welfare and the first woman to sit in the New Brunswick legislature, immediately flew to Tracadie, investigated some of the welfare homes owned by Breau Sr. and padlocked the welfare office until the books were examined.

Throughout this local furor, given prominent coverage in *L'Évangéline* as well as in the English dailies of the Irving-owned chain, the premier kept a discreet silence. He also took little part in the Kent-South by-election campaign, which the pundits assumed would result in an easy Liberal victory. One of the few local issues stemmed from dissatisfaction some Acadians had with settlement terms after their homes had been expropriated for the Kouchibouguac National Park.

The election results stunned most observers. The Progressive Conservative candidate, Omer Léger, piled up an early lead and went on to a landslide victory. The upset marked the first time that eighteen-year-olds could vote in New Brunswick elections. Léger thought this had been a factor in his victory: it was a case of the new youth vote exercising its first chance to strike at the established order. In Kent County, that meant the Liberal party. Hatfield could not have anticipated this when he lowered the voting age a few months earlier to comply with an 1970 election promise, but he took full credit for the upset.

Two days before the by-election ballots were cast, fate gave Hatfield's French support another boost. The Lieutenant-Governor, Fredericton contractor Wallace S. Bird, died suddenly of a heart attack. The Trudeau government acted with unusual speed to name his successor. On October 8, voting day in Kent South, the media caught the hitherto camera-shy Hatfield as he accompanied the new appointee back to Fredericton. The office would be filled by Hédard Robichaud, the long-time MP for Gloucester and federal fisheries minister before being named to the Senate. The media suggested he owed his appointment to Hatfield, but the decision had come from the Trudeau cabinet, probably acting on the recommendations of Louis Robichaud.

Regardless of how Hédard Robichaud got his latest recognition for long and distinguished service to the Liberal party, few better ways could have been found to strengthen Hatfield's image among Acadian voters. The Robichaud clan was a powerful force in Gloucester County. In Hédard's home town of Shippagan, the Robichaud fish plant (once owned by his father and later sold to another prominent Liberal family, the McLean's of Black's Harbour in Charlotte County) was the area's biggest employer. Its management remained in Hédard Robichaud's family: his brother Valerin was both plant manager and town mayor. Robichauds' also owned Shippagan's largest supermarket as well as a furniture store and a dry-cleaning establishment. Another brother was the town's secretary and a brother-in-law managed another fish plant.

Hédard's wife, the vivacious and fluently bilingual Gertrude, was a Légère from Caraquet, where she kept close ties with numerous relatives. All were staunch Liberals, but Hédard and Gertrude Robichaud's frequent public appearances over the next decade, often with Premier Hatfield at their side, strengthened his efforts to appear more sympathetic to Acadian aspirations than any of his Tory predecessors had been.[1]

Off-setting these fortuitous events in Hatfield's early years as premier were increasing signs of economic stagnation. Indeed, the predominantly French northeast sector seemed on the verge of total collapse. Despite massive sums of public money, most of it from the federal treasury, that had been poured into the region since the mid-sixties, all efforts to narrow the economic gap with the more affluent south seemed fruitless. If anything, this gap was growing.

While French and English civic and business leaders in Moncton were cutting ribbons opening a $1.4-million city hall complex, Place L'Assomption, the north shore reported shutdowns or cutbacks in the pulp mills and fish-packing plants. Fluctuations in the former industry were familiar, but the closing of the Gorton-Pew fish-processing plant at Caraquet just before Christmas, 1971, was a bitter blow.

The north shore malaise became a media event on January 16, 1972 when Gloucester County labour leaders staged "A Day of

[1] This and other information relating to citizens and events in the Acadian peninsula used in this and the preceding chapters came from countless interviews during the four years (1969-1973) the author resided with his family in Middle Caraquet and worked as a freelance journalist and part-time teacher.

Concern" at Bathurst. On the platform with Premier Hatfield were federal politicians Jean Marchand, Robert Stanfield and David Lewis. Facing them were 3,500 citizens, most of whom seemed ready to listen so long as the speakers spoke French. Anglophones like Hatfield were often drowned out by militant students from Collège Bathurst who quickly gained control of the meeting.

Pandamonium broke out when union organizer Mathilda Blanchard of Caraquet, the mother of former student activist Michel, yielded to the students' chant "On Veut Mathilda!" and mounted the stage. Pointing her finger at a startled Jean Marchand, the federal minister of regional economic expansion (DREE), she charged that the only thing Ottawa had done was study and re-study the region, tell the people they were illiterate and then suggest they should move to urban areas.

"You've destroyed our forests! You've destroyed our oyster beds ! You've ruined our farms with your property taxes. You've ruined our education system and reduced our unemployment insurance scheme to zero by moving everything to Moncton! But we're not moving!"[2]

The crowd roared its approval. The fact that Madame Blanchard ignored such distinctions as private and public or federal and provincial jurisdiction meant nothing to them. The colourful Mathilda, who a few years earlier had run a distant third to Hatfield when he won the Tory leadership, now had her inning. She left the arena carried high on the shoulders of cheering students.

Thus ended "A Day of Concern" so carefully organized by the conservative-minded New Brunswick Federation of Labour. Besides giving national media attention to the dwindling job opportunities at the aging Consolidated Bathurst mill, it had provided students from Collège de Bathurst with ways to express their militancy. They had already gone on strike against their own administration and were now watching its autonomy disappear

---

[2] Saint John *Telegraph-Journal*, January 17, 1972. See also the author's New Brunswick article in *The Canadian Annual Review of Public Affairs 1972* (Toronto, 1973).

as Université de Moncton assumed control of degree-granting role for all French post-secondary institutions. The rally also cemented their ties with several former student activists, including Michel Blanchard, now a full-time worker with CRAN (le conseil regionale d'amenagement du nord-est).

He had joined CRAN in September, 1971, as its information officer. Another staff addition was Father Yvon Sirois, a 60-year-old former parish priest at Tracadie, whose new mandate was to help organize (or animate) the pulp-cutters in the area. One week after his appointment, Blanchard issued a press release in which he criticized Herb Breau, MP, and other members of what he called the "patente" or gang, for failing to prevent the economic exploitation of their fellow Acadians.

Meanwhile, students at Université de Moncton were carrying on where Blanchard had left off — luring Mayor Leonard Jones into public debate in order to publicize the growing French fact in that city. The excuse for this new confrontation was the National Film Board's *L'Acadie L'Acadie*. This graphic portrayal of the Blanchard-led ruckus on the Moncton campus in 1968 had won first prize at an international film festival held in France in June, 1971. When Radio Canada announced its plan to show it to Moncton viewers as well as to those on the north shore, Mayor Jones threatened to sue for libel.

The New Brunswick première aired January 8, 1972, sent jubilant students into the streets and they staged a demonstration on the mayor's front lawn. One was arrested and charged with loitering. Jones must have known he was being used to provide more grist for the militant young Acadians' mill.

A few days after the incident on Jones' lawn, five hundred students held a massed rally on their campus to form a "common front" — a popular term in Québec at this time — to get bilingual services in Moncton. They were strongly supported editorially by *L'Évangéline's* editor Claude Bourque.[3] Other support came from three of Moncton's eight councillors and from a Citizens' Committee for Bilingualism formed with a young Acadian lawyer, Sylvio Savoie, as its president.

[3] *L'Évangéline*, January 13, 1972

On February 21, the Société Nationale des Acadiens added to the pressure by presenting Mayor Jones with a French plaque to match the English one already on the new city hall complex. Jones' refusal to accept the French plaque and his decision to return the honorary Acadian citizenship certificate sent to him from Louisiana, Moncton's "twin," prompted Gérard Pelletier, the Secretary of State, to call him a bigot.

In May, 1972, the student charged by Jones demanded through his Acadian lawyer that both Prime Minister Trudeau and Premier Hatfield uphold the constitutionality of New Brunswick's Official Languages Act, still only partially proclaimed. He also wanted a French trial. Jones' lawyer objected and the case was suspended until a ruling from the New Brunswick Supreme Court. The decision in mid-December upheld the act and the Minister of Justice, J.B.M. Baxter, said he would recommend that cabinet immediately proclaim that section of the act making French language trials legally available.

When he signed the proclamation on December 20, Lieutenant-Governor Hédard Robichaud must have had a great sense of satisfaction. He and other charter members of the New Brunswick chapters of l'Ordre de Jacques Cartier could remember back to those frustrating days in the early 1930s when they began plotting their course toward cultural autonomy. By 1972, many of their major goals had been realized.

For younger francophones, indoctrinated with daily television accounts of the Parti Québécois and its independence movement, New Brunswick's pace of change was too slow. On February 6, 1972, a scant three weeks after the well-orchestrated "Day of Concern," Bathurst spawned the Parti Acadien. It was not really the town of Bathurst, but a small core of articulate young Acadians, most of them recent graduates or junior staff members of Collège de Bathurst, known back in Louis Robichaud's student days there as Collège Sacré-Coeur.

They had developed their *esprit de corp* while organizing protests to reform their own institution. Then, under the CRAN umbrella, they had moved off the college hill to press for local French television and radio outlets. It was this last issue that drew

Euclide Chiasson, a young philosophy teacher, onto the larger public stage.

In 1970, Chiasson had helped organize l'Association des Francophones du Nord-Est to lobby for an end to Québec's domination of the area's radio and television programming. The president and chief spokesman for that short-lived group was Jean Gauvin, an education student who would become, before the decade ended, Hatfield's high-spending fisheries minister. Chiasson remained at his college post, which gave him the financial base and the contacts to prepare for a new political party.

Why did Le Parti Acadien "come out" at this time? As Chiasson explained it later in his role as party spokesman, a group had been working behind the scenes for about a year, but the public viewing of the film *L'Acadie L'Acadie* plus the Day of Concern manifestation "made the time right."[4] He and Calixte Duguay, a colleague with a local following as a poet and a folk-singer, had teamed up with Michel Blanchard and four others to draft a party manifesto pledged to set up a separate Acadian province in northern New Brunswick.

A closed meeting attended by fifty invited delegates, probably chosen through the CRAN network and representing farmers and wood-cutters as well as students, quickly endorsed the manifesto. It was clearly an anti-establishment group, devoid of lawyers and businessmen. The most conspicuous delegates were two priests, Fathers Sirois and Thériault, formerly from the Tracadie parish but now either part or full-time workers from CRAN.

The majority of these charter members of the Parti Acadian were from that first generation of Acadians to benefit from newly accessible high schools and universities. They had also been reared on a steady diet of television — English as well as French

[4] Interview with Euclide Chiasson in Bathurst, February 2, 1972. The author also recorded interviews with Calixte Duguay and Mathilda Blanchard, which along with other material formed the basis for several CBC items, including one aired on "Maritime Magazine" in February, 1972, and a CBC "Commentary", aired nationally the week of February, 1972. See also an article that appeared about the same time in the now-defunct Montreal monthly *Last Post*.

— with the accent on violence in Viet Nam and confrontations in Québec. They hoped to make political capital from the many signs of dissatisfaction among ordinary New Brunswickers — people who probably knew little about the art of staging protests but who were becoming used to taking part in them. Many had attended the "Day of Concern" and participated in other less publicized confrontations in recent months throughout French New Brunswick.

In September, 1971, high school students and parents had chained up school buses at St. Leonard, near Edmundston. They kept their schools closed for several weeks until education officials in Fredericton bowed to their demands to use their school rather than a new one at Grand Falls twelve miles away.

In December, 1971, three hundred students at Tracadie held the minister of education, Lorne McGuigan, hostage for several hours to dramatize their concern over faulty heating and ventilation at their new high school. Four students threatened with expulsion for their part in detaining McGuigan were supported by a more orderly public meeting by about 100 students from l'Université de Moncton and a similar number from Collège de Bathurst as well as "representatives of the local CRAN committee and others from the Company of Young Canadians."[5] Throughout the spring of 1971, less dramatic protests against similar examples of poor workmanship and inappropriate school design were staged at St. Anselme, near Moncton, Dalhousie and Kedgwick and prompted a lead editorial in the *Telegraph-Journal* to ask "Are the Schools Safe?"[6]

Other disturbing questions were being raised by the Nutter-LeBlanc Task Force on Social Welfare. As noted earlier, its members had been appointed by Premier Robichaud in June, 1970, "to spearhead the stimulation of a dialogue within the New Brunswick community on the contents of the White Paper on Social Development and Social Welfare."[7]

---

[5] *Telegraph-Journal*, December 3, 1971
[6] *Telegraph-Journal*, May 6, 1971.
[7] *Telegraph-Journal* June 25, 1970; see also L'Évangéline of same date.

Of the nine other members appointed later, four were French-speaking: a Dalhousie lawyer, two welfare recipients from Sheila (near Tracadie) and Edmundston, and Father Pierre Poulin, "curé" for Collège de Bathurst.

They began their hearings just weeks before Robichaud called the 1970 general election and after a few meetings they suspended their tour until the ballots had been cast. Early in November, they resumed their deliberations in Bathurst and then travelled on to Caraquet, Tracadie, Lamèque and Sheila. The turnouts were small and the presentations usually oral and informal.

Everywhere, the message was the same: the poor were getting poorer; the system was not working for them. When the commissioners turned up at the colleges and universities, the students used the occasion to voice their concerns against assimilation into English society, the illiberal administrations and the lack of French radio and television. Their well-articulated views, especially at Collège de Bathurst, often showed the influence of CRAN's animation efforts.

It was at Bathurst that Euclide Chiasson first publicly discussed his view that the French should form their own political party. Father Pierre Poulin, in his dual role as a commission member and a colleague of Chiasson's, disagreed, saying that such a party would tend to isolate the French.[8]

Curiously, *L'Évangéline*'s report of this Collège de Bathurst session made no reference to Chiasson's statement or Poulin's response, although the *Telegraph-Journal*'s story did. Instead, the French version stressed the usual Acadian complaints about assimilation and the lack of French media outlets. There seemed to be a gentleman's agreement between Chiasson and *L'Évangéline* not to mention the new party until its creators had chosen the most opportune time for a public unveiling. Meanwhile, the often sensational stories of the poor people's complaints before the task force provided the mulch for the new party's seedbed.

[8] *Telegraph-Journal*, August 14, 1970; see also photographs, August 17 issue.

Another useful publicity vehicle was the Senate Committee on Poverty. It arrived in New Brunswick in August, 1970, just as the Nutter-LeBlanc entourage was getting started. Headed by Senator David Croll of Toronto, its New Brunswick members, Muriel Fergusson of Fredericton, Edgar Fournier of Edmundston and Dr. F.A. McGrand of Sunbury County, made up almost half of the seven-member Ottawa delegation. It almost seemed that this investigation had been formed primarily to study New Brunswick.

Their hearings had covered only Saint John, Moncton and Fredericton when they abruptly cancelled their swing through northeastern New Brunswick. Apparently, they decided their findings might be embarrassing to the Robichaud government during the election campaign. Before leaving the province, the senators did make a whirlwind car trip through Harcourt, Rogersville, Tracadie and Brantville, where they "saw poverty at its worst."[9]

Later in the year, after the general election, a Tracadie couple, Mr. and Mrs. Alfred Basque, were flown to Ottawa for a special appearance before the Senate Committee. The Acadian couple had impeccable credentials for representing their class.

He was a 46-year-old wood-cutter with a few months' formal schooling. According to his account, given in the regal splendour of the Red Chamber, Basque would leave his wife and six children early each Monday morning to drive about 100 miles to a lumber camp. He and his fellow workmen lived in shacks during the week while cutting for a private contractor. He earned less than $50 a week and had to accept welfare for part of the year to bring his annual income to about $3,000, the exact amount of the value of property one had to have in order to receive a Senate appointment. Madame Basque added that many others in the Tracadie area were far worse off.

She was in a position to know. As president of the local CRAN animation group, Madame Basque had been trying for two years to inform and inspire other poor people. A handsome woman with an impressive, even commanding presence, she told the

[9] *Telegraph-Journal*, November 25, 1970; also *L'Évangéline* of same date.

Senators about CRAN's recent budget cuts which had made it impossible to employ an animator "who had awakened the population."[10] She said that no one had ever explained why "the elite of Tracadie had declared war on those who were trying to lead the poor out of their misery."

"I am not here to overthrow or to criticize," Madame Basque declared, "but to find solutions to poverty. We must talk about solutions and not the facts. Down home we have been talking about poverty for two years .... Are we truly making war on poverty or simply repeating the same things? "

Her attentive audience could not answer her cold logic and blunt questions. Their report caused scarcely a ripple on a political scene immersed first in the FLQ crisis and its aftermath and then in the inevitable elections. As 1970 faded into history, so too did the politicians' interest in making permanent changes in Canada's economic and social structure. Perhaps that is slightly unfair: at least one member of the impoverished Basque family subsequently graduated from Université de Moncton, thanks to the educational revolution represented by student loans.[11]

The Nutter-LeBlanc Task Force on Social Development finally produced a 268-page report made public in September, 1971. It contained no fewer than 227 individual recommendations and followed on the heels of comments by Brenda Robertson, the minister of youth and welfare, accusing some areas' landlords of abusing the welfare system.[12] Expressing her concern that eleven percent of the people of New Brunswick were living on welfare, she did not comment on figures released in conjuncton with her interview that the welfare roles in Caraquet, Tracadie and Shippagan ranged from 29.74 to 33.46 percent — three times the provincial average.

[10] *Telegraph-Journal*, August 8, 1970
[11] *L'Évangéline*, October 28, 1970. [Over the next three years, the author had frequent talks, mostly on the telephone, with this indomitable woman.].
[12] *Telegraph-Journal*, September 28, 1971; Moncton *Transcript*, September 27, 1971.[The Moncton account was more comprehensive, reflecting the work of its associate editor, Angus MacDonald, who travelled with the Task Force and attended most of the sessions.]

Although the French fact was not its main thrust, the Nutter-LeBlanc Report made some pointed references to New Brunswick's duality. It called for a timetable for the full implementation of the Official Languages Act, more senior French administrators in the department of education, and more and better French language television programming.

Its main points dwelt with all New Brunswickers. "Most people do not feel involved in the governmental process .... Government programs do not really reflect the wishes of the people and do not meet their needs." As a result, "people feel more helpless in influencing policy and certain segments — the poor, the young and the elderly, tend to withdraw from society activities or become rebellious and even violent in demanding changes in the system."

The report acknowledged that some attempts, represented by organizations like CRAN, did exist to try and bridge the gap, but their functions were "poorly defined; they were not related formally to government; they suffered from inadequate funding and lacked professional staff."

Much of the problem was "communication isolation." Nowhere was this more evident than in northern New Brunswick, where the French citizens were served by one 5,000-watt radio station and a television station based in Moncton, "neither of which reaches two-thirds of the people." There was "more awareness about affairs in Québec."

New Brunswick's education system, centralized under Louis Robichaud's Program of Equal Opportunity, received sharp criticism. It was "too rigidly structured" and was administered by teachers and officials in an authoritarian manner. It stressed "values far removed from those of students and hence added to the tensions so evident today." Children of poor families were "poured into a school system based on middle class values of which they have no knowledge, with which they come into conflict and consequently frequently drop out and become candidates for social assistance and unemployment insurance." They were further disadvantaged because many lacked basic necessities such as food, adequate clothing and proper facilities at home.

In one important aspect, the Nutter-LeBlanc solution was similar to that proposed by the Byrne inquiry. It also wanted a new administrative structure that would be outside both the legislative and the existing departments of government. Despite its criticisms of the bureaucracy and the inadequacies of CRAN, the task force recommended a new bureaucratic structure that bore a striking similarity to CRAN's. Five regional development councils of from 10 to 20 members should be set up to identify regional needs, and to evaluate all government and community programs to see whether the people's needs were being met. These councils would also provide greater coordination of services and better cooperation among government departments.

A typical council would have two legislative members, one from each of the major parties; two welfare recipients and three students representing the universities, trade schools and high schools. Other citizen-representatives would be drawn from the chambers of commerce, the N.B. Federation of Labour, service clubs, the churches and associations from the primary producers (wood-cutters, farmers, fishermen). Three government appointees would compensate for gaps in representation: " several of these should be women."

What the Rev. Nutter, Emery LeBlanc and their fellow commissioners were recommending was an entirely new approach to governing and administering New Brunswick. Their councils would make the legislative assembly almost superfluous. Probably for this reason, plus the fact that the task force had been created by the Liberal regime of Louis Robichaud, the Hatfield government's response to its recommendations was cool.

Another reason, which became more apparent as the Hatfield rule lengthened, was the Tory leader's aversion to royal commissions and investigative bodies acting outside the legislature. Just as Robichaud rejected the Byrne report's suggestion that commissions should more or less replace government departments, so did Hatfield ignore the idea of regional development councils.

Yet, Hatfield quietly began implementing some of the Nutter-LeBlanc suggestions, especially those affecting French citizens.

The Official Languages Act was fully proclaimed, and as the task force had also urged, court proceedings were revised so that hearings could be held in either language. Over the next few years, more French administrators found places in the higher levels of the education department. An alcoholic treatment and prevention centre, another task force suggestion, was eventually established under the supervision of an early opponent to Hatfield's leadership, the outspoken but popular Dr. Everett Chalmers. Several out-patients' clinics were placed in smaller centres, but like Robichaud, Hatfield shied away from making substantial changes in the established order. He seemed even less willing to challenge the old adage: the poor are always with us.

Hatfield showed the same degree of caution — perhaps it was political sagacity — when the Parti Acadien finally struck its colours in February, 1972. He left it to his "French lieutenant" and minister of finance, Jean-Maurice Simard, to give the government's response. "The support of the entire French-speaking population of New Brunswick would not be sufficient to elect such a party." Former premier Louis Robichaud, from his Ottawa vantage point, had no doubts either: "They're doomed before they start; they won't get to second base." He thought the situation in northern New Brunswick was "going to be rectified, but it's never going to become a situation of full employment. If they're seeking this as part of their policies, they will be frustrated."

Robichaud's successor as provincial Liberal leader, Saint John lawyer Robert Higgins, was more cautious. He was pleased to hear Euclide Chiasson's comment that it was not his intention to form a party on an ethnic basis. "Anyone had the right to form a party if they desired," he added.[13]

Two powerful Acadian lobbies took advantage of the new party's appearance to remind English New Brunswickers that the French still had a long way to go to achieve equality in Canada's only bilingual province. The recently-appointed executive secretary of La Societé Nationale des Acadiens (SNA), Hector Cormier, had been a high school teacher who had gained prominence in the fight to get a francophone superintendent in Moncton. He had also led a more successful campaign to block

[13] *Telegraph-Journal*, February 8, 1972.

the construction of a bilingual school. (The Acadians wanted a unilingual one of their own.) For these efforts on behalf of the Acadian cause, Cormier lost his teaching post but was rewarded with the SNA job. He told an English reporter that the SNA had not been involved in the Parti Acadien's formation, but he thought its appearance was a sign of "a certain malaise" and a reaction "to what we are getting from the existing parties." Cormier noted that Acadians had "very little representation at the higher echelons of the civil service in Fredericton" and that this situation likely would not change without some action.[14]

He added that the SNA might discuss the Parti Acadien at its next meeting, but that depended on whether Chiasson and his party executive could supply official documents on party policy.

Judging by what editor Claude Bourque had to say in *L'Évangéline*, he had met both with Chiasson and Cormier before the new party's unveiling. The editorial published three days *before* the party's launching echoed Cormier's criticisms of the two old parties. Bourque noted the Acadians' continued under-representation in the Hatfield government and wondered whether those who were there could exert any meaningful pressure within the present system. Even in electoral districts with Acadian majorities, they gave up a seat to an English candidate. He was referring to the city of Bathurst, which was 85 percent French; it had elected two anglophones out of a total of six for Gloucester. "Is anything like this true of Metro Saint John?" Bourque asked.

Bourque's editorial concluded that the birth of an Acadian party should come as no surprise. "Nor should its backers be surprised that they may be unable to form a government or even elect a single member." But "was there any other solution for a better representation and a better advocacy of French-speaking Acadian interests in the Legislative Assembly of New Brunswick?" He thought the Acadian party would grow and thrive to the extent that the other parties refused to recognize the legitimate aspirations of the Acadians.

---

[14] *Telegraph-Journal*, February 8, 1972.

This initial assessment neatly summed up the Acadians' political dilemma — one they had been grappling with for years. It also accurately predicted the fate of the Parti Acadien. Over the next decade, it failed to elect a single member. Its greatest obstacle was Richard Hatfield. He took advantage of the changing political climate to "come out smelling of French roses". Again, it was an event beyond his control — the results of the 1972 *federal* election.

The Trudeau-led Liberals saw their "parliamentary majority reduced to a minority position with the party losing over thirty seats in English Canada and suffering some humiliating defeats in traditionally safe Liberal seats."[15] For the first time in a decade, Ottawa's Liberal establishment was on the defensive. Hence, it was willing, even anxious, to re-examine relations with provincial governments. As premier of Canada's only bilingual and bicultural province, Hatfield seized the chance to exploit his strategic position.

He was aided by federal Liberals anxious to strengthen their hold in Acadian New Brunswick. In May, 1972, the Secretary of State, Gérard Pelletier, was the keynote speaker at a weekend conference held in Fredericton by the SNA. Most of the 800 delegates, including Euclide Chiasson of the Parti Acadien, had their expenses covered by a $25,000 grant from Pelletier's office. The minister promised the delegates that northern New Brunswick would get regional television within two years. A few days later, Premier Hatfield announced that the provincial crown agency, the Community Improvement Corporation, would begin expropriating land for an Acadian Historic Village near Caraquet. He also promised provincial funds to aid students at Collège de Bathurst to create television programs for distribution over CHAU-TV, in New Carlisle, Québec. For years, it had been blanketting the Gloucester-Restigouche region with programs

---

[15] Donald A. Savoie, *Federal-Provincial Collaboration: The Canada-New Brunswick General Development Agreement* (Montréal, 1981), p. 25. This is essential reading for those seeking to understand the complex funding programs between the two levels of government.

originating in Montréal — programs that often reflected a strong separatist bias.

The average New Brunswicker, English or French, was either unaware or unconcerned about which government paid for what. The Hatfield announcements strongly suggested that these efforts aimed at benefitting the Acadian peninsula would be paid by Fredericton. In fact, the funds for the Acadian Historic Village came from a joint federal-provincial shared-cost effort with Ottawa bearing the lion's share. Being much closer to the scene, Hatfield took most of the political credit.

He quickly seized on another Ottawa decision to gain political ground when the Trudeau government named Bernard Jean, the long-time Liberal MLA from Caraquet, to the New Brunswick bench. Hatfield looked for a strong local candidate to carry the Tory colours in a by-election. He found his man in Lorenzo Morais, the mayor of Caraquet. It was really a marriage of convenience. Hatfield needed a high-profile candidate and Morais wanted to expand his political horizons.

Born in poverty, Morais was an Acadian success story. He gained his electrician's training in Montréal and then worked for three years in Halifax, perfecting his trade and his English. By the time he became Caraquet's mayor in 1969, he had his own plumbing and heating business which had profited from big contracts during the school and hospital construction boom. He also owned an apartment block, a hardware store and the town's only shopping mall. He had helped negotiate with a large Japanese firm to establish a textile plant in Caraquet, one of many short-lived ventures set up throughout the Maritimes to take advantage of generous federal and provincial incentive grants and loans aimed at industrializing the region.

Morais' Liberal opponent was Richard Savoie, president of United Maritime Fishermen's Limited, a cooperative. He was also a member of the SNA executive and a regent of Université de Moncton.[16] The Parti Acadien did not field a candidate, a decision that raised doubts as to its desire to challenge the

[16] See *Telegraph-Journal*, September 14, 1972. Other sources were the candidates' campaign material mailed to Caraquet residents.

political status quo. Its presence probably would not have affected the outcome. It was Morais all the way.

As Claude Bourque observed in his editorial following the September 18th results, the voters opted for political opportunism, going along with the idea that a member on the government side would help their region more than another Liberal opposition member. They also liked a good show and Morais, with his big blue-and-white rented helicopter flitting about the riding during the final three days of campaigning, provided one. He also gave them a victory party in the Caraquet arena they would remember for many a day.

Morais was a realist. "I don't know if this will be a long-lasting marriage," referring to his recent affiliation with the Tories. "It all depends on what I can get for my people ... The House in Fredericton will come down unless I get what I want."[17]

What Morais wanted was the tourism portfolio, vacant since Hatfield fired Charles Van Horne the previous August for uncontrolled spending. Morais would be disappointed. Hatfield probably realized from his newest member's campaign style that this bouncy five-foot-three Acadian might be as difficult to control as Van Horne. When the tourism job went to another Acadian, Jean Paul LeBlanc of Moncton, Morais did not hide his disappointment.

He rarely spoke in the House and toward the end of the 1973 session he was often absent. When Hatfield called the 1974 election, Morais did not re-offer. Whether he realized it or not, he had served Hatfield's purposes: he had helped improve the Tory leader's credibility among francophone voters.

The Parti Acadien made its political debut in mid-December, 1972 when it finally fielded a candidate to contest a Bathurst by-election to fill a vacancy caused by the death of the long-time Liberal member and former minister, H.H. "Bud" Williamson. This time there were no upsets. A young bilingual Liberal lawyer, Eugene McGinley, won easily in a light turn-out. The Parti Acadien candidate, school teacher Louis Boudreau,

[17] *Telegraph-Journal,* September 14, 1972.

received 435 votes, compared to McGinley's 3095 and 2558 for the Tory.[18]

Party leader Euclide Chiasson candidly admitted that the Parti Acadien had not realized the importance of mapping an effective campaign strategy. He made another point that might have caught Hatfield's attention: contending parties should be placed on an equal footing by changes in the electoral laws limiting campaign expenditures and providing some public funds. Shortly after the 1974 general election, Hatfield took steps along these lines, guaranteeing funds for all parties fielding a minimum of ten candidates.

It was left to René Lévesque to give the Parti Acadien one of its few lifts during its first year of life. In fact, the Québec leader gave the entire Acadian lobby an excuse to reassert its aims and remind New Brunswickers they were not separatists.

Late in November, Lévesque spoke at the University of New Brunswick, where he told his student audience that Québec's political independence was inevitable. During a lively question period, Lévesque was asked what effect this might have on New Brunswick's Acadians. "If Québec becomes a going concern," he replied with his familiar shrug, "young Acadians could become our privileged immigrants of the future. It is apparent that the French minority in areas of Canada away from Québec are a lost cause." [19]

Claude Bourque was moved to make an eloquent rebuttal.

> A people, it is said, has a soul. The Acadian people has a soul, has a destiny and has its dreams. If the past has failed to destroy the Acadians, no René Lévesque is going to order the Acadians to fade away and blend into the people of Québec, not even if Québec should become independent. Acadians have chosen New Brunswick as their

[18] *L'Évangéline*, December 12, 1972.
[19] *Telegraph-Journal*, November 25, 1972.

home — twice. We have every intention to stay here, to grow and flourish here.[20]

For the Parti Acadien, Euclide Chaisson was less poetic but equally emphatic. He rejected Lévesque's paternalistic and arrogant attitude. The PQ leader was "talking through his hat." Hector Cormier of the SNA thought Lévesque was dishonest for using such tactics to reach his goal of Québec separation. And he added: "The day Acadians decide to die culturally, they won't ask René Lévesque's permission. He doesn't determine the future of Acadians."

Who did? Judging by the 1971 census figures which began appearing in mid-1972, the biggest factor was the economy. A news release from Statistics Canada showed that the percentage of New Brunswickers speaking French had declined from 35.2 percent in 1961 to 34 percent a decade later. This contrasted with another set of figures showing that in the same period, those New Brunswickers whose mother tongue was French had increased from 210,000 to 215,000.

To Claude Bourque, the explanation for this apparent paradox was simple. Francophones had been migrating to the industrial centres of the United States while those remaining in New Brunswick were having fewer children. "Our young people are the ones who are leaving us," he warned. "If the socio-economic plight of the Acadians gets no better in the next ten years, then we must expect to read more such disturbing news."

More came in April 1973, in the form of so-called "yellow books" prepared for each of the Atlantic provinces in a revamped federal department of regional economic expansion (DREE). These policy study papers had been ordered when Don Jamieson was named late in 1972 to succeed Jean Marchand to the DREE portfolio. The yellow book predicted that New Brunswick's unemployment rate could reach "unacceptable levels" by the 1980s because of probable declines in agriculture and

---

[20] *L'Évangéline, November 27, 1972* and carried in translation by the *Telegraph-Journal*, December 4, 1972.

fisheries.[21] Furthermore, New Brunswick's socio-economic composition, an apparent reference to its biculturalism, "constituted a development constraint." Why? Because a number of Acadians from the northern part of the province preferred to live in a French-speaking area and were not willing to move elsewhere in the province "where employment opportunities are more readily available."

In 1966, when the original federal-provincial agreement (Fund for Regional Economic Development or FRED) was signed, 4,000 families in northeastern New Brunswick were to "benefit" from a government-assisted resettlement program. Six years later, after spending $1.6 million, the bureaucrats could report that only 165 families had moved "to more prosperous municipalities." This was one of the revelations of a five-part series on FRED carried by *L'Évangéline* in January and February, 1973 — a series quickly translated and published by the *Telegraph-Journal*.

Those interviewed for the series usually gave two reasons for opposing the resettlement scheme. Besides a natural reluctance to move from their home communities, they did not like being told they had to, or else face the withdrawal of basic services like electricity and health care. They also concluded that with their backgrounds and lack of training, they would find few jobs in the so-called growth centres. Some people found themselves caught in a bureaucratic tug-of-war.

Just north of Bathurst, Father Yvon Sirois, as a part-time worker for CRAN, had organized several communities to oppose any resettlement plans being promoted by recent university graduates like Bernard Gauvin, a former star in the film *L'Acadie L'Acadie*. He was now a key figure in the regional development board office at Bathurst. As he admitted to the *L'Évangéline* reporter, he was finding "spreading the word a challenge."

These well-researched newspaper articles revealed that the great expectations of the optimistic Sixties had been realized only by a few. Some like young Gauvin had found secure havens

[21] Donald A. Savoie, *Federal-Provincial Collaboration*, (Montreal, 1981) pp. 26-27

in the government bureaucracy. Others had followed the earlier example of Lorenzo Morais and acquired skilled trades now in great demand in the booming industrial south, notably Saint John.

The Irving-owned shipyard was working on its largest contract: four 35,000-tonne tankers for Esso. Just outside the city limits at Coleson's Cove, a workforce of 240 was building a $212-million generating plant. The economic prospects in the northeast were bleak, except for the base metal mines. The pulp mills were turning more and more to mechanical harvesters; fish plants were closing because of a massive decline in herring stocks due to overfishing.

One of the most disappointed figures in the DREE story, its original minister Jean Marchand, went so far as to call the original agreement "rotten." To improve or replace it would involve months of hard bargaining between Ottawa and Fredericton. Richard Hatfield, ever wary of his weak French flank, publicly expressed his determination to have Ottawa honour one part of the original bargain — to help rebuild Route 11 that ran along the perimeter of the Acadian peninsula. More than anything else, Route 11 symbolized the politicians' interest in this sprawling French community. By 1972, the highway was in a wretched condition, a fact brought home daily to every Acadian household faced with mounting repair bills for tires and shocks ruined by unavoidable pot-holes.

Hatfield's persistence won the Route 11 round. When the new federal-provincial agreements were signed, the first one contained over $13 million for highway construction. The terms would last only until March, 1975, but that was long enough for the Tory premier. He expected to have a new mandate by then. Times were always changing, but Hatfield stuck with one timeless New Brunswick truth: road work brings in votes.

In the meantime, the Acadian cultural lobby never ceased reminding the Hatfield administration that the French were not getting their share of jobs in Fredericton, especially in the education department. The government's answer was a minister's committee on educational planning, co-chaired by Malcolm MacLeod, assistant deputy minister, and A.A. Pinet, superintendent for the Edmundston district. A leaked version of their report appearing in *L'Évangéline* on October 23, 1973, was rejected by the SNA. The suggestions for more local authority did not go far enough. The SNA also disliked a recommendation that compulsory second language training should begin in grade three. What the SNA wanted was two school systems, one French, the other English.

As the Acadian cultural lobby postured and the bureaucrats worked over their yellow books, 200 woodlot owners and pulp-cutters chose a cold April day in 1974 to drive down from the north shore for a demonstration in front of Fredericton's Centennial and legislative buildings. Organized by a government-funded North Shore Forestry Syndicate, they demanded new legislation designed to help the ailing pulp and paper industry also give the small wood producer and private truckers the right to bargain with the big companies. The protest paid off: subsequent legislation included this demand. Even better in the short term, by December, 1973, the small woodlot owners were getting nearly $10 more a cord for their wood.

Acadian herring fishermen were less fortunate. Throughout the spring and summer of 1973, they watched in disbelief and anger as this historic mainstay collapsed. Old-timers like Martin Gionet of Middle Caraquet could remember carting waggon-loads of herring roe or eggs from the shore for use as field fertilizer. How could such a resource fail?

They all knew the culprits: large purse-seiners, most of them owned and crewed by British Columbians. They had started arriving in the Caraquet and Shippagan areas in the late 1960s, after their own herring stocks had reached the vanishing point from over-fishing. Federal fisheries experts had encouraged them to bring their vessels through the Panama Canal and up to the Gulf of St.Lawrence, where the herring stocks were "unlimited".

At the same time, a generous subsidy program had enabled some young Acadians to buy new seiners from two local boatyards at Lower Caraquet. One had been started by the Robichaud administration and the other, a steel-boatyard, was begun under Hatfield. Nearby herring reduction plants operated non-stop, churning out fertilizer and pet food. By 1973, the big seiners were returning empty and the west coasters began selling their aging vessels to Acadians, encouraged by generous government loans.

Down in Fredericton, where fishing problems rarely surfaced, the Hatfield forces were preparing for another election. A tax credit bill, passed December 4, 1973, during a short autumn session gave $45 to $75 to 120,000 home-owners and a $30 rebate to 300,000 tenants. In the March 1974 budget, the eight-percent sales tax on clothing and footwear was removed and a week later Premier Hatfield announced that 29,000 civil servants would get a special payment of $125 each to "help ease the impact" of steadily rising living costs, mostly from sky-rocketing oil prices.

Never one to leave elections to chance, Hatfield also fulfilled a 1970 election promise by creating 58 single-member constituencies. Two of these new ridings received their first test in September when by-elections were held in York South and Campbellton. The latter area had been represented by Van Horne until he resigned after being accused of unauthorized spending in his tourism department. His successor was another Tory and a bone fide francophone, Fernand Dubé, who promptly took over in tourism. York South also returned a government supporter, David Bishop, a Protestant minister. Hatfield needed no more indicators: two weeks after these results were in, he announced that a general election would be held November 19.

For the first time since 1920, four political parties were contesting, although only the Liberals and Conservatives ran a full slate of candidates. All parties attempted to present four distinct platforms, but in reality there were only three.

The Parti Acadien, competing in the thirteen ridings where the French voters dominated, issued a platform very similar to that of the New Democrats, whose 35 candidates included 5 French.

The Parti Acadian wanted two ministers of education — one French and the other English. The NDP wanted enough schools to serve the French community and mandatory regulations forcing municipalities to provide services in both official languages "where there is at least 20 percent of the population speaking the minority official language."[22] Both parties wanted more local control of education as well as a state-operated automobile insurance plan, a government take-over of the New Brunswick Telephone Company, and more aid to cooperatives.

The Progressive Conservative platform was the most general on the bilingual and bicultural issue but was far more specific about plans for developing the economy. Twenty percent of the existing off-shore fishing fleet and at least 30 percent of the inshore would be replaced; a $300-million highway program would include a modern highway connecting Campbellton and Moncton and residential property taxes would be phased out by 1979.

The Liberals under Robert Higgins considered "unity" the "cornerstone" of their platform. They promised financial help to those municipalities "where either English or French constitute a significant minority and thereby require service in their mother tongue." They would "reconstruct" the education department to provide "distinct programs for the two ethnic groups." They would provide second language programs in schools for any parent "choosing to do so" in order that their children "may strive for the second language." Liberals would also abolish the residential property tax, but by 1977, two years earlier than the Tories.

The six-week campaign was vintage New Brunswick politics: much talk about local issues and personalities rather than the English-French fact. Less attention was paid to the weak state of the forest resource, the Bricklin sports car venture or the nuclear power station. The latter would be built at Point Lepreau on the Bay of Fundy rather than at an alternative site near Caraquet on Chaleur Bay.

In the French ridings, the Parti Acadien provided little challenge to the two old parties. Francophone voters knew which side their "political bread was buttered on." With two exceptions they cast their ballots either for *les rouges* or *le bleus*. Only

[22] *Telegraph-Journal*, November 15, 1974, special supplement

Euclide Chiasson, the Parti Acadien president, kept his deposit. He collected 1, 011 votes in the new riding of Nigadoo-Chaleur just north of Bathurst. His support enabled the Tory candidate, Roland Boudreau, to defeat the incumbent Liberal.[23]

Gastien Godin, a young law student, made an even more impressive showing as an independent in Shippagan-Isles. His 1, 877 votes allowed the Liberal incumbent, André Robichaud, to squeak by his Tory opponent by a mere 67 votes. If village rivalries had not interfered, Godin might have won the Progressive Conservative nomination and given Hatfield another toehold on the Acadian peninsula. This happened the next time round, when Jean Gauvin, the former student activist at Collège de Bathurst, narrowly beat Robichaud and was rewarded with the fisheries portfolio.

The 1974 election results provided Hatfield with only five francophone winners out of 33. It would be inaccurate to conclude, however, that this meagre French support was proof that once again New Brunswickers had retreated behind their ethnic bunkers. On the contrary, a closer look at these results suggest that French voters were breaking from their Liberal tradition.

Caraquet did return to the Liberal fold, which was not surprising considering the poor performance of their Tory choice in the November 1972 by-election. Kent South and Campbellton, on the other hand, decided to stay with their by-election Tory members, probably because both Omer Léger and Fernand Dubé had cabinet positions. In the new riding of Madawaska-Lakes, Jean-Pierre Ouelett scored a Tory breakthrough, joining the finance minister, Jean-Maurice Simard, who won easily in Edmundston.

The Moncton results also indicated a shifting French vote. The chairman of the Treasury-Board, Jean-Paul LeBlanc, lost by a wide margin to another Acadian, Ray Frenette in Moncton East, while in Moncton North, Rev. Michael McKee, the Liberal standard-bearer won convincingly to become the first priest ever

---

[23] *Telegraph-Journal*, November 20, 1974. (Boudreau received the Natural Resources portfolio.)

to sit in the legislature. Times had indeed changed, but not to the extent that the French had foresaken the Liberals.

Out of 25 successful Liberal candidates in this 1974 election, 13 were francophone. Ridings like Kent North and Shediac remained as solidly *rouges* as Albert and Sunbury stayed blue. The shifts that did occur in predominantly French ridings suggest that Acadians in increasing numbers were following the lead of their Madawaska neighbours: voting for the man rather than the party. At the same time, they continued to give strong support to *federal* Liberals like Herb Breau in Gloucester and Romeo LeBlanc in Westmorland-Kent. They seemed to be striving, like French voters in Québec, for the best of both worlds: support the government of the day provincially and federally. Over the past two decades, that policy had paid off for French New Brunswickers. Much of their success was a spin-off from federal efforts to maintain Québec within Confederation.

Whatever the reasons, almost all the goals set by Calixte Savoie, Dr. Albert Sormany and other members of the Acadian lobby of a generation earlier had been achieved.

# CONCLUSION

After a 120-year struggle, French New Brunswickers have achieved three basic objectives in their determination to preserve their cultural autonomy. They have their own school system with the all-important university and professional faculties. They have their own French clerical leaders and French dioceses. They have become political power-brokers within New Brunswick's ultra-conservative political system.

As well, they have their own French associations and lobbying groups, their own state-financed cultural centres in Fredericton, Saint John and Newcastle to help stem the assimilation rate that inevitably occurs when a linguistic and cultural minority moves into an English milieu. Their efforts have created Canada's only officially bilingual province. As a result, countless public and legislative meetings become a translator's dream — and sometimes a nightmare. Be they farmers, fishermen or bureaucrats, the scene is the same: all the delegates are wired for instantaneous translations. Defendants' demands for court proceedings to be heard in their first language can and are being met.

Two other powerful factors vital in maintaining this French community are much less secure: their religious institutions and the economy. During the last third of the 19th century and the first quarter of the 20th, Acadian priests and nuns, teaching sisters and brothers, were the cultural shock-troops of the Acadian renaissance. Together, they led the assault against the English-minded Irish bishops.

After the French dioceses were created, they joined forces with French doctors, lay teachers, businessmen and administrators to press toward educational autonomy. In these efforts, they were sustained and supported by a French cooperative movement in the form of *caisses populaires* and la Société l'Assomption.

All the while, a powerful social change was sweeping North America: secularism. French New Brunswickers were no more able to withstand the lures of the market place than the English. And like the English, their young were more intent on accumulating material goods than adhering to the faith. And they were having fewer children — fewer even than *les anglais*.

Québec was being rocked by these same social upheavals, but their young could and did turn to the State as their replacement for the Church. That state in Québec had become entirely French; the English Québecker was a dwindling minority.

Furthermore, that Québec state was now the biggest economic generator, the largest employer. It created policies encouraging Québecois to invest in a French-oriented economy. With the help of Radio-Canada and the private communication sector, Québec has maintained and expanded the French television and movie industries. Taking advantage of federal politicians vying for their block of votes, Québec leaders fashioned a nearly autonomous state within a steadily weakening federal structure.

The founders of the short-lived Parti Acadien may have had similar goals. Some radicals-with-tenure, teaching at Université de Moncton, may still harbour such dreams, but for its French citizens the New Brunswick realities are a far cry from what has been or can be achieved in Québec.

Instead of a gigantic money-machine like Hydro Québec, New Brunswick has the Irvings and McCains, remarkably successful families that are resolutely English. And in the case of the Irvings, they control that massive cultural assimilator, television.

New Brunswick and Québec differ in yet another aspect. More New Brunswick young people whose first language is English are becoming bilingual, thanks to the popularity of the French immersion programs in the provincial school system. The edge that French New Brunswickers had in the competition for jobs requiring fluency in both languages is decreasing.

It could be argued that the French in New Brunswick have gone about as far as they can or will go. Perhaps they have reached a plateau in their climb toward equality; they may be slipping back.

Assimilation continues to take a huge cultural toll. And the birth rate remains below the replacement level as young French New Brunswickers vie with their English neighbours to accumulate more and to live "the good life," represented by point eight children, two cars, ten credit cards and four cats.

It is safe to say that these were not the goals perceived by Father Marcel-François Richard or Dr. Albert Sormany. Yet both these men and their contemporaries would have rejoiced at the official recognition of New Brunswick's French fact. It is firmly in place, thanks to the Official Languages Act and all its bureaucratic spin-offs, and even more so because of Université de Moncton.

This educational institution was the physical and cultural realization of all those who dared to dream big dreams away back when the first Acadian Congress was held at Memramcook in 1881. A university they could call their own — a place to train successive generations of francophone professionals — a place to keep alive the cultural torch rekindled a hundred years earlier by a handful of clerics and lay people. If anything could stem the tide of assimilation, it was this educational off-spring of Collège Saint-Joseph, where the Acadian renaissance began.

So goes the elitist view of history — the tale of how an intrepid few saved the Acadians from extinction and led them towards equality with *les anglais*. Yet would Father Richard have achieved anything without the support, numerical as well as cultural, of his scattered Kent County parishioners? What would l'Université de Moncton accomplish without the steady flow of students registering each year not only at its main campus but in those others located in the far purer French environments of Shippagan and Edmundston?

The true custodians of Acadian culture are not only tenured professors and bureaucrats shored up by government wage scales and fringe benefits. They also include lusty, fiesty fishermen truckers, woodsmen, fish packers and thousands educated more on the job than in stale classrooms.

Today's challenge is finding leaders who can bring them together — the North and the South, the villages and the towns. During the turbulent 1960s, Louis Robichaud somehow managed this feat. But times are forever changing, and time may not be on Acadians' side.

# BIBLIOGRAPHY

## BOOKS

Baker, William M., *Timothy Warren Anglin, Irish-Catholic, Canadian.* (Toronto, 1977).

Belliveau, J.E., *Little Louis and the Giant K.C.* (Hantsport, 1980).

Belliveau, J.E., *The Monctonians: Citizens, Saints and Scoundrels.* (Hantsport, 1981).

Belliveau, J.E., *The Monctonians: Scamps, Scholars and Politicians.* (Hantsport, 1981).

Camp, Dalton, *Gentlemen, Players and Politicians.* (Toronto, 1970).

Daigle, Jean (Ed), *Les Acadiens des Maritimes.* (Moncton, 1980).

Doucet, Camille-Antonio, *Une étoile s'est levée en Acadie: Marcel-François Richard.* (Ottawa, 1973).

Doyle, Arthur T., *Front Benches and Back Rooms.* (Toronto, 1976).

Hautecoeur, Jean-Paul, *L'Acadie de discours.* (Laval, 1975).

Hopkins, Castell (Ed), *The Canadian Annual Review 1907, 1916, 1917.* (Toronto).

King, Louis J., *The Scarlet Mother on the Tiber.* (St.Louis, Missouri, no date).

LeBlanc, Emery, *Les Acadiens: La Tentative de génocide d'un peuple.* (Ottawa, 1963).

Leger, Médard J., *Du Miel au Fiel: histoire de la Patente dans le comté de Gloucester.* (Ottawa, 1970).

Machum, Lloyd, A., *A History of Moncton.* (Moncton, 1965).

MacNaughton, K.F.C., *The Development of the Theory and Practice of Education in New Brunswick.* (Fredericton, 1947).

Mailhôt, Raymond, *La Renaissance Acadienne (1864-1888): L'Interprétation Traditionnelle et Le Moniteur Acadien,* Thèse de Diplôme en Études Supérieures. (Montréal, 1969).

Newman, Peter C., *Renegade in Power: The Diefenbaker Years.* (Toronto, 1973).

Savoie, Alexandre-J., *Un Siècle de revendications scolaires au Nouveau-Brunswick 1871-1971: les commandeurs de l'Ordre à l'oeuvre 1934-1939.* (Vol II) (Montréal, 1980).

Savoie, Alexandre-J., *Un siècle de revendication scolaires au Nouveau-Brunswick 1871-1971: Du français au compte-gouttes (1871-1936)* Vol. 1 (Montréal, 1978).

Savoie, Alexandre-J., *Un Demi-Siècle d'Histoire Acadienne.* (Montréal, 1976).

Savoie, Calixte, *Mémoires d'un nationaliste acadien.* (Moncton, 1979).

Savoie, Donald A., *Federal-Provincial Collaboration: The Canada-New Brusnwick General Development Agreement.* (Montréal 1981).

Saywell, J. (Ed), *Canadian Annual Review of Public Affairs for 1966.* (Toronto, 1967).

Stanley, D.M.M., *Au service de deux peuples.* (Moncton, 1977).

Thériault, Léon, *La Question du pouvoir en Acadie* .(Moncton, 1982).

Thorburn, Hugh G., *Politics in New Brunswick* .(Toronto, 1961).

Tremblay, Marcel, *50 Ans d'education Catholique et française en Acadie.* (Bathurst, 1949).

Trofimenkoff, S.M., *The Dream of Nation: A Social and Intellectual History of Québec.* (Toronto, 1983).

Wade, Mason, *The French Canadians.* (Toronto, 1956).

Young, R.A., *"Planning and Participation in the Northeast New Brunswick FRED Agreement,"* doctoral dissertation (Oxford University, 1975).

## GOVERNMENT DOCUMENTS

*ARDA Task Force Report for the Pilot Rural Development Area in Gloucester-Restigouche-Northumberland Counties New Brunswick.* (January, 1966).

Canada, House of Commons, Debates.

Canada, Senate Debates.

Fraser, Hon. J.J., Report Upon Charges relating to the Bathurst Schools and other Schools in Gloucester County (Fredericton, 1894).

Johnston, J.F.W., Report on the Agricultural Capabilities of the Province of New Brunswick (Fredericton, 1850).

*Journals of the Legislative Council of New Brunswick.*

Pépin, Pierre-Yves, Life and Poverty in the Maritimes, *ARDA Research Report No. RE-3, Project 15002,* Ministry of Forestry and Rural Development (Ottawa, 1968).

Public Archives of New Brunswick, (Railway Files).

Report of the New Brunswick Committee on Reconstruction (Fredericton, 1944).

Royal Commission on Finance and Municipal Taxation in New Brunswick (Fredericton, 1963).

Synoptic Report of the Legislative Assembly of New Brunswick.

## NEWSPAPERS

Chatham Gleaner.

Fredericton Head Quarters.

L'Évangéline.

Le Moniteur Acadien.

Le Madawaska.

Moncton Transcript.

New Dominion and True Humorist.

Saint John Telegraph.

Saint John Standard.

Saint John Morning News.

Saint John Telegraph-Journal.

Saint John Globe.

Saint John Morning Freeman.

## ARTICLES/COMMENTARIES

Alexander, David, "Literary and Economic Development in Nineteenth Century Newfoundland," in *Acadiensis,* (Autumn, 1980).

Andrew, Sheila, "Spreading the Word: The Development of the Antigonish Movement in Acadian New Brunswick, 1935-1940", a graduate paper, University of New Brunswick.

*Atlantic Advocate* (Fredericton).

Beck, Murray, "Flamboyant Charlie versus Acadia's Hero" in *Commentator,* December 1967.

Glendenning, Burton, "New Brunswick's expanding pulp and paper industry" (Concordia, University, Montréal, 1974).

Hatfield, Michael, "H.H. Pitts and Race and Religion in New Brunswick Politics," *Acadiensis* (Spring, 1975).

LeBreton, Clarence, Les Blackhall: Histoire d'une famille et son influence. (Fisher and Sager, (Eds) *The Enterprising Canadians* (Newfoundland, 1979).

Poirier, Bernard, "William End," Dictionary of Canadian Biography, Vol. X (Toronto, 1982).

Stanley, George F.G., "The Caraquet Riots of 1875", *Acadiensis* (Autumn, 1972).

Stanley, George F.G., "The Flowering of the Acadian Renaissance", in D. Bercusson and P. Buckner (Eds), *Eastern and Western Perspectives* (Toronto, 1981).

*The Mysterious East* (various editions) (Fredericton, 1970-73).

Wilbur, Richard, "Acadians at the Cross-Roads" in *Soundings,* National Network, CBC radio (August 5, 1970).

Wilbur, Richard, "What Ever Happened to CRAN"?, *Rule and Revolution,* National Network, CBC radio (February 3, 1971).

Wilbur, Richard, *Maritime Magazine,* Commentary, CBC radio (February, 1972).

Young, R.A., "and the people will sink into despair: Reconstruction in New Brunswick" 1942-52" in *Canadian Historical Review,* LXIX, 2, 1988.

# INDEX

L'Acadie L'Acadie (Film) 218, 236, 238
Agricultural Rehabilitation and Development Act [ARDA] 211, 212, 213
Albert, André 27, 28
Anglin, Timothy Warren
  Bishop Rogers support 58-59
  Caraquet Riots 26
  election victories 18
  enters politics 3-4
  Speaker of Commons 10, 36, 58
Antigonish Movement 213, 214
L'Association Acadienne d'-Education
  Blakney speech 152
  first conference 139
  founded 138
  goals 153, 180, 182
L'Association Canadienne-Française d'Education 138, 143
L'Association Catholique de la Jeunesse Canadienne 128, 130, 132, 135
L'Association des Francophones du Nord-Est 218
Atholville, Town of 119, 120
Banks
  Bank of St.Stephen 9
  Commercial Bank of Saint John 9
  fishermen 108
  Montréal 9
Barry, J. Paul, Judge 221
Barry, Mgr. Thomas 72, 73, 80, 100, 191
Basque, Mrs. Alfred 241-242
Bathurst
  Day of Concern 235-237
  Electric and Water Power Company 117
  Grammar School 7, 78
  mining 198
  new convent 21
  opposes common schools act 17
  paper company 112, 113
  politics 3, 246
  school controversy 75-96
  trial of Caraquet Rioters 31
Baxter, J.B.M. (Premier)
  1925 election 113, 116
  regulation 32, 127
Baxter, J.B.M. (MLA) 237
Beckwith, Charles (Surveyor) 41-43
Belliveau, Alphée
  family life in Fredericton 87-88
  influence on Acadians 88, 188
  Normal School 95
Biron, Father Eugène-Raymond 56-57, 62-66
Blackhall, James G.C.
  background 9-10
  Caraquet Riots 23-31
  influence 9-10
Bird, William, (MLA)
  1953 election 170, 172-3
  Irving interests 173
Blair, Andrew (Premier)
  background 87-88
  Bathurst meeting 84-85
  Bathurst school issue 78-96
  Central Railway 82
  debates with Pitts 87
  defeated by Pitts 82-83
  introduces resolution 92-93
  political support 78, 82

response to Fraser Report 95
1895 election 94
**Blakney, C.H. Ford (MLA) 134**
  appointments 147, 152
  background 157
  French education 152
  House speeches 151, 157-8, 165
  Million Dollar Fund 157
  political defeat 168
  religious education 165-6
  Son-in-Law 189
**Blanchard, Mathilda 216, 235**
**Blanchard, Michel**
  background 216
  Caraquet 228
  court case 220-221
  CRAN 223, 225-6, 226, 236
  U-de-M Activist 217-220, 235
  Parti Acadien 238
**Blanchard, Théotime**
  Bathurst schools issue 92
  Caraquet Riots 23-38
  debate on Riots 35-36
  first elected 14, 16
  first opposition to Schools Act 17
  settlement motion 44-45
  1874 election 19
**Borden, Sir Robert 104, 106**
**Boucher, Gaspard**
  cabinet minister 148, 152, 164, 165, 167
  death 170
  education 139-140, 141, 167
  La Petite Boutique 124, 126
  MP for Restigouche-Madawaska 170, 177
  1952 election defeat 170
**Boudreau, Dr. Alexander 192, 193-4, 213-214**
**Bourassa, Henri 75, 175**
**Bourque, Claude (Journalist) 236, 246, 248, 250, 251**
**Breau, Herb (MP) 232, 236, 257**
**British North America Act**
  Manitoba 58
  negotiating 7

Section (93), 15
Section (133) 181, 199
**Buchanan, Norman (MLA) 181-182**
**Bûcherons**
  working conditions 155, 163, 196-197, 241, 253-4
**Burchill, Percy (Lumberman) 156**
**Burns, Kennedy**
  closure Collège Saint-Louis 69
  defence for Caraquet Riots 36
  opposes School Act 17
  Orange Lodge Bill 34
  1874 election 19
**Byrne, Edward J. (Lawyer Royal Commission)**
  192-4
**Caisses Populaires 153, 161, 167-68, 187, 213-214, 223, 229, 259**
**Campbell, William M. 140-141**
**Campbellton, Town of**
  Dr. George Dumont 190
  Fraser companies 119
  L'Ordre de Jacques-Cartier 129-130, 138
  political representation 91
  poverty 225
**Caraquet**
  caisses populaires 167-8, 213-4, 223
  convents 21
  CRAN 223
  Eudistes 99-100
  fishing 9, 150, 214, 234, 254
  Historic Village 232, 247, 248
  opposition to Schools Act 17
  politics 3, 156, 248-9
  settlement 40
  shipbuilding 160
**Chatham Gleaner**
  bank failures 9
  elections 3, 13
  opposes school Act 16
**Chalmers, Dr. Everett 205, 245**
**Chiasson, Euclide 218, 238, 240, 245-6, 247, 249, 250, 256**

Chiasson, Joseph 25, 37
Chiasson, Mgr. Patrice-Alexandre (Bishop of Chatham) 130, 138, 141
Collège de Bathurst 218, 235, 237, 240, 247
Collège Sacré-Coeur
 education conference 141-142
 enrollment 167
 established in Bathurst 126, 177
 established in Caraquet 99-100
 grants 176
 Louis J. Robichaud 178, 187, 190
 Summer School 143
Collège Saint Joseph, Memramcook (also Université Saint-Joseph)
 Acadian Congress 61
 beginnings 2
 celebration Expulsion Bicentennial 175
 Collège Saint-Louis 69
 graduates 52, 88
 growth 38, 58, 76
 impact of Common Schools Issue 21
 Irish students 52
 politics 91, 147, 172, 184, 229
 Société l'Assomption 126, 127
 staff 56
 Summer School 143-4
Collège Saint-Louis (Kent County)
 Biron 56-57, 62-64
 closure 68-69
 rivalry with St Michael's College 6, 57
 opens 56
Collège Saint-Louis (Edmundston)
 established 152, 167
 grants 176
Common Schools Act
 Bathurst schools issue 79-96
 constitutionality 33
 1875 Compromise 82, 85-95
 final Act 13, 15
 introduced 12

reaction to 11-30 Passim
 regulations 20
Compromise of 1875
 Bathurst Schools Issue 76-96
 Caraquet Riots 20
 revealed by Blair 94-95
Confederation
 Irish bishops 7
 negotiating 7
 opposition 8
 reaction 40
Congress, Acadian National
 Arichat 72-73
 Church Point, N.S. 71, 73
 Memramcook 60-61, 88
 Miscouche 68, 88
Connolly, Joseph E (MLA)
 150, 151, 172, 180, 181, 182
Conscription of 1917
 102
Cormier, Clarence (MLA) 231
Cormier, Hector 245-6, 250
Costigan, John (MP)
 Common Schools Act 18
Courrier des Provinces Maritimes 69, 81, 91, 106
CRAN (Conseil Régional d'Aménagement du Nord-Est)
 Blanchard, Michel 236
 Collège de Bathurst 240
 communication 243, 244
 efforts and responses 223-4, 241-2, 252
 1970 election 225-6, 228
 origins 214-5
 Parti Acadien 237-8
Crocket, James 102, 103
Dalhousie, Town of
 financial problem 148-9
 International Paper 118, 119, 120
Danish Settlements
 education 88
 origin 44-45
Day, George (Editor) 19, 26
DeGrâce, Gérald (Educator) 188
DesBrisay, L.G. (MLA) 189, 206

**Deutsch, Dr. John 191**
**Diefenbaker, John 210, 211**
**Doucet, André (MLA)**
  Acadian support for Conservatives 160
  Caisses Populaires 161
  education 145, 146
  Fisheries Loans Board 160, 167, 170
  hardships of Acadian pulp-cutters 163
  religious education 166
  1953 session 170-171, 173, 176
**Doucet, J.F. Gloucester School Inspector 90**
**Doucet, Stanislas-Joseph 54, 60, 66, 71**
**Douglas, James (Surveyor) 40, 41**
**DREE (Department of Regional Economic Expansion) 235, 251, 252**
**Dubé, Fernand (MLA) 255, 257**
**Dugal, Auguste (MLA) 94, 102, 104**
**Dumont, Dr. George (MLA)**
  background 130, 190-191, 199-200
  Byrne Report 196
  death 207
  L'Évangéline 199
  Minister of Health 189
  Québec 199-200
**Dysart, A.A. (Premier)**
  French education lobby 140, 146
  1935 election 137
  1939 re-election 146
**Eaton, T. Company (Eatons) 132, 134**
**Edmundston, Town of**
  Collège Saint-Louis established 152
  education 123-125, 138, 149-150
  Fraser Companies 119, 125, 148
  hospitals 177
**Education (General)**
  Byrne Commission 193, 195-6
  enrollment 88
  illiteracy 153
  New Schools 167
  Nova Scotia 7
  Program of Equal Opportunity 202, 206, 208-11, 215, 243
  reform 7
  school inspectors 8, 11, 88, 100
  teachers' salaries 94-95
  under-financing 148, 151
**Elections (Federal, Provincial and Bi-Elections)**
  1830, 3; 1867, 3, 6; 1870, 13-15; 1872, 18-19; 1874, 19-20; 1877, 58-59; 1891, 81; 1892, 82-83; 1917, 102, 104, 106; 1920, 107; 1925, 112-116, 123; 1930, 127; 1935, 136-137; 1939, 146, 147; 1948, 166-167; 1952, 165, 171-172; 1956, 180; 1960, 182, 186-7; 1963, 197; 1967, 207-209, 225; 1970, 225-227; 1971, 232-233; 1972, 248-49; 1974, 250, 254-257, 1982, 231
**Eudistes, Congrégation des 99, 143, 152**
**L'Évangéline**
  Acadian nationalism 8, 218, 219-220
  CRAN 224
  difficulties 168, 199, 229
  education 139, 219, 220
  end 231
  founding 70-71
  French diocese 72, 75
  Kent County elections 81, 233
  parti Acadien 224, 240
  prohibition 102
  refrancisation 131-2
  students 236
  translator's contract 91
**Fairweather, Gordon (MLA) 174, 182**
**Fédération Acadienne des Caisses Populaires 213-214, 223**
**Ferguson, Senator John 25, 30**

Index 283

Fergusson, Senator Muriel 241
Fishing
  boats 160-161
  Loans Boards 160, 167
  lobster canning 51
  relations with processors 3, 10, 37
  state of 9, 153-4, 155, 254
Flemming, Hugh John (Premier)
  appeals for French support 160
  elected Premier 164-5
  first Cabinet 170
  Irving expansion 162
  1953 session 171, 175-6
  1956 session 180
  1960 election 182
  1960 session 185, 186
Flemming, James Kidd (Premier)
  Valley Railway Scandal 94, 102
Foster, Sir George 78
Foster, Walter (Premier) 103, 105, 111
Fortin, Lucien
  education 178-9, 180
  first elected 170
  French-English relations 175, 180, 181
Fournier, Edgar
  attacks Louis Robichaud 186
  Chairman Hydro Commission 170
  clashes with Gallant 171, 176-7, 183
  Senator 199, 241
  1953 Session 171, 174-6
Fournier, Michael (MLA) 184, 189, 197
Fowler, George 86-87
Fraser Companies 113, 118-120, 125
Fraser, Donald (Mill Owner) 113, 136
Fraser, J.J.
  Bathurst Schools issue 83-93
  Common Schools compromise 38
  Provincial Secretary 46

FRED (Fund for Regional Economic Development) 251-252
Fredericton, Gleaner 102-103, 184
Frenette, Ray 257
Gallant, W.J. (Tony) (MLA)
  background 178
  clashes with Fournier and Pichette 176-7, 183
  conduct in House 171, 180, 182
  Escuminac disaster 184
  hospital premiums 183, 184-5
  Liberal leadership 182
  Municipal Affairs' Critic 172
  quits Liberal caucus 185
Gauvin, Bernard 220, 252
Gauvin, Jean (MLA) 238
Gibson, Alexander "Boss" 44. 93
Gifford, John 29, 31
Gionet, Martin 254
Girouard, Antoine 14, 69
Gloucester County
  Caisses Populaires 161, 213-4
  communication 247
  CRAN 214
  education 11, 57, 88-90, 140, 145, 146
  family allowances 158
  financial problems 151, 164, 180, 183, 184, 201, 234-5
  fishermen disasters 92
  mining 172, 198, 201
  politics 3-4, 14, 26, 59, 148
  reaction to schools Act 20
  settlement 38-46
Godin, Gastien 219, 256
Gorton Pew Ltd. 150, 236
Grand Falls Hydro Project 92, 112, 117, 119, 120
Guerrette, Phillippe (MLA) 199-200
Guibord, Joseph 33, 36
Guthrie, Lt Col Percy 101
Hatfield, Richard B. (Premier)
  CRAN 225

"Day of Concern" 235
education 253
electoral laws 249, 254-5
Kent-South by-Election 232-3
languages policies 237, 243, 244, 245
Program of Equal Opportunity 204
promoting French fact 231-2, 234, 247, 248, 249, 253
Van Horne 249, 255
1970 election 227
1974 election 249-250, 254, 256-7
**Hawkes, John (Publisher) 105**
**Higgins, Robert (MLA) 245, 255-6**
**Highways 106, 107, 116, 253, 255**
**Hospitals 167, 183**
**Hubbard, Colson 25, 27**
**Hubert, Jean (Editor) 168**
**Humphrey, John A (MLA) 31-32**
**Imperial Order, Daughter of the Empire (IODE) 181**
**Inch, J.A. (Chief Supt Ed) 88, 95-96**
**Inches, C.F. (Lawyer) 149, 150**
**Institut Canadien 32-33, 60**
**Irish**
 clergy 4
 Collège Saint-Louis 64-66
 conflict with acadiens 56-70, 95, 191-192
 emigration 95
 management 2
 politicians 2-3
 1916 riots 102
**Irish Bishops**
 Common Schools Act 18, 191
 language issue 12, 15, 52-76, 259
 Lateran Council 19
 1st Acadian Congress 61
**Irving, K.C.**
 Bay Steel Company 201-202
 Byrne Commission 194, 202
 expansion World War II 104, 162-3

 in praise of 181, 260
 J.C. Van Horne 207-208
 Program of Equal Opportunity 202-3, 206
 shipyard 252
**Jack, Edward 47-48**
**Jean, Bernard (MLA) 197, 214, 223, 224, 248**
**Jesuit Order 57**
**Johnson, Urbain 19, 60, 90**
**Johnston, Prof James F.W. 39**
**Jones, Leonard (Mayor) 217, 226, 236, 237**
**Judicial Committee of Imperial Privy Council 20, 33**
**Kelly, William 25, 27, 28-30, 35**
**Kent County**
 education, state of 11, 151,-152, 172
 elections 14, 81
 exodus 16, 38
 opposes Schools Act 18, 20
 poverty 212
 settlement 39-50
 supports Collège Saint-Joseph 21
**King, George (Premier)**
 Attorney-General 20, 36
 first elected 11
 Common Schools Act 13, 15, 21
 Orange Lodge 19
 School Act compromises 37-38, 93
 1st School Bill 12
 1870 election 14
 1872 election 15
 1874 election 18-19
**King, Louis Joseph 92-93**
**King, W.L.M. (Prime Minister) 112, 116**
**Knights of Columbus 114, 115**
**Kouchibouguac National Park 212-213, 233**
**Ku-Klux-Klan**
 1925 election 112, 113, 114, 115
 1935 election 136-137

LaBillois, Charles (MLA) 81, 82, 91
LaForest, Fred (MLA) 90-91
Landry, Alexis 221, 222
Landry, Dr. D.V. (Provincial Secretary) 94
Landry, Israel
 attempts politics 4-5
 begins *Moniteur Acadien* 4, 15
 Correspondence with Rameau 8
Landry, Pierre-Amand
 common schools issue 14, 15
 defeat in 1874 election 19
 La Société Nationale l'-Assomption 72
 Minister of Public Works 93
 MLA 12
 Richard-McGuirk Affair 54, 55
 Senate appointment 81
 trial of Caraquet Rioters 36-47
 1st Acadian Congress 60-61
 2nd Acadian Congress 68
 3rd Acadian Congress 73
Landry, Valentin 20, 72, 75
LaPorte, Dr. P.H. (MLA) 139, 141, 142
Lateran Council 19, 55
Laurier, Wilfrid 33, 104
LeBlanc, Arthur T. (Judge) 133
LeBlanc, Emery (Journalist) 222, 244
LeBlanc, Father Edouard (Bishop) 75, 100, 102
LeBlanc, Jean-Paul (MLA) 227, 249, 257
LeBlanc, Joseph (MLA) 173-174, 176, 189
LeBlanc, Roméo 257
Lefebvre, Père 2, 21
Leger, Antoine J. (MLA) 116, 133, 142
Leger, Médard 137
Leger, Omer (MLA) 233
Leger, T.J. (Moncton Merchant) 132-134
Légère, Martin J. 213, 214, 223

LeGresley, Léandre (Educator) 145, 168
Lejeune, J.T. (School Inspector) 140-141, 144, 152
Lévesque, Adrien (MLA) 189, 190
Lévesque, Rev Dr. Georges-Henri 178
Lévesque, René 67, 217, 221, 250
Losier, W.A. 145, 146, 148
McElman, Charles 187, 205, 206
MacFarlane, Dr A.S. (Chief Superintendent) 127, 128
McFarlane, P.G. 100-101
McGrand, Dr Frank (MLA) 164, 241
McGuigan, Lorne (MLA) 239
McGuirk, Father Hugh 55-56
McInerney, Dr George 183
McIntyre, Peter (Bishop of Charlottetown) 54, 57, 66-68
MacKay, Hugh (Conservative Leader) 147, 159
McKee, J.K. (MLA) 151
McKee, Rev Michael (MLA) 257
McKenzie, Alex 34-35
MacKenzie, Dr N.A.M. 152, 153
MacKenzie, Dr W.H. (Educator) 174
McKernin, Harold 216
McLean, Angus 112, 113, 117
MacLeod-Pinet Committee (on Educational Planning) 253
McManus, P.J. 17
McNair, John B. (Premier)
 named to bench 171
 post-war policies 162-163, 164
 Redistribution Bill 159
 Resources Development Board 156
 sales tax 164
 wartime economy policies 151, 155, 157
 1935 election 137
 1939 begins Premiership 147

1948 election 166-7
1952 election Defeat 165, 171
**Madawaska County**
　created 21
　education 21, 88, 124
　financial problems 164
　patronage 91
　politics 170
　settlement 21, 38-49, 97-98
**Madawaska, Le 124, 136, 139**
**Maillet, Antonine (Novelist) 130**
**Mailloux, Louis 25, 30, 37**
**Manitoba**
　cultural clashes 15, 58, 72
　comparison with Bathurst School Issue 77, 79, 81, 84, 91
**Marchand, Jean (MP) 235, 251, 252**
**Melanson, Mgr L.J.A. 142, 143, 191**
**Meldrum, Wendall W. 206, 220**
**Mersereau, George (School Inspector)**
　88-89, 90, 140
**Michaud, Benoît 130, 138**
**Michaud, J.E. 116, 142, 190**
**Michaud, Dr Marguerite (Educator) 174, 188**
**Middlemore Home Corp 98**
**Moncton**
　assimilation of French 135-6
　church activities 58
　commercial growth 99, 234
　economy 161
　education 182, 200-1
　politics 170, 226, 227
　refrancisation 132-134, 137
　settlement/growth 40
**Moniteur Acadien, Le**
　beginnings 4, 15
　Collège Saint-Louis 66-67
　Common Schools issue 18
　coverage of Caraquet Riots 24-34
　declining influence 71
　editors 4, 6
　legislative debates 12-13

　lotteries 58
　Rameau de Saint Père 8
　supports Collège Saint-Joseph 21, 38
　translation contracts 91
　1917 conscription 102
**Morais, Lorenzo (MLA) 248-9, 252**
**Morning Freeman (Saint John Newspaper)**
　Common Schools Act 15-16, 18
　coverage of Caraquet Riots & trial 24-30, 36
　founding 3
　Guibord affair 36
　language issue 12
　1874 election 19
**Napier, Samuel 14, 16**
**N.B. Committee on Reconstruction 152-155**
**New Brunswick Hydro Commission 112, 147, 148, 167**
**New Brunswick Reporter and Fredericton Advertiser 78, 79**
**New Brunswick Teachers' Association 182**
**New Democratic Party 255**
**Normal School (Fredericton)**
　(Also Teachers College) 60, 88
　Acadian lobby 139
　Belliveau, Alphée 87-88
　French enrollment 88, 95, 124, 145
　general 128
　Summer School 144
**Northumberland**
　financial problems 151, 152, 164
　opposes Schools Act 20
**Nutter, Harold L. (Anglican Dean) 222, 244**
　(See Task Force on Social Development)
**O'Brien, Archbishop of Halifax 68, 72, 73**
**O'Brien, Edward**
　Bathurst Schools Issue 89

Index 287

O'Brien, J. Leonard (Lt Governor) 189, 191-192
O'Leary, Father Henry 74
O'Leary, Henry (MLA) 19, 34-35, 45, 63-65
Official Languages Act 220, 237, 243, 244, 261
Orange Lodge
  decline 189
  Herman Pitts & Bathurst issue 78-95
  incorporation debate 34-36
  L'Ordre de Jacques Cartier 129
  political influence 19, 28, 33
  regulation 32, 127, 128
  1925 election 114
Ordre de Jacques Cartier
  Bathurst Conference 141-142
  Campbellton 129-131, 191
  education 137, 138, 139, 141, 146, 175, 177
  influence 187, 191, 237
  Moncton 132-134
  origins 128-129
O'Sullivan, James 192, 193, 194
Ouellette, Jean-Pierre (MLA) 257
Paper Companies
  Ability Power & Paper 156
  Bathurst Paper 112, 113, 118, 192, 193, 235
  Fraser companies 113, 118, 119, 120, 125, 149-50, 162
  general 117, 119-120, 123, 155
  International Paper 118, 119, 120, 148, 149
  paper towns 117, 118, 119, 120
  Price and Pierce 156
  Port Royal Pulp and Paper Company 162
  Rolland Paper Company 147
  Rothesay Paper Mill 186, 197
  South Nelson Forest Products 197
Paquetville
  settlement 40-50
Parkin, George 7, 78
Parti Acadien, Le
  election participation 246, 248, 249-250, 255
  formation 224, 230, 232, 237-9, 240
  policy 246, 249, 250
  support 245
Parti Québecois 221, 237
Peacock, Dr Fletcher (Dep Min Ed) 143-144
Pelletier, Father Joseph 26-27
Pelletier, Gérard 237, 247
Pelletier, Roderique 223
Pépin, Pierre-Yves 211, 212
Petite Boutique, La 124, 125, 126, 139
Petrie, J.R. (Economist) 153-155
Pichette, Roger (MLA) 170, 171, 176, 183
Pitts, Herman H.
  attempts resolution 94
  Bathurst school issue 78-96, 155
  enters politics 82-83
  maiden speech 85-87
  summary of role 95
Poirier, Joseph (MLA) 90, 99
Poirier, Pascal (Senator) 36, 37, 53, 60, 69, 73
Pokemouche 40, 66, 71
Program of Equal Opportunity 202, 203, 204, 206, 208, 209, 210, 215, 243
Progressive Conservative Association 226
Prohibition 108-111
Pugsley, Dr William
  railway promotion 94
Québec
  coverage of Caraquet Riot trials 37
  response to Common Schools Act 18, 19
  settlers to N.B. 41-42, 45
Québec Quiet Revolution 199, 215, 218
Railways

Canadian National Railway (CN)
131, 134
Central 82
construction 8
C.P.R. 94
Eastern Railway extension 46
grants 13, 44, 46, 95
Intercolonial 8, 48, 50
International 94, 95
Kent-Northern 50
Moncton-Buctouche 50
National Transcontinental 94
NB Railway 44, 97, 162, 173
Valley Road 44
**Ralliement de la Jeunesse Acadienne, Le 216, 217**
**Rameau de Saint-Père 1, 2, 4, 6, 8, 57, 64, 70**
**Rand, Ivan C. 112, 113, 114**
**Rand, Théodore 20**
**Redistribution Bill of 1895 94**
**Regulation 17 (Ontario) 141**
**Regulation 32 127, 138**
**Renaud, Auguste 6, 18**
**Restigouche, County of 151, 170, 196**
**Richard, André (MLA) 180, 189, 224**
**Richard, Camille 216, 217**
**Richard, Clovis T. (Prov Sec Treas) 137, 142**
**Richard, Ernest (MLA & Speaker) 189, 190, 224**
**Richard, Dr Léon 216**
**Richard, Father Marcel-François**
  Biron Association 56-57, 62, 64, 66
  clashes with Bishop Rogers 56-73
  Collège Saint-Louis 56-69
  death 76
  early years 54
  influence 190, 261
  Le Moniteur Acadien 59-60
  McGuirk Affair 55-56
  Relations with Rome 71-76
  Rogersville 68

settlement efforts 50
1st Acadian Congress 60-61
2nd Acadian Congress 68
3rd Acadian Congress (Church Point) 71
4th Acadian Congress (Arichat) 72-73
**Richards, Charles D. (Premier) 128**
**Richibucto 6, 63-64, 161**
**Riel, Louis 37, 67-69**
**Roberts, Dr William F. (MLA) 110, 140**
**Robertson, Brenda (MLA) 232, 242**
**Robichaud, Gilbert (MLA) 190, 200**
**Robichaud, John (MLA) 108, 190**
**Robichaud, Hédard**
  background 233-4
  L'Association Acadienne d'-Education 138
  Lieutenant-Governor 233
  L'Ordre de Jacques Cartier 237
  MP Gloucester 183, 190
  Secretary Fisheries Loan Board 160
  Senator 232
**Robichaud, Louis J. (Premier)**
  Advisory Staff 205-6, 210, 215
  background 177-8, 187
  Byrne Report 196, 244
  CRAN 224
  education 174, 184
  elected leader 182
  first Cabinet 189
  first election 168-169
  first session as Premier 188
  general 76, 146
  maiden speech 172
  Nutter-LeBlanc Task Force 222-3, 239-40, 244
  Parti Acadien 245
  Program of Equal Opportunity 202-5, 206, 207, 243
  resignation 232

1953 session 171, 176-7
1956 session 179, 180
1960 election Campaign 186-7
1960 session 184, 185-6
1965 election 197
1966 White Paper 201
1967 election 207-9
1970 election campaign 186-7
200th Anniversary Expulsion 173
**Robidoux, Fernand (MLA) 18, 59**
**Rogers, Bishop James 6, 15, 18, 38, 52-73, 80, 95, 191**
**Rogersville 68-71, 73**
**Roy, Alfred (Ed L'Évangéline) 132, 148**
**Royal Commissions**
  Biculturalism & Bilingualism 135, 220
  Finance and Municipal Taxation 96
  hearings 193-4
  members 192-3
  recommendations 195-196, 243
  responses to 196-198, 201
  school financing 174, 179, 180-181, 182
**St. Cyr, Dr Gérard 214, 223**
**St. Louis de Kent 21, 52, 62**
**St. Michael's College (Chatham) 57, 60, 62, 100**
**Savage, Father 74, 75**
**Savoie, Alexandre-J. 145**
**Savoie, Calixte (Educator, Senator)**
  Bathurst Education Conference 142-3
  Dysart 137
  goals 258
  L'Association Acadienne d'Education 138-140
  La Petite Boutique 124
  La Société l'Assomption 125-126, 132, 168
  L'Ordre de Jacques Cartier 129
  letters to editor 141
  Moncton refrancisation 132-134

NB Committee on Reconstruction 153
principal in Edmundston 123, 124, 125
regulations 32, 127-128
teachers' Summer Schools 143-4
200th Anniversary Expulsion 173
**Savoie, Richard (Manager) 248**
**Savoie, Roger 216, 217, 220**
**Scarlet Mother on the Tiber**
  See King, Louis Joseph 92-93
**Seivewright, John (MLA)**
  Bathurst School Issue 83, 87, 91
**Sellers, Rev J. 84, 90**
**Senate Committee on Poverty 240-241**
**Settlement**
  Act to facilitate settlement 43
  Blue Bell Tract 97-98
  Danish settlements 44-46, 50
  Free Grant Land Act 44
  French Settlers hardships 44-46
  Hemlock Harvester boom 49-50
  Johnston Report 39, 48-49
  Middlemore Home Corporation 98
  NB & Nova Scotia Land Company 43
  new areas opened 40-41, 97-98
  ratio of English & French Settlers 42
  reports of Edward Jack 47-49
  Scottish settlements 45-46
  Surveyor's Reports 40-42
**Sherwood, Cyrus B. (MLA) 204, 207**
**Simard, Jean-Maurice (MLA) 226-7, 245, 257**
**Sirois, Father Yvon 236, 238, 252**
**Sisters of Charity 86, 88, 92, 95**
**Smith, Albert J. (Premier) 4-5, 56**
**Société d'Assurance Caisses Populaires Acadiennes, La 167-8**
**Société Nationale des Acadiens (SNA), La**

216, 218, 220, 237, 245-6, 250, 253
Société Nationale l'Assomption, La
72, 73, 74, 75, 125, 128, 131, 132, 133, 138, 153, 168, 200, 259
Société Mutuelle l'Assomption, La 73-74, 76, 98, 228-9, 230
Société Saint-Jean-Baptiste, La 60, 131
Soeurs de la Congrégation de Notre-Dame, Les 21, 69, 80
Somers, Fred (MLA) 185
Sons of Temperance 82, 85
Sormany, Dr Albert M.
    Bathurst Conference 142
    Dysart 137
    early years in Edmundston 123
    Fraser Companies 119, 120, 123, 136
    Goals 258, 261
    La Petite Boutique 124, 126
    La Société l'Assomption 126
    L'Association Acadienne d'Education 138-140
    L'Ordre de Jacques Cartier 129, 137
    regulation 32, 127-128
    Teachers' Summer School 143-4
Stanfield, Robert 217, 235
Stockton, A.A. (MLA) 81-82, 90
Sweeney, Bishop John 5, 6, 15, 18, 20, 21, 26, 38, 52, 76
Taché, Bishop 15, 58
Taillon, Brother Léopold 144
Task Force on Social Development and Social Welfare 222, 223, 224-5, 239-240, 242-244
Taylor, Austen (MLA)
    Tory leader 171, 180
Taylor, Claude (MLA) 174, 200-201
Teachers' College 174, 188, 200
Television 215, 222, 228, 237-8, 239, 243, 247, 260

Têtu, F.A. 41-42
Thériault, Léon (Professor) 230
Thériault, Norbert (MLA) 197, 206
Thomson, Rev A.F. 81, 84-85, 89-90, 93
Tilley, L.P.D. (MLA and Premier) 116, 136-137
Trudeau, Pierre E. (Prime Minister) 120, 233, 237, 247, 248
Tupper, Charles 7
Turgeon, Onésiphore 59
Tweedie, L.J. (MLA & Premier) 90-91
Université de Moncton 76, 184
    Blanchard affair 216, 221, 226
    education lobby 220, 239, 261
    expansion 235
    founding 191-192, 210
    Le Parti Acadien 7, 224,
    misc 242
    Québec influence 200, 215-6
    secularization 229, 230, 260
Université de Québec à Montréal (UQAM) 218
University of New Brunswick 78, 204, 217, 250
Vail, Sheriff 25, 27, 28
Van Horne, J. Charles (MLA) 206-7, 207-9, 249, 255
Vautour, Jacques 56, 212-213
Veniot, Dr Clarence (MP) 140, 142
Veniot, Peter J. (Premier)
    Angus McLean 117
    becomes premier 111
    death 116
    early years 105-106
    first elected 1895 94
    French education 140
    Grand Falls power project 112-117
    Kent County Election 1891 81, 82
    Ku Klux Klan 112, 113, 114, 115
    Minister of Public Works 105-110
    prohibition 109-111
    Pulp and paper industries 112
    1917 election Role 103, 104

1920 election 107
1925 election 112-116, 123
**Victoria County 20, 43, 88**
**Wardell, Michael 79, 184, 203-4, 206**
**Westmorland County**
 elections 5, 14
 family allowances 158
 French schools 174, 184
 media 184
 reactions to schools issue 21
 settlement 39-49
**Williamson, H.H. "Bud" (MLA) 197, 200, 228, 249**
**Wilmot, Lt-Governor L.A. 13, 15**
**Young, Aurèle (Professor) 229**
**Young, Fred (MLA) 150**
**Young, John (MLA) 90-91**
**Young, Robert (MLA) 3, 10, 17, 23, 36, 37, 38, 156, 161**